Janet Aldis

The Queen of Letter Writers Marquise de Sevigne

Dame de Bourbilly (1626 - 1696)

Janet Aldis

The Queen of Letter Writers Marquise de Sevigne
Dame de Bourbilly (1626 - 1696)

ISBN/EAN: 9783744738026

Printed in Europe, USA, Canada, Australia, Japan

Cover: Foto ©Lupo / pixelio.de

More available books at **www.hansebooks.com**

THE QUEEN OF LETTER WRITERS

MARQUISE DE SÉVIGNÉ
DAME DE BOURBILLY
1626-1696

BY

JANET ALDIS

"Quelle femme aimable ! quel adorable écrivain !
Nulle, parmi les femmes françaises, n'a possédé
à ce degré l'imagination et l'esprit"
SAINTE-BEUVE

WITH EIGHTEEN ILLUSTRATIONS

METHUEN & CO.
36 ESSEX STREET W.C.
LONDON

PREFACE

MADAME DE SÉVIGNÉ, said Sainte-Beuve, wrote her *Letters* "during twenty-seven years of the most delightful period of the most agreeable French society"; and no other writer gives so complete a picture of that vivid and fascinating epoch as the famous Marquise. It was the Augustan Age of France, when modern manners and modern culture passed swiftly from their bright dawn to a brilliant noontide. In literature, there were Corneille, Molière, Racine, La Fontaine, Madame de Sévigné, and La Rochefoucauld; the rivals Mignard and Le Brun were painting their wonderful portraits; Pascal was stirring society with his anonymous *Lettres provinciales*; Bourdaloue and Bossuet were pouring forth to crowded congregations their eloquent thunders of denunciation, and the funeral orations which have since become classics; Saint Francis de Sales was founding convents and monasteries, and preaching and living the holy life; while the humble Saint Vincent de Paul was steadfastly devoting his energies and talents to the service of the unregarded poor, and by the example of his simple and sincere enthusiasm, making it fashionable for high-born ladies to minister with their own delicate hands to the sufferers in prison and in the Hôtel Dieu.

We can only realise the charm of that wonderful century by comparing it with the arid century that followed; by contrasting its spontaneous and fertile flow of genius, its natural romance and colour, its genuine religious ardour, with the stultified and absurd self-consciousness of straining mediocrity, the formal picturesqueness and paraded infidelity which were so conspicuous in the more sophisticated eighteenth century. The people of Madame de Sévigné's day lived and breathed romance. Duelling and abductions, deeds of high daring, and pious self-renunciation were in the air. The city was gay with frequent religious processions, when, mingling with priests and people, friars in their brown, white, and grey habits marched through the streets barefoot or in sandals, and devout citizens draped windows and balconies with their choicest carpets and tapestries, and lent their most valuable pictures and treasured *articles de virtu* to decorate altars in the public squares where the Host rested when the priest was wearied with its weight. On Midsummer Day, Saint John's fire flared up from the Grève, and those whose name was John lighted his fire on their doorsteps with superstitious precaution, for fear of misadventure. Brutal and frequent executions took place, not only on the Grève, but in the public streets; and by night, in those same dark and narrow streets, bands of mysterious figures in mask and domino swept silently by, or played tricks on gay cavaliers with clanking swords, or on the humbler citizen going home from tavern or wineshop. The Seine was then the principal highway of traffic for the city, and ponderous barges, laden with oil and wood and wine, glided slowly into the capital; the Champs Elysées were veritable and delightful fields, a fashionable rendezvous where the gay promenaders along the Cours-la-Reine might walk or meet their friends; and the Bois de Boulogne was a dense wood outside Paris, through which people usually travelled in companies as a protection against the brigands who made their haunts in its deep recesses.

And in the Letters of Madame de Sévigné we get brilliant and detailed descriptions of all this life and glow and colour; truthful and impressionist pictures of the moment, which, written to amuse her idolised daughter in Provence, have delighted countless thousands in the centuries that have followed. The Marquise did not dream that she was writing for posterity. Though some of her letters were handed about among friends, and admired during her lifetime, it is evident that she and her daughter made a compact before they parted that their letters to each other should be private. When, occasionally, she showed a part of her daughter's letters to Madame de la Fayette, she assured the Comtesse de Grignan that she was not indiscreet, that she knew exactly how much to show, and to what friends to show it; and once, when she had greatly enjoyed one of her daughter's letters, she exclaimed: "Bon Dieu! my dear child, how charming your letters are! There are passages in them that deserve to be printed; one of these days you will find that a treacherous friend will betray you"—with no thought that her own letters would eventually be given to the world by her granddaughter Pauline, the Comtesse de Simiane.

But no author, writing for a large and appreciative public, could have given more care to his work than did Madame de Sévigné, writing only for the eyes of her daughter, for whose amusement and pleasure she was never tired of giving her best. There was nearly the length of France between Madame de Sévigné and the Comtesse de Grignan, but in spirit the Marquise was always with her daughter, and whatever happened in Paris or Brittany, Livry or Vichy, or wherever she chanced to be, she always sent an account of it to Provence. She wrote almost daily those vivid and life-like chronicles of the gossip of the Court, the news of the town, interesting details concerning intimate friends, her own thoughts, aspirations, religious sentiments, and philosophy of life, and all in such graceful, easy, piquant and varied phrases, that there is amazingly little repetition throughout the two thousand letters. These letters were the chief occupation of her days. It is noticeable that when she was with her daughter, she wrote to her other friends much more frequently; but when she was separated from Madame de Grignan her first care was always to write to Provence, and if, as occasionally happened, there was not enough of interest to fill her letter, she would lay down her pen and "run round the town" to see if she could gather any news to send her.

"I give you," she once told her daughter, "the top of the basket; that is to say, the flower of my head, of my eyes, and of my mind."

It has not been attempted in the present volume to give a resume of her complete correspondence. It has been written mainly with the idea of giving the personal history of the Marquise in its relation to her times, and of showing how intimately she was connected with the great events of her day, and how closely she came into contact with the great personages who were, consciously or unconsciously, occupied in making history: her uncle the Cardinal de Retz, the Duc de la Rochefoucauld, Foucquet, Maréchal Turenne, and many others. The letters have, however, been freely used in this endeavour to picture the private life of a *grande dame* in Parisian society and at Versailles, at the Baths and at her country-house, or travelling in France two centuries and more ago.

By a fortunate chance, the chief houses in which Madame de Sévigné lived have been spared by Time and the Revolution. The house where she was born in the Place des Vosges still stands, marked by a tablet in her honour; only a few paces away, in the Rue de Sévigné, is the fine Hôtel de Carnavalet, which she occupied for the last twenty years of her life; her beautiful country-house Les Rochers, in Brittany, is almost untouched by time, amid the park and gardens which she planted, and loved with such a genuine passion; and at Gargan-Livry, a few miles from Paris, may still be found the grey old Abbaye where she spent her tranquil girlhood with the good Abbé de Livry.

Among the many authorities which I have used, I am especially indebted to Monmerqué's valuable edition of the *Lettres*, with Mesnard's *Notice biographique*, in the *Collection des grands écrivains de la France*; Walckenaer's *Mémoires touchant la vie et les écrits de la Marquise de Sévigné*; *Mémoires* of the Comte de Bussy, Madame de Motteville, Cardinal de Retz, and La Grande Mademoiselle; *Journal du Voyage de deux jeunes hollandais à Paris en* 1656–1658, publié par A. P. Faugère; and Dr. Martin Lister's account of his visit to Paris in 1698.

For the place of Madame de Sévigné's birth, and the date of her daughter's birth, I have followed Mesnard, who has given a copy of the *acte de baptême* in each case.

J. A.

CAMBRIDGE, *July* 9, 1907

CONTENTS

CHAPTER I

The duel on Easter Sunday morning at the Porte Saint-Antoine—The scandal in Paris, and its consequences—The birth of Madame de Sévigné—Her celebrated grandmother Sainte-Chantal, the disciple of Saint Francis de Sales—A twofold inheritance 1

CHAPTER II

A family council—The Abbé de Livry chosen as guardian of Marie de Rabutin-Chantal—Her life at the Abbaye—Walpole's "Notre Dame de Livry"—An amorous tutor—A shabby man of letters 13

CHAPTER III

Her "portrait" by the Marquise de la Fayette—The young Burgundian heiress is betrothed to Henri, Marquis de Sévigné—The bridegroom fights a duel and is dangerously wounded—An old chateau in Brittany—The furniture of Madame de Sévigné's room—The birth of Françoise Marguerite de Sévigné 24

CHAPTER IV

The Hôtel de Rambouillet, the pioneer of Parisian salons—The Marquise de Rambouillet—A lady's bed-chamber in the seventeenth century—Julie d'Angennes—*La Guirlande de Julie*—A polished society of *précieux et précieuses*—The Duchesse de Longueville—Mademoiselle de Scudéry . 35

CHAPTER V

The dissipated young Marquis de Sévigné openly neglects his wife—The birth of Charles de Sévigné—Madame de Sévigné has many admirers—The Comte de Lude, Segrais, the Abbé de Montreuil, the Comte de Bussy-Rabutin—A daring abduction 49

CHAPTER VI

A visit to the Bishop of Chalon—The Marquis and his wife return to Paris—The beginnings of the Fronde—The flight of the Court to Saint-Germain—Paris besieged by the Queen—"Mazarins" and "Frondeurs"—The Duchesse de Longueville at the Hôtel de Ville 61

CHAPTER VII

The "Princes' Fronde"—The Sévignés give a supper-party to the Duchesse de Chevreuse—The *appartement* of the crippled poet Scarron—The Marquis de Sévigné and Ninon de l'Enclos—An intercepted letter—The Marquis conducts his wife to the solitude of Les Rochers—The diamond earrings—The Marquis de Sévigné is killed in a duel . . . 71

CHAPTER VIII

Madame de Sévigné's widowhood at Les Rochers—She returns to Paris and gradually re-enters Parisian society—Rival suitors—The quarrel between the Duc de Rohan and the Marquis de Tonquedec in her *ruelle*—A haughty Duchess—The battle of Saint-Antoine 83

CHAPTER IX

The Comte de Bussy pays court to the Marquise—He gives a fête in her honour in the Temple Gardens—Madame de Sévigné at the height of her charm and popularity—A period of temptation—Dangerous gallants—The Prince de Conti ; Nicolas Foucquet 93

CHAPTER X

The escape of Cardinal de Retz—His relative, Madame de Sévigné, acts as intermediary—A letter to her old tutor Ménage—The Comte de Bussy leaves Paris to go to camp—A lively correspondence between the two cousins 105

CHAPTER XI

The Queen of Sweden visits Paris—Her impression of Madame de Sévigné—An infant prodigy—La Fontaine's verses on the Marquise—A ball in her honour—Wax-candles carried off by the maskers 114

CHAPTER XII

The Comte de Bussy in difficulties—He desires to borrow money of the Marquise — A misunderstanding — Madame de Montglas pledges her diamonds—Bussy's mean revenge on his cousin—Molière gives *Les Précieuses Ridicules* 124

CONTENTS

CHAPTER XIII

The last fête at Vaux—A startling arrest—Letters from Madame de Sévigné found among the private papers of Foucquet—A Parisian scandal—The Comte de Bussy defends his cousin's good name 131

CHAPTER XIV

Foucquet's trial—Madame de Sévigné writes a daily account of it to the Marquis de Pomponne—The Chancellor Séguier—A period of suspense—Foucquet is sent to Pignerol under the escort of d'Artagnan and his famous Musketeers 140

CHAPTER XV

Madame de Sévigné introduces her daughter at Court—"A beauty who will set the world on fire"—Mademoiselle de Sévigné dances with the King—Verses in her honour 151

CHAPTER XVI

A reconciliation between the Marquise and her cousin Bussy—Letters of explanation—The Marquise writes a clear summing-up of his offences—The Comte finally sues for mercy, and is pardoned by his cousin . . 161

CHAPTER XVII

Suitors for the hand of Mademoiselle de Sévigné—A vain young beauty—The Duc de Caderousse—The Marquis de Mérinville—"The prettiest girl in France" unmarried at twenty-three—She is betrothed to a widower with two young daughters 169

CHAPTER XVIII

Mademoiselle de Sévigné is married to the Comte de Grignan—An ancient and honourable family—An imprudent mother—Charles de Sévigné—His campaign in Candia against the Turks 178

CHAPTER XIX

The Comte de Grignan is appointed Deputy-Governor of Provence—Madame de Sévigné's grief and disappointment—Model letters from a mother-in-law—The Comtesse de Grignan remains a year in Paris with her mother—The Bishop of Marseilles 185

CHAPTER XX

A celebrated letter—La Grande Mademoiselle and M. de Lauzun—A royal love-story—Madame de Sévigné visits the Tuilleries, and is the confidante of La Grand Mademoiselle—A Princess in tears 193

CHAPTER XXI

A bitter parting—The perilous journey to Provence—A tender mother—"A pretty pagan"—Spring at Livry 202

CHAPTER XXII

Baron de Sévigné—His dissipated life in Paris—"He wears the chains of Ninon"—An actress' love-letters—"A fool in heart but not in head"—Description of a fête at Chantilly—The death of Vatel . . . 211

CHAPTER XXIII

The Marquise and her household go to Brittany for the *belle saison*—Her cavalcade of carriages, pack-horses, and postilions—The tenantry assemble on the wrong day to welcome the young heir—Dancing Bohemians—Sévigné leaves for the camp in Lorraine 221

CHAPTER XXIV

The States of Brittany—A seventeenth-century town—The Duchesse de Chaulnes visits the Marquise at Les Rochers—A humorous criminal—A grand banquet at the Castle of Vitré—A doorway heightened to admit pyramids of fruit—Guests at Les Rochers—A collation in the garden . 229

CHAPTER XXV

The "Fête de Marie" at Vitré—A drinking province—The Marquise takes refuge at Les Rochers—An exhausted hostess—Madame de Sévigné is escorted back to Vitré by the Governor's guards 239

CHAPTER XXVI

Wolves in the woods at Les Rochers—The birth of a grandson—The Marquise and her household return to Paris—A warm welcome given to the *mère-beauté*—A charming society—A brilliant group of writers . . . 247

CHAPTER XXVII

The Marquise visits her daughter in Provence—Madam de Sévigné at Marseilles—Her return to Paris—A midnight walk with Madame Scarron—The death of Turenne 256

CHAPTER XXVIII

The Marquise has an attack of rheumatic fever—She is tenderly nursed by her son and the Bien-Bon—Rival beauties at the Carmelites—The Marquise goes to Vichy for the waters—A coquette at the Baths two hundred years ago—Appalling remedies prescribed by physicians—The hanging of a countess 268

CHAPTER XXIX

The Marquise at Versailles—Madame de Montespan at cards with the King—The Hôtel de Carnavalet—The reckless extravagance of the Grignans—A clever stepmother—A sarcastic letter 279

CHAPTER XXX

The Marquise visits Les Rochers with the Bien-Bon—The rough roads of Brittany—Madame de Grignan comes to Paris for a long stay—Company at the Hôtel de Carnavalet—The marriage of Charles de Sévigné—The death of the Bien-Bon in 1687 289

CHAPTER XXXI

The young Marquis de Grignan at Philipsburg—Madame de Sévigné at the performance of *Esther* by the young ladies of Saint-Cyr—Her last visit to Les Rochers—The marriage of the Marquis de Grignan—The marriage of Pauline—The death of Madame de Sévigné 298

INDEX 309

LIST OF ILLUSTRATIONS

The Marquise de Sévigné . . . . *Frontispiece*
  By permission of Messrs. Hachette, Paris

                                                                                  FACING PAGE

Place des Vosges (Place Royale), Paris 6
  From a Photograph by Mons. Sauvanaud, Paris

The Abbaye de Livry 18

Henri, Marquis de Sévigné 30
  By permission of Messrs. Hachette, Paris

Christophe de Coulanges, Abbé de Livry . . . 84
  By permission of Messrs. Hachette, Paris

The Comte de Bussy 100
  From an Engraving after the Original Portrait at Versailles

Nicolas Foucquet 118
  From an Engraving after the Original Portrait at Versailles

Charles de Sévigné 152
  By permission of Messrs. Hachette, Paris

The Comtesse de Grignan (Françoise de Sévigné) . . 158
  By permission of Messrs. Hachette, Paris

Henriette, Duchesse d'Orléans 194
  From a Miniature by Petitot in the South Kensington Museum

The Duchesse de Montpensier ("La Grande Mademoiselle") . 194
  From a Miniature by Petitot in the South Kensington Museum

The Comtesse de Grignan 206
  From the Portrait by Mignard in the Musée Carnavalet, Paris
  From a Photograph by Mons. Moutet, Paris

Les Rochers, Madame de Sévigné's Home in Brittany . 222

Maréchal Turenne 260
  From an Engraving by Nanteuil, after Champaigne in the Bibliothèque Nationale, Paris

xv

	FACING PAGE
THE MARQUISE DE MAINTENON	272
From a Miniature in the South Kensington Museum	
THE MARQUISE DE MONTESPAN	272
From a Miniature by Petitot in the South Kensington Museum	
THE HÔTEL DE CARNAVALET, COUR D'ENTRÉE	282
From a Photograph by Mons. Moutet, Paris	
THE MARQUISE DE SÉVIGNÉ	294
From a Portrait at Versailles	
From a Photograph by Messrs. Neurdein, Paris	

THE QUEEN OF LETTER WRITERS

CHAPTER I

The duel on Easter Sunday morning at the Porte Saint-Antoine—The scandal in Paris, and its consequences—The birth of Madame de Sévigné—Her celebrated grandmother Sainte-Chantal, the disciple of Saint Francis de Sales—A twofold inheritance

IT was the morning of Easter Day of the year 1624, and the devout and faithful of the parish church of Saint Paul in the Marais, the most fashionable quarter of Paris, had gathered together to "make their Easter." The priests in gorgeous vestments, with little white-robed acolytes in attendance, were celebrating High Mass to a great congregation, for the Church's festivals were at this period strictly observed by almost the whole population.

Among the crowd was the young Baron de Chantal, afterwards the father of Madame de Sévigné, who had come with his recently married wife, Marie de Coulanges, and her family. The Baron had just communicated, when a lackey, hurriedly entering the church, found his way to where the young noble sat, and gave him a message from his friend, Bouteville de Montmorency.

"Monsieur le Marquis," whispered the servant, "was waiting for Monsieur at the Porte Saint-Antoine, where he was about to fight a duel with Monsieur Pont-Gibaud, and he begged him to come immediately and act as his second."

It might have occurred to some people that church-going clothes with black velvet slippers made scarcely a suitable costume to wear as second, but this ardent duellist did not give

I

a thought to such trifles. Without hesitating an instant, he left his wife and her relatives,—who doubtless wondered what had called him away so suddenly,—and, traversing the short distance along the Rue Saint-Antoine, in a few minutes reached the Porte, where the combatants were awaiting him in hot, impatient anger.

Chantal was eagerly welcomed by his friend, and so fierce was the quarrel that they did not even wait to send for swords. Knives were borrowed from a neighbouring tavern, and in the shortest possible time principals and seconds were fighting with the reckless bravery and practised skill of that duelling age, under the grim shadow of the Bastille.

Fortunately no one was killed, but such an extraordinary affair was not likely to remain a secret. It was a choice piece of gossip for Easter Day, and before night the news had spread over court and town, and everyone was talking of the scandalous occurrence. It reached the ears of Richelieu, the powerful minister of Louis XIII, who had determined to suppress duelling, which, it was said, was yearly robbing France of more of the bravest of her young nobility than the most disastrous wars. The minister was gravely offended. Was his famous Edict to be regarded as a dead letter? To be set aside as an idle form? The Church, too, was scandalised. A duel on Easter Day! Such sacrilege and profanation were unheard of! And Church and State united their clamours for punishment for this outrageous defiance of civil and ecclesiastical laws.

Swift retribution followed the offence. Shortly after, on the 24th of April, the Parlement of Paris in solemn conclave declared that Bouteville de Montmorency, Pont-Gibaud, and their seconds were convicted of *lèse-majesté* both human and divine. A decree pronounced them to be "ignoble, vulgar, and infamous," and condemned them to be hung and strangled on a gallows in the form of a cross, which must be erected in the Place de Grève. Furthermore, the same decree ordained that their houses were to be razed to the ground and their goods confiscated.

But laws that could sanction such stringent and brutal sentences had necessarily to be slackly administered—at least in the case of nobles who had powerful friends to avenge them

—and before this terrible sentence was pronounced the young men had promptly taken flight. The Baron de Chantal was forced to leave his wife, to whom he had been married only a few months, and to take refuge in Burgundy, his native province, where for some time he hid in the house of his brother-in-law, the Comte de Toulongeon.

The law had to take its course, however, notwithstanding the non-appearance of the culprits, and a gruesome little farce was enacted for its satisfaction. As the condemned had disappeared, vengeance was wreaked on them by means of their effigies. A gallows was duly erected in the Place de Grève, and figures representing the four duellists were hung in front of the Hôtel de Ville. What followed reads like an incident from a romance, but was nothing more than a common occurrence of the time. The *Mercure François* records that on that same night, as darkness fell, a company of lackeys, well protected by a band of horsemen, came stealthily to the Place de Grève, and while some kept a keen lookout for the watch, others hurriedly cut down the gruesome caricatures of their masters and carried them off.

Gradually the scandal died down, and no further efforts were made to punish the culprits. Their goods were not confiscated, their houses were not razed to the ground, and by cautious degrees the young men began to appear among their friends and at Court again, though Richelieu kept an eye on their conduct that was by no means friendly. But their peril had not taught them a great deal of wisdom! Bouteville de Montmorency was a born swordsman, with such a passion for duelling that nothing could keep him from it long; while the Baron de Chantal was one of those brilliant young men, endowed with all the talents, who by some trick of inherent perversity take pleasure in offending those people they ought to conciliate.

His nephew, the Comte de Bussy, who figures so largely in Madame de Sévigné's life, has left a slight pen-sketch of him which gives a suggestion at least of his charm and varied accomplishments; which indicates also that his daughter must have inherited not a little of her wit, fascination, and delight in life from her reckless and ill-fated father.

"He became," writes Bussy, "one of the most accomplished cavaliers of France, not only for the graces of his person, but for those of his mind also. He danced with an incomparable grace, he fenced well, and his courage was of a rare quality. He was very lively and animated, giving to every word he said such an original and graceful turn that it was a pleasure to hear him converse. But he did not charm by this alone; it was by the air and grace with which he spoke; in him all was playful."

Unfortunately this young cavalier, in addition to his other accomplishments, had a habit of plain-speaking which by itself was sufficient to gain him many enemies. Madame de Sévigné, more than half a century later, briefly referred to an incident in her father's life which throws an illuminating flash on his whole career, and makes it easy to understand why this brave and witty young noble, of good birth and powerful connections, never gained preferment at Court. When Schomberg, one of his friends, was made Maréchal de France in 1625, the Baron de Chantal wrote this laconic note of congratulation—

"MONSEIGNEUR,—Qualité, barbe noire, familiarité."

Madame de Sévigné thus explains to her daughter this sole item of her father's correspondence that had been preserved. "You understand that he wished to say to M. de Schomberg that he had been made Maréchal de France, because he was a man of quality, because his beard was black like the King his master's, and because he was admitted to familiarity with the King.

For a time the Baron settled down quietly in his house in the Place Royale with his gentle young wife, Marie de Coulanges, who was the daughter of Philippe de Coulanges, Conseiller du Roi, and Marie de Bèze, "people of great honour and virtue," said their aristocratic connection the Comte de Bussy, "though not of noble birth." But it seemed impossible for this rash and impetuous young man to keep out of mischief long. Six short months after he had been hung in effigy with his friends, he again arranged to fight another duel as second to his fire-eating friend Bouteville, but, by a fortunate chance, the King was warned of the affair in time to prevent it.

Louis XIII, who had always found this witty young noble

amusing, began to look coldly on him when Richelieu pointed out that he was an intimate friend of the Prince de Chalais, who, for high treason, was beheaded in 1626, and of the Marquis de Toiras, who had also offended the powerful and vindictive Richelieu. Indeed, the Baron had the misfortune to displease the great Cardinal, which was infinitely worse than displeasing the King, as he was soon to discover in a most startling fashion.

Some two years after his marriage, on February 5, 1626, a little daughter was born to the Baron and his wife—not the first, for a child who died at birth had preceded her—a daughter who afterwards, as the Marquise de Sévigné, brought more fame to her house and race by her pen than all her valiant fighting ancestors had brought by their swords. For a year after her birth all went well with the household in the Place Royale; we may even suppose that the young Baronne, with her bright baby and her handsome and fascinating husband, enjoyed for a brief space a semblance at least of that domestic tranquillity of which she had experienced so little during her short wedded life.

But this tranquillity was not of long duration. On the 12th of May 1627, Bouteville de Montmorency, the incorrigible duellist, arranged a meeting with Beuvron; and their two seconds—seconds always fought in those days—were Bussy d'Amboise and des Chappelles.

The affair took place in the Place Royale, that fine square which is now called the Place des Vosges, the very heart and centre of the Marais Quarter. Strangely enough, though eighteenth-century Paris has been so effectually swept away by civilisation and Baron Haussmann, this spacious "Place" of red-and-white brick mansions, after three hundred years of natural and political storms, looks not very different from when it was built by the bluff Henri Quatre, and considered one of the finest squares in Europe.

Standing in the Place des Vosges, we are back again in the seventeenth century. In that corner mansion lived the haughty des Rohan; near by, the beautiful intriguing Duchesse de Chevreuse kept the watchful Mazarin on the *qui vive* with her ceaseless plottings; under those quaint, cool arcades, some of France's greatest men have paced, deep in earnest converse on the burning questions of their day,—Sully, Richelieu, Corneille,

Molière, La Rochefoucauld, Turenne; and, so strange is the fortune of war, in those same arcades horses were stabled during the Fronde! Here, in the square, the favourite game of "running the ring" was played by gallant young nobles; on fête days those long straight windows were gay with rare carpets and priceless tapestries; lackeys and waiting-women gossiped in those attics with mansard roofs, or quarrelled in the "Place" below as they waited for their masters. But chance and inevitable change have metamorphosed those shady promenades into sordid little shops, now given over to menders of broken china, dealers in second-hand clothes, and vendors of iced drinks; there is the inevitable cheap sweet-store, and an emporium of tawdry *garnitures* for humble funerals; while the panelled and decorated rooms above, where Court beauties swept in and out in trailing garments of silk and brocade, attended by gallants in plumed hats and richly embroidered mantles, are now let out in suites of rooms or business offices.

The Baron de Chantal lived with his wife and little daughter Marie in the house which is now number one, where a tablet records the fact that Madame de Sévigné was born there. One may be quite certain that, on the day of the fateful duel, the young Baron was either looking from an upper window or standing near his friend in the square while the fight was progressing. Indeed, there is little doubt that faces were peering from most of the many windows giving on to the "Place," all keenly interested in a duel of any kind, but especially a duel in which the notorious Bouteville de Montmorency was a principal.

It was a day of disaster for this young noble and his friends. One of the seconds, Bussy d'Amboise, was killed by Bouteville's second des Chappelles. Bouteville, knowing that he could expect no mercy from Richelieu, fled hastily across the square to the house of his friend Baron Chantal. The latter had horses in waiting, and the two offenders galloped hastily away by one of the narrow back streets, hoping to escape into hiding till the affair should be condoned, if not forgotten.

But there was to be no farce of hanging in effigy this time! Richelieu, whose consistent policy was to bring lawless nobles under the law, determined to make an example that should

effectually deter others from disobeying his edict. The fugitives were followed up at once and arrested at Vitry-le-Brûlé, where, with the least delay possible, they were beheaded by Richelieu's command, amid the astonishment and fervent execrations of the French nobility.

This duel and its fatal consequences had a serious effect on the fortunes of Madame de Sévigné's father. The Baron found, to his consternation, that, in the warrant of arrest issued against Bouteville, the unfortunate duel of Easter Day two years before was recalled; and worse, his name was mentioned as being concerned in it!

It was a sinister omen to be thus distinguished by Richelieu in such a connection; it was something of a warning, or even, it might be, a threat, and he felt that his head would be safer if he removed from Richelieu's near neighbourhood for a time. So, bidding good-bye to his wife and baby daughter, who was then a little more than a year old, he set out to join his friend the Marquis de Toiras, at that time governor of the Isle of Rhé. Toiras gladly welcomed the Baron as a gentleman volunteer, and when news of this reached his mother, the Blessed Chantal, she wrote to her daughter-in-law in the Place Royale—

"Oh, my dearest daughter, ₁I do not doubt that your poor heart must be in pain at the thought of your husband exposed to the chances of war. . . . I pray that God may preserve you with your dear little one. . . ."

The forsaken young Baronne needed all the support that Sainte-Chantal's prayers could give her. A few weeks after her husband had joined the army of the Marquis de Toiras, the Duke of Buckingham landed with two thousand English troops on the Isle of Rhé. The Baron de Chantal, at the head of his company of volunteers, was soon in the midst of the fight, where among brave men his bravery was conspicuous. Three horses were killed under him, and during the engagement, which lasted six hours, he received twenty-seven wounds. He lingered for two hours in mortal pain, then, having received the sacraments, —a sad consolation to his mourning wife and mother,—this gallant young noble died at the early age of thirty-one.

This was the first of that series of deaths which left his little daughter, Marie de Rabutin-Chantal, so peculiarly an orphan. The Marquis de Toiras, grieving for the loss of his friend, sent the Baron de Chantal's heart home to his young widow, who placed it in the Church of the Minims, which has since been destroyed. It is said too, that, after her years of mourning were over, he offered himself to her in marriage, but that the gentle, heart-broken Baronne resolved to devote her life to her little girl.

She did not, however, long survive her husband. She moved from the house in the Place Royale, so full of bittersweet memories of her short and anxious wedded life, and for the six years of her widowhood lived with her parents, Philippe de Coulanges and his wife, sometimes at their mansion in the Place Royale, sometimes at Sucy, the country-house which her father had built a few years before. Then she too died, and her bright and lovely little daughter was left to the care of her grandparents de Coulanges.

The Blessed Chantal, fully occupied with the cares of her new Order, wrote to thank Philippe de Coulanges and his wife, not only for the incomparable love which they had for her son, "but for the care which they had lavished on '*cette pauvre petite pouponne.*'" "But what can be said when God speaks?" she writes on the death of her daughter-in-law. "Let us hope that His sweet goodness will be father, mother, and all things to the little one that the dear departed has left."

Madame de Coulanges was a gentle guardian to her daughter's little girl. She taught her herself, she gave her wise and constant care, and we learn from one of Sainte-Chantal's letters that, at the early age of eight, she was presented for her first communion.

"The news you give me of that poor little orphan consoles me greatly," she writes to Philippe de Coulanges. "How happy she will be if God preserve you and my poor, very dear sister, to continue your wise and pious guidance! In truth I love that child as I loved her father, and all for God. I am rejoiced to hear that she is to communicate at Easter. I shall keep it well in mind, and pray God that at the reception of our sweet Saviour it will please Him to take entire possession of that little soul."

Scarcely two months after her first communion—that great

epoch in the life of a Roman Catholic child—little Marie de Chantal lost her pious and wise grandmother de Coulanges, who died in May 1634, at the age of fifty-seven, and was buried beside her daughter, the Baronne de Chantal, at the Convent of the Visitation in the Rue Saint-Antoine, one of those founded by the Blessed Chantal. Two years and a half later, Philippe de Coulanges, then an old man of seventy-five, was taken also, and Marie de Chantal, not yet eleven years old, was robbed by death of all her nearest kin. There was her paternal grandmother, Sainte-Chantal, it is true, but that holy woman, who had abandoned her own children for the love of God, was too absorbed by the duties of her Order to undertake the care of a young granddaughter, and never even saw her, though she came to Paris in 1641, at the command of Anne of Austria, while Marie de Chantal was a young girl.

Many years afterwards, Madame de Sévigné wrote to her daughter a brief confession of her spiritual difficulties. " I desire to be devout, but my mind is naturally worldly. . . . I am neither of God nor of the devil, and this state troubles me, though between ourselves I find it the most natural state in the world. One does not belong to the devil, because one fears God, and at bottom has the principles of religion; one does not belong wholly to God, because His laws are so strict, and no one loves self-denial."

In these days, when we place so much to the account of heredity, when we do not consider genius as a "sport" but regard it rather as the choicest flower of racial tendency, it is interesting to trace in two of Madame de Sévigné's immediate ancestors those well-defined, but opposing strains of devotion, and an intense joy in all the good gifts and pleasures of life. It is clear that from her father, the handsome, witty, gay and gallant courtier, she derived much that was brightest and most arresting in her genius, the qualities to which she herself gave the generic term, *Rabutinage.* But there was another side to her character that charmed the circle of friends who knew her best, a side which gives a peculiar *cachet* to her letters, which attracts the sympathy of her readers, which shows her to be truly human, most truly woman, as no mere hard brilliance of wit or felicity of phrase could ever have revealed her; which gives a softening, an atmosphere so to speak, to her letters and her life; that half mystic, half devotional instinct which she probably inherited from her famous grandmother, the " Blessed Chantal."

This well-known saint had a strange story. Jeanne Françoise Frémyot was the daughter of President Frémyot of the Parlement of Burgundy, a man of staunch moral and physical courage, who had been a valiant supporter of the King during the troublous times of the League. Christophe de Rabutin-Chantal, the grandfather of Madame de Sévigné, a Burgundian noble of ancient race, married her in 1592. Like all the Rabutins, he was brave, sarcastic, free of speech and life, with the habit of answering all adverse questions with the sword. He fought eighteen duels, but, strangely enough, he escaped all the perils of his numerous affairs of honour, to die, while out hunting, from a blow given accidentally by a friend. He was only thirty-seven when he died, leaving his widow with four children; three girls and one boy, Celse Bénigne, the youngest, who was then four years old.

Madame de Chantal went to live with her husband's father, Guy de Rabutin, and gave all her leisure to good works. At Bourbilly, a castle and estate which was part of Madame de Sévigné's inheritance, there is still shown a large oven where the pious widow used to bake the bread which she made for the poor with her own hands. At another place she was called the Saint of Monthelon, and there is no doubt that, but for her children, she would have become a *religieuse* on the death of her husband.

After some years of widowhood, Madame de Chantal had a vision in which she saw an ecclesiastic in soutane and rochet, who, she divined, was to be her spiritual director and guide.

Singularly enough, Saint Francis de Sales, while in retreat, preparing for his Lenten course, had a vision also, in which it was revealed to him that he was to be the founder of a new Order, and that a widow and certain others whom he saw were to be its first members.

When Madame de Chantal was at Dijon, staying with her

father for the Lenten season, she heard Saint Francis de Sales preach for the first time in her life, and immediately recognised him as the ecclesiastic who, in her vision, had been indicated as her spiritual guide. At the same time, Saint Francis, seeing the Baronne among his congregation, at once saw in her the widow who was to be the head of his new Order.

Could there be any doubt after this as to what would be the result? Her children were still young, and for some years longer she stayed with them. But in due time one of her daughters was married; the two other daughters took the veil; and her only son, Celse Bénigne, who was afterwards the father of Madame de Sévigné, was then fourteen. Madame de Chantal, all this time under the spiritual influence of Saint Francis, ever drawn with a more potent attraction towards the holy life, finally resolved to leave her son and her relatives, to found the new Order which the Bishop of Geneva had dreamed of years before.

She told her father of her intention, and the President asked her mildly, as he shed bitter tears—

"What, my dear daughter, does a father who has always loved you so well count for nothing? At least let me die before you go, then do as you will."

Her young son, the Baron de Chantal, did not take the news so calmly. He implored her with all the strength of his passionate nature not to desert him.

But the pious widow was firm. Doubtless she thought it more meritorious to establish convents for the glory of the Church than to stay in the world with her young son, and such a matter was between herself and God, however it might appear to human eyes and hearts.

The lad of fourteen, however, could listen to no reasons, could not be persuaded that any call, however holy, could take precedence of his crying need for his mother, and, beside himself with hot-hearted, boyish grief, he threw himself across the threshold, passionately declaring that if she went she would have to step over his body, vainly hoping that he might thus prevent her going. Her mother's heart must surely have been torn with anguish, but she did not swerve from her purpose. She left the house with her son's cries ringing in her ears, and from that time onward she cut herself adrift from her family, and steadfastly set her face towards the religious life. Under the direction of Saint Francis de Sales, she founded eighty-seven convents of the Order of the Daughters of the Visitation of Saint Mary.

Madame de Sévigné never saw her famous grandmother, but she always wrote with reverence and affection of her saintly and illustrious relative, and occasionally in jesting mood would refer to Saint Francis as her "spiritual grandfather." Whenever she was in grief or trouble, she would retire to the Convent of the Visitation in the Rue Saint-Antoine as to a home, and wherever she stayed as she travelled in France, she would always visit the Convent of the Visitation of Saint Mary if there happened to be one in the town. The Sisters, who respected her for her connection with their revered founder, called her "the living relic," and always gave her a cordial and affectionate welcome.

Madame de Chantal died at Moulins in one of the convents she had founded. Soon after her death a selection of her letters was published, and just one hundred years later she received the honours of canonisation and beatification.

CHAPTER II

A family council—The Abbé de Livry chosen as guardian of Marie de Rabutin-Chantal— Her life at the Abbaye —Walpole's "Notre Dame de Livry"— An amorous tutor—A shabby man of letters

THE little Marie de Rabutin-Chantal, now about ten years old, and "a beauty who attracted all hearts," as Madame de Guette tells us in her *Mémoires*, was orphaned indeed by the death of her grandfather. A family council was held for the purpose of choosing a guardian for the young Burgundian heiress, and it was then that her cousin, Roger de Rabutin, afterwards too well-known as the Comte de Bussy, played his first part, so to speak, in the drama of her life, in which he was so frequently and not always creditably an actor. His father, Léonor de Rabutin, was prevented by his affairs from attending the meeting of relatives, and Roger, then a handsome youth of eighteen, was sent as his representative.

Christophe, the second son of Philippe de Coulanges and consequently her mother's brother, was chosen as the child's guardian. He was the Abbé de Livry, a staid, grave young man of twenty-nine, as complete a contrast to her brilliant and reckless father, who would have been her natural protector, as could possibly be imagined. There was not a sparkle of wit, not a glint of humour among the whole range of his virtues. He had, in fact, not one of those dangerous and glittering qualities which were so conspicuous in the Rabutin ancestry, but the child could not have had a better guide and adviser, or one who was more wholly devoted to her interests. From that time forward, to the day of his death some fifty years later, he was her truest friend, her most reliable counsellor, and always an actively beneficent influence in her life. Circumstances had made him an abbé, vowed to the Church, but nature and inclination had surely destined him to be, like so many of his ancestors, "a gentleman of the long robe." He had an inborn passion for calculation, an intuitive caution in all business dealings, an innate probity of character, qualities which made him an excellent trustee of the property of the young heiress; indeed, he managed his niece's affairs so skilfully during her minority, that her wealth had increased considerably by the time she married.

Besides nursing her estates during her girlhood, and giving her the best advice on money matters after her marriage, he taught her to pay her debts with as much care and rectitude as if she had been nothing but a good and honest bourgeoise; he cultivated her intelligence so that she had a thorough knowledge of all business relating to her property; and he showed her how to regulate her expenses, and how to manage her own and her children's fortunes, in such a capable fashion, that her spendthrift cousin the Comte de Bussy sneered at her as being "too good a woman of business for a lady of quality."

Madame de Sévigné's wit, and genius, and charm came to her direct from nature, but there is little doubt that the wise guidance and counsel of the "Bien-Bon," as she always called her uncle, trained her faculties in the direction of prudence and wisdom, and instilled into her from youth that rectitude and probity which, in the Marquise, is so greatly a part of her many-sided, amazing charm. She often mocked affectionately at her uncle's love for *les beaux yeux de la cassette*, at his continual calculations, at his love for arithmetic; but she recognised nevertheless what a great part these very unromantic qualities had played in procuring the happiness of her life.

But his affectionate care was not all expended on her material interests. It is probable that for some time he educated her himself; then, as she grew older, he engaged two excellent masters, Chapelain and the Abbé Ménage, both men of high literary reputation, who gave her that solid and thorough education which proved a staunch support to the genius which afterwards found such matchless expression in her letters.

She studied Latin sufficiently "to be able," as she wrote, "to read Virgil in all the dignity of the text." "Italian," she says, "I have learned very well; thanks to the good masters I have had." And Ménage, who was a clever linguist, taught her Spanish, which was a quite fashionable language among the nobility, for was not the Spanish princess, Anne of Austria, Queen of France? Marie de Chantal also learned dancing, though, to the Rabutins, dancing was almost a natural instinct; and her voice was so well trained, that besides taking an intelligent interest in music, she sang "little Italian songs," which she loved for their passionate fervour. She acted delightfully in private theatricals; she composed little *chansons*; she had a keen and vivid interest in all current literature as well as in the works of the dead masters; and by her manners, as well as by her accomplishments, she grew up to be one of the most charming and distinguished women in a polished and world-renowned society.

It was, one cannot doubt, a new and absorbing interest in the life of the young and serious Abbé to watch the development of the mind and to train the amiable character of his lovely and intelligent little niece. The Abbaye de Livry still stands, hardly touched save by Time's defacing fingers, and it is not difficult to imagine the bright-eyed, fair-haired little Marie de Chantal, playing, studying, and laughing in the meadows and woods which lie around it, during the happy and healthful girlhood which she spent under the wise care of the Bien-Bon.

Horace Walpole, whose passionate admiration for the letters of Madame de Sévigné provoked the jealousy of his letter-writing friend Madame du Deffand, wrote to George Montagu, in 1766, describing a visit to this early home of "Notre Dame de Livry," as he calls the Marquise de Sévigné. It is of especial interest to those who have seen the Abbaye as it exists to-day, for the little pavilion that he mentions as having been built by the Abbé for his niece is no longer there.

" . . . Livry is situated in the Forêt de Bondi," he writes, "very agreeably, on a flat, but with hills near it, and in prospect. There is a great air of simplicity and rural about it, more regular than our taste, but with an old-fashioned tranquillity, and nothing of *colifichet*. Not a tree exists that remembers the charming woman, because in this country an old tree is a traitor, and forfeits its head to the crown; but the plantations are not young, and might very well be as they were in her time. The Abbé's house is decent and smug; a few paces from it is the sacred pavilion built for Madame de Sévigné by her uncle, and much as it was in her day; a small salon below for dinner, then an arcade, but the niches now closed, and painted in fresco with medallions of her, the Grignan, the Fayette, and the Rochefoucault. Above, a handsome large room, with a chimney-piece in the best taste of Louis the Fourteenth's time; a Holy Family in good relief over it, and the cipher of her uncle Coulanges; a neat little bed-chamber within, and two or three clean little chambers over them. On one side of the garden leading to the great road is a little bridge of wood, on which the dear woman used to wait for the courier that brought her daughter's letters. Judge with what veneration and satisfaction I set my foot upon it! If you will come with me to France next year, we will go and sacrifice on that sacred spot together."

This was written by Walpole about eighty years after the death of the Abbé de Coulanges, before the Revolution began its work of devastation among religious houses. Even now, more than two hundred years since Madame de Sévigné had any connection with Livry, this spot, where she spent some of the happiest hours of her life, is practically unchanged in all its broader aspects. The village of Livry, and the beautiful Forest of Bondi, have, it is true, in these days of easy communication become suburbs of Paris, and are now portioned out into gardens and smart villa residences, all asleep behind close-shut *persiennes* during the white glare of the burning summer sun. The tiny lake, in compliment to Walpole's "Dame de Livry," is called the Lac de Sévigné; the Abbé's house is alluringly but mistakenly described for the benefit of literary pilgrims as the "Demeure de Monsieur de Sévigné"; even the hostess of the little wine-shop a few yards from the lake gives voluble misinformation concerning the haunts of the illustrious lady whose memory bestows such distinction on the suburban village.

But happily the Abbaye, with its adjoining chapel, is some

distance away, and remains undisturbed in solitude and the peace of desolation. It is approached by a long avenue of trees, in which a tall crucifix stands half-hidden among the thick foliage. At the end of the avenue is the long, low house, with no striking architectural features, dismantled, falling into ruin, with nothing but painted wainscot walls and dusty floors to be seen through the closed windows, though, annexed to the east wing, is the chapel, kept in good repair and used for village service.

The pavilion mentioned by Walpole, to which she often came with her daughter and her dear friends, the Marquise de la Fayette and the Duc de la Rochefoucauld, as a refuge from the summer heat of Paris, has entirely disappeared; gone, too, is the little bridge of wood on which "the dear woman used to wait for the courier that brought her daughter's letters." Some straight and formal chestnut walks, however, remind one of her home at Les Rochers, and look as if at some time she may have planted their early predecessors; and though fruit-trees and fertile fields have taken the place of the lovely gardens that used to abut on the Forest of Bondi, the old house, set in its green solitude, is still eloquent of the presence of the serious Abbé and his beautiful young ward.

We hear strangely little of the Brothers who inhabited the Abbaye, and their days were probably too occupied with their devotions, too monotonous in their religious calm, to take much place in the life of the young girl whose thoughts and desires were trending towards the great world she was so soon to enter. But we get a glimpse of one Brother many years after this, which is almost the only indication we find that there was actually a Brotherhood of monks living in the Abbaye. In May 1672 the Marquise writes to her daughter: "Here is a very tragic story from Livry. Do you remember that pretended devotee who dared not turn his head? I said that it seemed as if he were carrying a glass of water on it. Devotion has turned his brain. One fine night he gave himself five or six stabs with a knife, and then fell on his knees in the middle of his room, naked, and covered with blood. Someone went in and found him in this state. 'Ah! Mon Dieu! brother, who has treated you thus?' 'My father,' he replied coldly, 'I am doing penance.' He then fainted, and was put to bed, and his wounds, which were dangerous, were dressed. With much care and attention he recovered at the end of three months, when he was sent back to his relatives at Lyons."

It was by no means a solitary life that the young girl led with her uncle the Abbé. Her aunt, Madame de Coulanges, would often visit Livry with her son, the little cousin Emmanuel, just eight years younger than Marie de Chantal, who was afterwards so witty, so gaily irresponsible, so incurably frivolous, that his friends all agreed that he never grew up to the end of his days. Other relatives came to visit the charming young orphan, and there were neighbours, too, who remained her friends all her life. Among these was Denis Saint-Pavin, whose father, the Prévôt des Marchands at Paris, was the seigneur of Livry. This young man, unfortunately a hunchback, was an intimate friend and welcome guest at the Abbaye, and as Marie de Chantal grew older he celebrated the young beauty in frequent verses. Both were young and gay-hearted, and evidently found much pleasure in the companionship; but Saint-Pavin had no hope of ever being any dearer than a friend. "I am her friend, but not her lover," he writes, and then whimsically points out the contrast between them. He extols her charms, and enumerates his own defects; his dwarf-like body, his long arms and legs, which, he says, cause him to be taken for a windmill.

Here too, to Livry, came Ménage and Chapelain, her tutors in languages and literature. The young Abbé Ménage, then in the early thirties, did more than give her lessons in Spanish and Italian, more than point out to her the beauties of the Italian poets; he lost his heart to his lovely young pupil, who, in addition to her complexion of cream-white and roses, her eyes sparkling with youth and genius, her shining masses of wavy fair hair, had a joyous wit and a brilliant intelligence that, by themselves, would have been a sufficiently dangerous charm. It is not surprising that the Abbé should be the humble and persistent worshipper of this young girl, just merging into the woman who was to fascinate and charm some of the bravest and wisest of the men of her generation; but his laughing pupil would never take his passion seriously. Perhaps, with those

THE ABBAYE DE LIVRY

clear-seeing eyes of hers, that put such a just value on most of the things that came across her vision, she divined that Ménage was one of those men—they are not all dead to-day!—who bring their worship to shrines that throw reflected glory on the devotee. Mesnard has truly said of him—

"It was the habit of Ménage to adore his pupils. He sighed by turns for Mademoiselle de Chantal and for Mademoiselle de la Vergne (who afterwards became Madame de la Fayette). He sang the praises of both in all languages. He loved them before and after their marriage, he loved them when they became widows."

Sometimes, as she grew older, there were little misunderstandings between master and pupil, and from two of her early letters to Ménage we gather that the Abbé had written her a sarcastic and wounding letter. But in her reply she shows such a frank amiability, such a desire of keeping his friendship, that he would have been a churl indeed to have resisted such friendly overtures.

"Once again," she writes, "I say to you that we do not understand each other. You have the good fortune to be eloquent, otherwise all that you have written to me would not be worth much, though it is wonderfully well put. I am not alarmed, however, and I feel my conscience so clear of all that you accuse me, that I have not lost the hope of compelling you to acknowledge my innocence. But this will be impossible if you will not visit me for half an hour, and I cannot understand why you so obstinately refuse to do this. I beg you once again to come and see me; if you will not come to-day, I entreat you to call to-morrow. If you will not come here, perhaps you will not close your door to me, and I shall follow you up so closely that you will be forced to admit you are in the wrong. You wish to make me appear ridiculous by saying that you have only quarrelled with me because you are sorry at my departure. If such were the case I should deserve *les Petites-Maisons* and not your hatred; but it is so different, and I cannot understand why, when losing a friend and regretting her, one should, because of that, treat her at the last interview with the utmost coldness. It is a most extraordinary way of behaving, and as I am not accustomed to it you must excuse my surprise. However, I beg you to believe that there is not one of the old or new friends of whom you speak that I esteem and love as I do you; this is why, before losing your friendship, that I beg you to give me the consolation of proving you to be in the wrong, and of saying that it is your affection that has ceased, CHANTAL"

Though this letter is signed " Chantal," it is thought by her biographers that it was probably written soon after her marriage, when the circle of her friends considerably increased, and that Ménage, accustomed to a very large share of her time and interest, was piqued at the division of his pupil's regard. The vanity of the Abbé was well known; has not Molière cruelly preserved him for all time as Vadius? but his pupil knew that beneath all his affectations there was a true and loyal heart, and she writes to him again on the same subject—

"It is you who have taught me to speak of our friendship as dead; as for me, caring for you as affectionately as I do, I should never have supposed it. Accuse yourself then of those disagreeable words which have so displeased you, and believe that I can have no greater joy than to know that you still feel for me the friendship which you promised me, and that it has had a glorious resurrection.—Adieu, CHANTAL"

But the young lady was not always so sweet and humble in her dealings with her tutor. Doubtless they were both fully aware of the wide social gulf between her rank and that of the man who had climbed into the great world up the ladder of literature. There was always in her treatment of Ménage a disregard of him as a possible lover, a sisterly and familiar attitude in which one might imagine her replying to any remonstrance, "Why, it is only Ménage!" an attitude that must have been peculiarly irritating to the vain young Abbé, whose weakness it was to pose as the adorer of charming ladies of rank, and who allowed neither her nor his friends to be ignorant of his passion for his lovely pupil.

The Comte de Bussy relates that one day after her

A WITTY RETORT

marriage, when she was driving out to make some purchases, her maid-companion was unable to come, and as it was not the custom then for a lady to drive out alone, she asked Ménage to accompany her, adding that she did not suppose anyone would remark on the circumstance.

The Abbé was deeply wounded at being treated so disdainfully, but Madame de Sévigné replied with scant ceremony—

"Get into my carriage, and if you are troublesome I shall come to see you at your house!"

Tallemant tells the story, that once, soon after her marriage, she kissed Ménage in the presence of several young gallants.

The young men were surprised, for though manners were very free at that period, and it was the usual custom to kiss the hostess and maids on arriving at an inn, this, they thought, was carrying the habit of kissing to an unusual limit.

Madame, seeing their astonishment, gaily explained her action.

"It was thus that they kissed in the primitive church!" she laughingly told them as she turned to go.

She was not even invariably submissive to him in his character of tutor, and on one occasion, having asked him how he was, Ménage replied, "Madame, je suis enrhumé."

"Je la suis aussi," answered Madame de Sévigné.

Ménage, who could not forget that she had been his pupil, conscientiously pointed out that, according to the rules of the language, she should have said "Je *le* suis."

"You may say it if you wish," she retorted with vivacity, "but if I said it like that I should think I had a beard on my chin!"

In spite, however, of her little impertinences to her tutor, which were usually the outcome of her vigorous and buoyant spirit, she had the utmost confidence in him, and sometimes told him of her most private affairs. Once, after a conversation of this kind, the Abbé, always anxious to edge in a little word of his devotion, remarked sentimentally—

"I am indeed your confessor, and have been your martyr."

"And I your virgin!" she promptly retorted.

It was during the first years of Madame de Sévigné's married life, when she was a popular and brilliant beauty in Parisian society, that Ménage was more than ever anxious to show his world on what familiar terms he was with his late pupil. He relates with a good deal of satisfaction that one day, at the Hôtel de Rambouillet, "I held one of Madame de Sévigné's hands in mine, and, when she had retired, M. Peletier said to me, 'There goes the finest work that ever came out of your hands!'"

Well might Madame de Sévigné treat his passion lightly, for he was evidently of the type who feel it a pleasing duty to be gallant to any lady in whose company they find themselves. But he had so advertised his passion for Madame de Sévigné that he occasionally received a lesson from ladies who were amused at his pretensions.

When the Marquise de Lavardin and he were both travelling in the same carriage to Brittany, on their way to visit Madame de Sévigné, Ménage, hoping to make himself agreeable, took one of her hands to kiss, doubtless adding some gallant little speech.

"Monsieur Ménage," said the Marquise laughingly, while drawing her hand away, "are you rehearsing for Madame de Sévigné?"

These anecdotes of Madame de Sévigné and her tutor indicate her greatest fault at this youthful, unformed period of her life, the only fault that even Tallemant des Réaux, the society spy, who set down all the failings, and faults, and mischances of his friends and enemies with such appalling industry, could find in the beautiful young Marquise,—a habit of brusque and thoughtless speech, which probably the wise and careful guidance of a mother might have pruned into gentleness. This want of a woman's training was, however, made up in some measure when she came under the influence of one of the most extraordinary women of her day, the Marquise de Rambouillet.

Her other tutor, Chapelain, was an entire contrast to the vain young Abbé Ménage, who dressed neatly and well in becoming black, and endeavoured to make the most of his personal charms in the eyes of the ladies he desired to please. Chapelain was an excellent scholar; he was in correspondence with most of the savants of Europe; and, as a literary guide, the young Mademoiselle de Chantal could not have had a better master. But his appearance was almost ludicrous; his chief passion was saving, and he probably thought good money wasted on clothes. Tallemant declares that he made a veritable sensation when he first visited the Hôtel de Rambouillet, wearing garments that looked as if they must have been purchased at the Marché de Friperie, a great gallery near the Halles, where second-hand finery was sold on Wednesdays and Saturdays by the Jews. His boots, said Tallemant, never matched each other, and were laced with string; his handkerchiefs were terrible, and his wigs were fit for nothing but to crown scarecrows. "I believe," wrote Tallemant with conviction, "that Chapelain never had anything absolutely new."

His long intercourse at the Hôtel de Rambouillet had probably taught him a few elementary lessons in the art of dress before he became the tutor of Mademoiselle de Chantal, but to the end of his life he always had the miser's deep-rooted objection to squandering money on clothes. In spite of this, however, he gained much respect by his literary attainments, and was held in honour by the habitués of the Hôtel de Rambouillet; and for twenty years at least he was looked on as a great poet, who, when he should publish his poem, *La Pucelle*, would be celebrated wherever the French language was spoken. Unfortunately, he was one day persuaded to publish *La Pucelle*, and then the lovely Duchesse de Longueville, who, for no especial reason except her beauty perhaps, was considered quite an authority on literature, said out loud the heresy that others only dared to whisper: "It is doubtless a charming poem," said the young Duchesse, "but isn't it rather wearisome?"

CHAPTER III

Her "portrait" by the Marquise de la Fayette—The young Burgundian heiress is betrothed to Henri, Marquis de Sévigné—The bridegroom fights a duel and is dangerously wounded—An old chateau in Brittany—The furniture of Madame de Sévigné's room—The birth of Françoise Marguerite de Sévigné

FOR eight happy years Marie de Rabutin-Chantal had been the cherished ward and companion of her uncle at Livry, when he decided to give her in marriage to a suitable husband. So many of the young girls of her day were married at sixteen, or earlier, that one may consider it part of the wisdom of the good Abbé in all that concerned his niece that he had not chosen to establish her sooner. It certainly was not because of a lack of suitors. Marie de Chantal was not faultlessly beautiful, with regular features and perfect contours, but she had in full measure that first exquisite bloom of girlhood which the French, with their love of paradox, so falsely call *beauté du diable*.

Years afterwards, her cousin Bussy, when describing her in a fit of pique, gave a detailed list of her imperfections, with a searching after malicious truth that would have been fatal to any but the most mathematically correct beauty of feature. He dwelt at length on her nose, which was "square at the tip"; he pointed out that her eyelids were "mottled"; that the pupils of her eyes were of different colours; that, like her forehead, her jaw was too square; but he was compelled in honesty to acknowledge that "she had the most beautiful complexion in the world, fresh and rosy lips, an exquisite figure, and thick wavy fair hair."

But how misleading is a catalogue of a woman's perfection or imperfection of feature! Is it not a truism that the elusive quality called "charm" can irradiate a plain face into something more alluring than beauty, while the lack of it leaves perfect features a mere dull mask of cold inanity? Contemporary evidence assures us repeatedly that Madame de Sévigné, without regular beauty, was one of the most singularly charming and attractive women of her day. She herself, with too much good sense to be vain, makes one light allusion to her appearance, when in after years, as a grandmother, she might speak of her attractions in the past tense. "People used to say I was very pretty," she once wrote to her daughter, which was an exceedingly modest way of referring to the numberless flattering things that had been said and sung of her.

Her defects might be catalogued, but it was more difficult to translate adequately her charm into words, it was so much the inexpressible attraction of innate grace of mind and joyousness of spirit, in addition to her distinctive personal beauties. Fifteen years later, when she was thirty-three, her friend the Marquise de la Fayette wrote this pen-portrait of her, and from it we gather at least an impression of her vivid and lovable personality. Madame de la Fayette, wishing to mystify her friend, sends her the portrait, pretending that it is from "l'Inconnu," the Unknown Gentleman.

"All those who attempt to paint pretty women take infinite pains to flatter them in order to please, without daring to mention a single word of their defects. But I, Madame, thanks to the privilege of being unknown to you, shall paint you with a bold hand, and tell you the truth without fear of incurring your anger. . . .

"I do not wish to overwhelm you with compliments, or to waste time by telling you that your figure is admirable, that your complexion has a bloom and beauty which assures us you are only twenty; that your mouth, your teeth, your hair are unrivalled. I will not point out these things to you, because your mirror will tell you them equally well, but as you do not fritter away your time in consulting it, it cannot tell you how charming you are when you speak, and this is what I must reveal to you.

"Know then, Madame, if by chance you do not know it already, that your mind so greatly adorns and beautifies your person, that there is nothing on earth so charming as you when you are animated by conversation from which constraint is banished. All that you say has such a charm, and is in such harmony, that your words attract the smiles and graces round you; the sparkle of your wit gives such a brilliance to your complexion and to your eyes, that though it appears that wit should reach only the ears, it is certain that yours dazzles the eyes, so that as we listen to you we forget that your features lack regularity, and we declare that you are the most perfect beauty in the world. . . .

"Your mind is great and noble, formed to dispense wealth, and incapable of the baseness of hoarding it. You love glory and ambition, and you love pleasures equally well; you seem to have been born for them, and they appear to have been made for you; your presence adds to diversion, and diversion increases your beauty. In short, joy is the natural state of your soul, and nothing is more contrary to you than sorrow. . . . You are by nature tender and passionate; your heart, Madame, is doubtless a treasure that no one could deserve; never was there one so generous, so true, and faithful. . . . You are the most courteous and obliging person that ever was known, and by the frank and sweet manner which is shewn in all your actions, the simplest compliments of good-breeding when said by you have the air of protestations of friendship; and all who leave your presence are persuaded of your esteem and goodwill without being able to explain what proof you have given them of either. In short, Heaven has endowed you with charms such as have never been given to any other person, and the world is under an obligation to you for having exhibited so many agreeable qualities which were never before known. I will not begin to describe them, else I should be breaking my resolve not to overwhelm you with praise, and furthermore, Madame, to say of you what is worthy, I ought to be your lover, and that I have not the honour to be!"

Under the somewhat tedious formality of the "portrait" we gather an impression, at least, of Madame de Sévigné's unusual charm, and if this is how she appeared in the eyes of her friends at the age of thirty-three, can we not imagine something of the brilliance of her presence when heightened by the exquisite unconsciousness of dawning womanhood, the freshness and delicate bloom of eighteen? In addition to her dazzling complexion, her perfect mouth and teeth, her masses of shining fair hair, and blue eyes that sparkled with goodwill, wit, and gaiety, her whole personality was tingling with joyous life to the finger-tips, and she possessed an extraordinary charm of manner "which persuaded everyone of her esteem and goodwill," a social gift in itself of the first importance.

Besides these attractions of mind and person, she had other charms which often count for so much in marriage, and in French marriage especially. Her *dot* amounted to one hundred thousand crowns, equal in modern money, it is said, to £24,000, in addition to which she had valuable expectations that ultimately came to £16,000 more. This Burgundian heiress had, in truth, "all the attractions," for she was also of an ancient and honourable race. Near Samur was Bourbilly, an old castle which she inherited, with the title of Dame de Bourbilly, from the Rabutin family, who could trace their ancestry back to the twelfth century. "I yield to the Montmorenci for honours, but the family is not of earlier date than ours," wrote Bussy de Rabutin with his inflated pride, at which her nobler spirit was occasionally a little scornful.

It has been thought a little strange that Bussy should not have at least asked for his cousin in marriage. He frankly tells us in his memoirs that his father was anxious for him to marry the young heiress, as her wealth would have been particularly welcome to his impoverished branch of the Rabutins. The gasconading Bussy gives us clearly to understand that though he was poor his personal attractions were of no mean calibre.

"Roger de Rabutin," he writes of himself, apparently without a blush, "had large soft eyes, a well-formed mouth, a large and nearly aquiline nose, a pleasing expression, and fair waving light hair." Though he could so minutely analyse his cousin's shortcomings, there was not a word of any defect in his own "portrait," but he might with truth have added that an absolutely unscrupulous disposition, allied to the most shameless hardihood, marred not only his character, but even the expression of his handsome face.

Notwithstanding his father's wishes, he made no offer for his cousin's hand. Long after, it pleased him to write that "he thought her the most charming woman in the world to be the wife of another." And he may have been quite sincere when he says that her light-hearted gaiety, so attractive to other men, would have been a source of disquiet to him had he married her. It is to be feared that to faithless husbands like himself no attractions, save those of the most dove-like domesticity, would have been entirely safe from suspicion. It is quite probable, also, that their very similarity of tastes, wit, and intellect made the two cousins unsuited to each other, for does not perfect marriage always demand dissimilarity? It might be, too, that the Bien-Bon, so watchful of his niece's interests, so clear-sighted in all that concerned her well-being, did not encourage the Comte de Bussy, who, just a year before Marie de Chantal's marriage, was united to another cousin, Gabrielle de Toulongeon.

While the Abbé de Coulanges was looking for a suitable alliance for his niece, Paul de Gondi, the Coadjutor of the Archbishop of Paris, and afterwards so notorious as the Cardinal de Retz, made overtures to the Bien-Bon on behalf of his young nephew, Henri, the Marquis de Sévigné. After due consideration, the Abbé thought it would be a suitable marriage. The connection with a powerful noble like Gondi counted for much, and de Sévigné was young, good-looking, with a substantial inheritance, and a descent that was entirely satisfactory. When Bussy, in exile, was occupying his leisure in making a family-tree, Madame de Sévigné sent these concise facts of her husband's ancestry—

"Fourteen contracts of marriage from father to son; three hundred years of chivalry; the fathers sometimes of considerable importance in the wars of Brittany and of distinction in its history; sometimes living at home as good Bretons; sometimes having great wealth, sometimes with only moderate possessions, but always making great and good alliances. In three hundred and fifty years, beyond which we can only find their Christian names, are du Quelnec, Montmorency, Baraton, and Château-giron. These are great names, and the women of these families married des Rohan and des Clisson. Since these four there are des Guesclin, des Coetquen, des Rosmadec, des Clindon, and des Sévigné of their own house. . . . "

Documents remain which show that the young Marquis owned considerable property; and when he came to sign the marriage settlement at the house of d'Ormesson, the family lawyer, who was also a connection of the bride through the de Coulanges, her relatives, greatly interested in the future husband of their charming young connection, remarked that "he was a fine cavalier of good figure, and apparently witty as well."

The arrangements for the marriage were interrupted by an occurrence that was not particularly auspicious for the bride's future happiness. The marriage contract was drawn up on the 27th of May 1644, but the signing of it was postponed by a quarrel, in which the hot-headed young Marquis was the chief offender. Henri de Sévigné, on the eve of his wedding, so to speak, whilst walking on the Pont Neuf met a young Breton, Paul Hay, du Chastellet, who, he had heard, had been saying certain things to his discredit. Without a moment's thought of his position as bridegroom, he struck du Chastellet with the flat of his sword. In any place there would have been but one answer to such an insult, but on the Pont Neuf, one of the most public thoroughfares of Europe, crowded like a daily fair, the affront was peculiarly irritating, and a meeting was at once arranged. They met soon after, and de Sévigné was wounded in the thigh, so severely that his life was for some time in danger, and it was not till the month of July that the marriage contract could be signed.

On the 4th of August 1644 the religious ceremony took place in the church of Saint-Gervais-et-Saint-Protais at two o'clock in the morning. The ceremony was performed by a relative, a nephew of Sainte-Chantal, Jacques de Neuchèze, Bishop and Count of Chalon-sur-Saône, who gave the bride a wedding-gift of ten thousand crowns.

Shortly after the marriage the Marquis took his young wife with him to Les Rochers, his estate in Brittany, which was to become such a dearly-loved home of the Marquise. In these days of swift and luxurious travelling we can only with an effort realise what discomfort and impedimenta were inseparable from a long journey in the seventeenth century. There were comparatively few inns in provincial France, and these were almost inconceivably bare of furniture and the necessaries of life. When the Queen Regent, Anne of Austria, was wandering in the provinces with the young King during the upheaval of the

Fronde, she came to an inn where there was no bed, and as her own had not arrived, she had to sit on the only chair the place could provide, her aching head supported by one of her ladies of honour! Every person of quality in those days carried his own bed while travelling, and this was generally strapped upon a pack-horse or mule. In addition to the travelling carriage for the seigneur and madame his wife, another carriage had to be provided for dependants and waiting-women, so that, with postillions, the whole cavalcade made quite a gay procession as it whirled swiftly along through the dull country villages and provincial towns.

The young Marquis and his wife were probably about eight or ten days on the road to Les Rochers, the nearest town to which was then, as now, the quaint little Vitré, which still contains several streets whose houses remain apparently untouched since Madame de Sévigné saw them as a bride, though probably they were then in better repair. The four and a half miles from thence to the chateau has not been greatly changed since her day, though on each side there were dense woods and plantations where there are now cultivated fields, bordered by cider-apple trees and chestnuts.

The Chateau of Les Rochers is situated in a thickly wooded country, sloping away in dark green hollows and rising again in green crests. The tiny church on a distant hill,—where Charles de Sévigné was baptized,—looks like a toy building half smothered in foliage. The chateau was already three hundred years old when Madame de Sévigné was first taken there, and in externals, at least, is not greatly altered to-day.

Did those gloomy forests, where wolves and other wild animals had their haunts, look somewhat savage and forbidding to the eyes of the young girl who had been brought up amid the gracious and cultivated beauty of the gardens and meadows of Livry? There is no record of her first impressions, but we know that it became one of her greatest pleasures, almost a passion indeed, to lay out gardens and to plant allées. "I have bought land, to which I have said, as usual, I shall convert you into a park," she once wrote to her cousin Bussy; and in her letters from Les Rochers she makes constant reference to her improvements on the estate; her labyrinth, her mall, and the

HENRI, MARQUIS DE SÉVIGNÉ

many walks to which she gave the names of her best loved friends.

Fortunately for the literary pilgrim who finds a satisfaction in seeing the *entourage* of Madame de Sévigné, her bed-chamber at the chateau has been left as it was when she occupied it, and passing over the threshold we step at once into the seventeenth century. On entering, the eye is struck by the date 1644 in brass letters over a door, which reminds us that this was the year in which she was brought here as a bride. A portrait of her father hangs just above the date; not a good painting, but it gives an indication of the wild and reckless spirit of that dashing cavalier, with just a soupçon of wistful regret underlying the painted bravado, as if his better self were conscious of wasted opportunities.

The bed, which is a half-tester, is especially interesting, for the faded hangings of biscuit-coloured silk, and the coverlet to match, are said to have been embroidered by Madame de Grignan, the idolised daughter of the Marquise; and the pale-tinted, delicate arabesques, leaves, flowers, and birds, carry us back to the far-away days when patient stitchery was the chief outlet for woman's talent of every kind. Opposite to the bed is the huge open fireplace with big brass dogs and irons, and in the slab of polished granite forming the arch of the mantel are three large Roman capitals in mosaic, M. R. C. (Marie Rabutin-Chantal.)

As we look at the appointments of the room, we are reminded how scarce and costly was furniture in the days when Louis Quatorze was king. Not only did private individuals carry their beds and toilet necessaries from town to country house, but even the royal family, when they journeyed from the Louvre to Saint-Germain, carried beds and cooking utensils; guests, though of the most exalted rank, were expected to bring their own; and when, after a time, the natural taste for luxury and ostentation of Louis XIV caused him to provide furnished rooms for certain privileged courtiers, his thrifty minister Colbert felt very serious at this unheard-of extravagance!

For a marquise, a lady of great position, with wealth and large estates, the little draped toilet-table looks singularly unpretending. The toilet set, too, of red lacquer, painted, not very artistically, with groups of flowers, is modest to the point of shabbiness; the looking-glass, in red-lacquer frame, would hardly be considered adequate for the waiting-woman of a marquise to-day; and the two upright brass candlesticks remind us of the semi-gloom in which people of the seventeenth century, in the provinces at least, passed the dark months of the year. On a tall chest of drawers are all that remain of her washing accessories—most probably all there were—a pewter ewer holding perhaps two pints of water, and one of those quaint porcelain vessels of beautiful old Breton pottery—rarely seen even in museums to-day—the front part barrel-shaped, the back flat for hanging close to the wall, holding perhaps a gallon or so of water. A shallow, stoup-like basin beneath served for washing bowl, into which the water was turned from the upper part of the vessel by a rudimentary tap.

A few old chairs of beautiful forms are standing about the room, most of them covered with tapestry whose colours are fresh and vivid; her ink-stand is kept in a glass-case, and near it is an account-book, very neatly kept, of some of her gardening expenses, but it is not in her own handwriting. Perhaps the most interesting part of the whole room is the deep recess near the window, in which she so often sat while she was penning those charming letters to her daughter and her many friends. We know, too, that she must frequently have laid down her pen to step out on to the terrace among the fragrant orange trees which still stand as they were in her day, or to wander yet farther among those formal gardens laid out by Le Nôtre, which she loved with such a genuine passion; or to muse, perchance, by her sun-dial on the happy hours it once recorded for her. "There are some pleasant recollections," she once wrote of Les Rochers, "but there are some so vivid and tender that one can hardly bear them."

But she had no mournful musings, no painful memories when her young husband brought her to his ancestral home as its mistress. The future was all theirs, a bright alluring future in tints of gold and *couleur de rose*. Both were young, of a joyous and happy disposition; they had wealth, a great name, and good health to enjoy the gifts with which Fortune had so generously dowered them. For the first two years after their

THE BIRTH OF FRANÇOIS DE SÉVIGNÉ 33

marriage they rarely visited Paris, spending most of their time in the solitude of Brittany, perhaps planning improvements and alterations, as is the custom of the newly wed; and, besides visiting their friends and country neighbours, making the acquaintance of their retainers and peasantry—those uncouth, primitive Bretons whose very language she did not understand, but to whom she was, one cannot doubt, a kind and gracious Lady Bountiful.

The first definite news we get of them is in March 1646, when her cousin Bussy and his friend Lenet, just preparing for a campaign, wrote a joint letter, in verse, imploring Sévigné and his wife not to waste the best years of their life among country neighbours, and begging them to come to Paris to their many friends again. In the autumn of the same year the Marquis and his wife did return to Paris, to their house in the Rue des Lions, where, on the 10th of October 1646, about two years after their marriage, their first child was born, Françoise Marguerite de Sévigné, the daughter to whom the Marquise wrote those wonderful letters which have gained for her a place among the world's men and women of genius.

The de Sévignés were kept in Paris for some time by a lawsuit, but they were quite willing and eager to enjoy the delights of the capital after their long sojourn in Brittany. The Marquise had indeed, till then, seen very little of the gay town since her marriage.

These were the few halcyon years before the storm of the Fronde. Anne of Austria, guided by the clever Mazarin in her state policy, brought up with pious care the handsome boy-king and his little brother the Duc d'Anjou. Never was the idle world of Paris more tranquil, more gaily devoted to simple pleasures. Daily drives along the Cours-la-Reine, the excitements of the Foire Saint-Germain from Epiphany to Lent; suppers, balls, and occasional comedies; these formed the amusements of wealthy aristocrats; and the Marquis and his young wife, then scarcely more than twenty, were welcomed in the best society. Besides their many friends, two of their relatives were influential officials in the great world: Gondi the Coadjutor, who was on the eve of greater power and notoriety, the relative of the Marquis; and the brusque Hughes de Rabutin, the Grand Prieur of the

Temple, the uncle of Madame de Sévigné, whom her husband used to call, presumably in private, "my uncle the Pirate."

"It was the time of polished conversation, of gallantry, and, in a word, of that which they called the *ruelles*," wrote Saint-Simon of this period; and it was in this atmosphere of old-world gallantry and polite conversation that Madame de Sévigné's talent was developed, that her mind and manners were formed. It was then that, as a young married lady, she was first introduced to a salon famous in the history of French literature, famous, indeed, in the polite society of Europe, the world-renowned salon of Madame de Rambouillet.

CHAPTER IV

The Hôtel de Rambouillet, the pioneer of Parisian salons—The Marquise de Rambouillet — A lady's bed-chamber in the seventeenth century — Julie d'Angennes — *La Guirlande de Julie* — A polished society of *précieux et précieuses*—The Duchesse de Longueville—Mademoiselle de Scudéry

"I HAVE still something remaining of that fine manner which made me a précieuse," once wrote Madame de Sévigné to her daughter from Les Rochers in the depths of Brittany, to prove that she had not lost all the polish of Paris by living for some time in the provinces.

This title of Précieuse, which, after Molière had delighted Paris with *Les Précieuses Ridicules* and *Les Femmes Savantes*, became a word for scorn and laughter, was, in the early days of Madame de Sévigné's married life, the highest commendation that could be bestowed on a woman. It represented delicacy of mind, of manners, of morals; the polished ease which can only be acquired in good society; and an extreme refinement of language and expression, which afterwards, in the *mauvaises ruelles*, as Madame de Sévigné called them, degenerated into affectation and all the mincing absurdities recognised under the name of "preciosity." When Scarron praised Mademoiselle de la Vergne to her mother, he called her *toute lumineuse, toute précieuse*; Mademoiselle de Mancini was called *la perle des précieuses*; and Madame de Sévigné was, as we have seen, like many another of her contemporaries, proud of her claim to the title.

At this time the headquarters, so to speak, of these *précieuses*, was the Hôtel de Rambouillet, in the Rue Saint-Thomas du Louvre, not far from the Tuilleries. It was the pioneer of Parisian salons, and without question the most celebrated in French social history. From 1630 till the year 1648, when the Fronde practically closed its doors, it was the centre, not merely of the literary and artistic life of Paris, but of its most polished social intercourse; and its mistress, under a sweet and exquisitely cultivated grace of manner, ruled her subjects with a charming and imperious power to which they were all willingly submissive.

The salon of the Hôtel de Rambouillet is so singularly interesting because of the coarse and dark background of manners and morals from which it gleams like a picture of fine-woven, many-coloured tapestry. In its early beginnings France was only just emerging from the primitive days of chivalry. Almost every gentleman was a soldier, more accustomed to life in camp than in court, with an absolute scorn for all intellectual accomplishments. An "Academy" then meant a riding-school; and the sons of gentlemen were taught how to ride well, to be adepts in the use of the sword, to play at running the ring, at mall, or at tennis, and if they excelled in these accomplishments their education was thought to be complete. The Prince de Condé, nephew of Henri IV, was considered quite exceptional, because, in addition to all these bodily exercises, he had his two young sons taught Latin; educated well, in short, especially the Prince de Conti; who was brought up at the College of Clermont.

But civilisation was gradually evolving by its usual and natural processes, and while the great Richelieu, under Louis XIII, was devoting his energies to the curtailment of the feudal power of the turbulent nobles, the salon of Madame de Rambouillet became the centre of an intellectual and social influence whose far-reaching effects it would be impossible to calculate. It was the splendid dawn of a recognised homogeneous society in Paris which reached its zenith in the latter half of the eighteenth century. It must not be forgotten that though Paris under Louis XIV was foremost among the cities of Europe in all the elegancies and arts of refined civilisation, yet, in the early days of the seventeenth century, Italy and Spain were far ahead of her in these respects. Spain had already formulated its code of strict and immutable etiquette, and Italy was the home of art and letters, and of a polished delicacy in matters of gallantry as yet unknown in France.

And it was from Italy that the young Marquise de Rambouillet brought her inherited taste for letters, art, and all the refinements of civilised life. Catherine de Vivonne was the only daughter of the Marquis de Pisani, who, while ambassador at Rome, married Julia de Savelli, a lady of the illustrious house that had given popes and cardinals to the Church. Their daughter was born at Rome, and in 1600, at the age of twelve, was married to Charles d'Angennes, Marquis de Rambouillet.

Her life in Paris that followed, fashioned in a large measure by herself, reads like that of a princess in some impossible fairy-tale. By the time she was twenty she had grown tired of the coarse and licentious society of the Court of Henri IV, and with that determination which was not the least conspicuous of her remarkable qualities, she decided to withdraw herself in a measure from the world, to devote herself to her family, and to the cultivation of art and letters in a society with tastes similar to her own.

As a beginning, the young Marquise built for herself a beautiful dwelling. She had inherited the Hôtel de Pisani from her father, and as this was dilapidated and falling into ruin, she had the old house pulled down and another mansion erected on its site from her own designs. In this new building the stairs were placed in an angle, suites of rooms opened from one into the other, and windows of the pattern that we now call French windows let in light and air in a manner that had hitherto been unimagined in Paris. The grounds stretched away to the Tuilleries, and, though they were in the midst of Paris, were so large that the neighbouring gardens did not disturb the privacy of the Hôtel de Rambouillet.

The furniture of this remarkable house was the choicest that could be designed or procured. Just as in our own dark days red rep curtains represented the highest height of the upholsterer's imagination in draperies, so, in the dawn of the seventeenth century, brown or red hangings were considered the only possible mode in France. But the original young Italian lady changed all that in her own house at least. The Blue Salon of the Hôtel de Rambouillet became nearly as celebrated as its beautiful and cultivated mistress. The Blue

Chamber was the bedroom of the Marquise (the "sanctuary of the Temple of Athene" her visitors called it), who, suffering from a malady that made excessive heat, whether of sun or fire, unbearable, was obliged to spend a great part of the day in the cool seclusion of her room; and on this, which was her reception chamber also, she lavished the costliest and most elegant decoration. Blue silk draperies shaded the windows, for, as a poet of the time remarked, ladies had discovered that the clear, untempered light of day was not too becoming to their complexions; the arm-chairs, the chairs without arms, and the stools or tabourets, were upholstered in blue velvet; finely-worked inlaid cabinets, wrought perhaps by those cunning Italian artificers whom Marie de Medicis had brought to Paris, made a dignified decoration for the room; and rare tapestries, Venetian lamps, pictures, and fresh flowers in exquisite crystal vases, gave to the salon an elegance and distinction that had till then been undreamed of in Paris.

A lady's bedroom in the seventeenth century was a singularly important part of the house. It was there that she often received her visitors, not necessarily in bed, though if she had the slightest ailment, or even only a fit of indolence, she would welcome her friends of both sexes from among her pillows with as little embarrassment as if she were receiving them in the garden. These bedrooms were frequently divided into two parts by a balustrade, in the fashion that may still be seen in the chamber of Louis XIV at Versailles. The bed, placed in the middle of the wall, had thus a space on each side—spaces that were called *ruelles*, a word in constant use during the seventeenth century. On one side, ladies interviewed their servants, or persons who came on business; the other was reserved for their closest intimates, or people they most delighted to honour. Occasionally the *ruelle* would be formed into an "alcove," Spanish fashion, by means of columns that reached from floor to ceiling, which made a still more private bower than that enclosed by the mere balustrade; and frequently in contemporary literature the ladies who received in their bedrooms are referred to as "*alcôvistes*." People who gossiped were said to be talking *à la ruelle*, for all the news of the town circulated through the *ruelles*, just as, a century later, current events were discussed in the salons. Madame de Sévigné, as we shall see, had her *ruelle*, and she was a constant visitor to that of La Grande Mademoiselle, who, because she was a Princess of the Blood, had her bedstead raised on an *estrade*, and ladies who came to pay their respects knelt on the steps leading up to her bed, "to kiss hands" as the phrase went.

The celebrated Blue Room was divided by gilded columns which reached from floor to ceiling. The vault of this alcove was decorated with allegorical pictures representing Love, Marriage, Summer, and Study. The blue draperies, the elegant furniture, the unusual adornments of the room, gave Madame de Rambouillet's guests a naïve surprise, it was all so new, so delightfully unlike anything they had ever seen before; and we must not forget that society was then in its fresh, early youth, and had neither lost the faculty of being surprised, nor adopted the worn dictum of Solomon that nothing is new under the sun.

There is no picture remaining of the mistress of this "Temple of Honour," as Bayle called it, but we gather from the evidence of her guests and friends that, besides being a beautiful and graceful woman, born for social empire, she had a singularly well-balanced mind, which so harmonised her various gifts that there is nothing distinctive by which to remember her; she remains a gracious presence, an inspiring influence, an embodiment in her own person and life of the beauty she so passionately worshipped with her beauty-loving, Italian nature. "She was revered, adored," said Madame de Motteville, "a model of courtesy, wisdom, knowledge, and sweetness." Segrais, a poet who was very intimate with Madame de Sévigné, writes of her: "She was amiable and gracious, of a sound and just mind; it was she who corrected all the bad customs which were common before her time. She taught politeness to all those of her period who frequented her house. She was also a good friend, and kind to everyone." Mademoiselle de Scudéry tells us, in one of the rhapsodical "portraits" brought into fashion by her facile and sentimental pen, that Madame de Rambouillet "is tall and her figure is excellent; all the features of her face are perfect; the delicacy of her complexion cannot be expressed, the dignity of her person is worthy of admiration, and from her eyes beam I know not what fire, which imprints respect in the mind of all those who behold it."

The Marquise de Rambouillet had seven children, but of these only two were associated with her in her salon. These daughters, Julie and Angélique, shared their mother's social duties and pleasures, while adding to the many attractions of their home. The more celebrated of these was Julie, the elder, who was, says Cousin, "without being absolutely beautiful, the most perfectly finished feminine type of the period." No woman, said a contemporary, had been so praised or sung since Helen of Troy. Her manners were so sweet, so amiable, so caressing, that all the many minor poets who frequented her mother's salon were inspired to write *chansons* or madrigals on the fair Julie. She charmed women as well as men. The Marquise de Sablé, herself a clever and remarkable woman, said that she could imagine no greater happiness on earth than to spend her life with Julie d'Angennes. The beautiful Anne de Bourbon, sister of the great Condé, and afterwards so well known as the Duchesse de Longueville, was her intimate and affectionate friend, and when she had the small-pox it was the courageous and devoted Julie who nursed her. But this graceful and winning girl refused the many suitors who sighed in vain for her. It was her opinion, and that of many others, that there was nowhere such a paradise on earth as the Hôtel de Rambouillet. One, however, among her suitors, persistently refused to take no for an answer. The Marquis de Montausier met her when she was in the full bloom of her beautiful girlhood, at the age of twenty-four, and for long years he urged his suit in vain. Eventually she accepted him, at the age of thirty-eight, when the fairest bloom of her youth was long past, because urged to do so by her mother, who probably thought it was time for her daughter to be established in life. It was to this patient, adoring suitor that the world of book-lovers owes that literary curiosity, *La Guirlande de Julie.* It is composed of nineteen leaves of parchment, and on each is a flower exquisitely painted by Robert, with a verse beneath written in praise of the fair Julie by the Marquis de Montausier and other gallants who frequented her mother's *ruelle.* It is interesting to note that

Angélique, the other daughter of Madame de Rambouillet who remained "in the world," married the Comte de Grignan, who afterwards married as his third wife the daughter of the Marquise de Sévigné.

How interesting would have been a glimpse into this famous salon at the time when the young Marquis and Marquise de Sévigné were introduced there after their marriage! In the mornings — for it was then that Madame de Rambouillet frequently received—the most distinguished ladies and gentlemen of the Court, as well as the most clever and famous men of letters, would assemble in the celebrated Blue Room. The ladies, clustering round their hostess in the beautifully decorated alcove, would be seated according to their rank on arm-chairs, chairs without arms, or tabourets, all toying with tiny canes, which, let it be whispered, was a little affectation *à la précieuse*! The gentlemen, in embroidered coats, with curls falling on their lace collars, would throw their rich cloaks on the floor, and, seating themselves in the most approved attitudes of gallantry, would trifle with the big plumes in their hats, while they gaily repeated the last new story from Court, criticised the last new play, or made an impromptu *chanson*, epigram, or *bon mot*, which would be quickly repeated from mouth to mouth with laughter and approval. Beyond the balustrade the less intimate or less important visitors walked about or sat on tabourets; abbés, poets, literary men, who held no brevet of rank save the uncertain and fluctuating rank bestowed by intellect. Chief among the visitors was the beautiful Princesse de Condé, who, though a Princess of the Blood, and forbidden by Court etiquette to visit anyone beneath the rank of duchess, made an exception to this rule in favour of Madame de Rambouillet. She had brought her lovely daughter Anne de Bourbon since girlhood, and this royal lady, world-renowned afterwards as the Duchesse de Longueville, was, among those fair women, the most supreme, triumphant beauty. She had been married only a year before Madame de Sévigné, and was then in the most brilliant prime of her dazzling loveliness, which Voiture poetically declared was made of "stars and pearls and flowers." Her large eyes of turquoise blue, the extraordinary white fairness of her complexion, her masses of silvery blonde hair, gave an ethereal look to the young Duchess who became so celebrated in the Fronde, and all her loveliness was heightened by a languorous grace which was one of her most potent charms. A few years before, she had passionately desired to vow herself to a religious life; all her thoughts were turned towards devotion, till one evening she was induced to go to a ball. She was a vision of loveliness on that, for her, fateful evening; and as she entered the room all eyes were turned towards the young beauty who looked so ethereal, so angelic in her brilliant fairness; and as she danced it may be safely assumed that more than one cavalier found the courage to tell her so. When she left the ballroom that evening, she trod on air, she was intoxicated with the new-found power of her beauty. Nothing more was said of a life of devotion; all such thoughts and aspirations were choked and hidden under the most worldly ambitions, till, years later, after having sinned and suffered, and wrought incalculable harm to her country, she strove to expiate her sins among the Carmelites.

Her husband was more than twice her age, but his rank was only one degree below that of the Condé family, and by a special privilege it was arranged that the young Duchess should keep all the prerogatives of her position as Princess of the Blood. It mattered not at all that hers was a loveless marriage, from which a host of evils to herself and others was to be the result, for rank was the most superlatively important question of the day, as may easily be gathered from the memoirs of Saint-Simon.

She was not the only victim in her own family of this arrogant pride of position. Even the great Condé, her elder brother, who everyone declared was a modern Cæsar; who vanquished the enemies of his country at Rocroy when a mere youth; before whose wonderful military genius armies fell defeated and dismayed; even he was forced to yield to his father in the matter of marriage. It was probably in the salon of Madame de Rambouillet that he met the gentle and charming Mademoiselle du Vigean, whom he learned to love with the ennobling and worshipping passion that comes only once in a lifetime. But there was such a wide, impassable gulf between the Duc d'Enghien, a Prince of the Blood, and one who was merely a lady, with charm, beauty, and intelligence, it is true, but no rank to speak of! And the Prince de Condé, the shabbily-dressed, astute old noble, with unkempt beard and slovenly habits, forgetting the hot-headed, tumultuous days of his own young passion, when in terror he had carried off his fair princess from the covetous eyes of his licentious uncle, Henri Quatre, decided that the marriage must not be dreamed of. There was a heart-rending separation, when the brave young Duc d'Enghien, the greatest hero of his age, fainted as he bade good-bye to the gentle girl whom he desired with all his being, and who, not long after, hid her broken heart among the Carmelite Sisters.

The Prince de Conti, the youngest of the Condé family, was also a visitor to the *ruelle* of the Marquise, and he may have met Madame de Sévigné there, for a few years later we find him among those who were especially attracted by her brilliant social charms.

But what a crowd of other visitors was welcomed at this hospitable salon! In Richelieu's time, some years before, it had become such a social centre that the suspicious Cardinal once suggested to Madame de Rambouillet that she should report to him any adverse comments on himself or his policy. With supreme tact the Marquise assured him that her guests needed no such espionage; her sentiments towards him were too well known, she said, for any of them to speak a disparaging word of him in her presence!

As in all such gatherings, some faces, some names, some personalities stand out conspicuously, forcibly arresting attention; while others are mere phantoms, powerless to stir even the most passing interest. Prominent among the dainty dames who fluttered in and out the Blue Room was Mademoiselle Paulet, the honorary secretary to the Marquise, whose mane of thick tawny hair, brilliant eyes, and fearless character, gained for her the title of *la Lionne*. La Lionne often entertained the company by her singing; which was so exquisite that nightingales were once found dead by a fountain where she had sung the night before—at least so said one of the many poets of the salon!

There was Voiture, too, poet and ambassador, the son of a wine merchant. Like Ménage, he was always affecting to be dying of love for some great lady, and always thirsting to fight duels—on paper! In spite of his absurdities, however, he was a clever linguist and man of affairs, and was frequently sent on foreign missions, which probably helped to foster his pretty talent for letter-writing. Madame de Sévigné, supreme in that art, greatly admired Voiture's letters, and often recommended them to her granddaughter. He wrote verse too, and very impertinent verse it sometimes was, but he was the darling of the Hôtel de Rambouillet, and everyone, even Anne of Austria, excused his audacities merely because he was Voiture. The men, probably, were not always so indulgent, for the Prince de Condé one day remarked, "If he were one of us he would be intolerable," and he was probably intolerable to some people as it was.

But he must have had his good and interesting qualities, or how could he have so charmed those clever, discerning ladies of the Hôtel de Rambouillet? He was neither tall nor handsome, his hair and beard were grey, and more than one gentleman, better endowed with personal attractions, wondered wherein his charms lay. One of them said so one day to Madame Saintot.

"Ah!" she replied, "if you only knew how agreeable he can be to women when he chooses!"

When the young Bossuet, then only seventeen, was taken to the salon of Madame de Rambouillet, he was asked to preach an extempore sermon. It was evening, and the young heaven-born orator, carried away by his own eloquence, held his audience interested and charmed till midnight.

Voiture did not lack the witty word for the occasion. "I have never heard a preacher begin so early, or end so late," said he.

Sarrazin, another poet, was the buffoon of the company, who lives to-day in Molière as *Triboulet*. Sometimes Madame de Longueville would say to him, "Preach like a cordelier, or a capuchin"; and Sarrazin would imitate these friars so well, that it was said of him that if he had only lived till the time of the eloquent Bourdaloüe, he would have preached like Bourdaloüe.

Balzac, scarcely remembered to-day, eclipsed in fame by his

greater namesake of the *Comédie Humaine*, was also a visitor at the salon. What a glimpse of the condition of the *porte-plume*, that expressive synonym for a literary man! we get in Richelieu's annoyance at not having one of Balzac's books dedicated to him. The independent Balzac had, in fact, not dedicated it to anyone.

"Does he imagine himself *grand seigneur* enough to dispense with a dedication?" asked the Cardinal in haughty displeasure.

As one calls to mind those interminable, basely flattering "dedications" to the *grands seigneurs*, who looked on them as payment for the support they gave to the literary man, the humble being who only lived, so to speak, in the smiles of their countenances, it is not surprising that George de Scudéry, impoverished descendant of a noble house, should proudly declare that though adverse circumstances had made him a *porte-plume*, the only plumes his ancestors carried were worn in their hats!

But George de Scudéry is hardly remembered to-day, except as the gasconading brother of his wonderful sister, Madeleine de Scudéry, that unmitigated literary woman. A descriptive phrase from Tallemant brings her vividly before us, the "tall dark person with the very long face," and Madame de Cornuel finishes the sketch with her witty *mot*, "She was destined by Providence to blot paper, for she sweated ink from every pore." Why is it that Mademoiselle de Scudéry, with every virtue under the sun, and not one of them hidden under a bushel, awakens an instinctive protest? Is it that her virtues are too terribly blatant, her accomplishments too obvious and paraded? Her attainments are almost appalling; in their universality one is inclined to wonder "how one small brain could hold so much." Conrart, who was her great friend, and a regular attendant at her *samedis*, writes that "she had a prodigious imagination, an excellent memory, an exquisite judgment, with a natural disposition to understand everything curious that she saw done, and everything praiseworthy that she heard of." She learned about agriculture, gardening, housekeeping, cooking, and a life in the country; she also turned her attention to the causes and effects of maladies, and the composition of an infinite number of remedies; she distilled perfumes and scented waters; and in addition to all these housewifely arts she learned to play the lute, to talk Spanish and Italian, and, more important than all, she wrote a number of novels, the chief of which is the *Grand Cyrus*, where she represents all the principal society of the time of the Fronde.

Here too, in this salon, the young Marquise de Sévigné would often meet her former tutors, the Abbé Ménage and the thrifty Chapelain; and the latter, with his absurd dress and miserly habits, not infrequently served as a target for the wits, one of whom, conscious of his own correct costume, once scornfully declared that the philosopher in his many-coloured garments looked like a mackerel!

The Duc de la Rochefoucauld, then the Prince de Marsillac, met at the Hôtel de Rambouillet both the famous women with whom his name is chiefly associated; the lovely Duchesse de Longueville, to whom he paid assiduous court more from interest than from any deeper feeling; and Mademoiselle de la Vergne, then a child of twelve or thirteen, who, some twenty-five years later, as Madame de la Fayette, became the supreme interest of his declining, gouty age; while Madame de Sévigné was the intimate and affectionate friend of both.

How impossible it is to give any idea of the numberless visitors who each thought it a great distinction to be admitted to this famous circle! But one at least must not be overlooked, the brilliant Madame de Cornuel, "who could never open her mouth without some sparkle of wit escaping." She is an abstraction of clever sayings. "Every sin she confessed was an epigram," said one of her friends, and almost every remark she made possessed some germ of originality that caused it to be repeated with delight. Of the ill-mannered Duc de Rohan she said, "He is very well-born, but he has been very badly whipped"; while of the devout James II of England she shrewdly remarked, "The Holy Spirit has eaten his understanding."

One of her lackeys fell down in her presence "on all fours." "I forbid you to rise," said his mistress, "you were intended by Nature to walk like that."

There was generally a quite perceptible sting in her wit, though perhaps it was fortunately not always apparent to the victim. Madame de Sévigné was delighted with the retort she once made to the somewhat foolish little Comtesse de Fiesque, who declared of a friend that he was not so stupid as he was said to be. "Why," said Madame de Cornuel pointedly, "you are like those people who have been eating garlic!"

Madame de Sévigné's intercourse with the Marquise de Rambouillet and those who visited her famous salon must have been of invaluable service to the young married lady who had not long made her début in Parisian society. Madame de Sévigné, like all daughters of Eve, was not free from faults, and those who admire her to-day as a sweet and fascinating woman, with almost every feminine grace, cannot but admit that in early youth her wit was somewhat boisterous. It was a kind of flamboyant joyousness, the outcome of magnificent health and high spirits, which now and again overflowed into imprudent speech; never, the most scandal-loving of her contemporaries agree, into imprudent action. Tallemant says leniently, " She had the habit of saying everything she thought was pleasing, though it was often a little free"; but even this industrious scandal-monger could find nothing worse to say of her. Indeed, with this exception, he has nothing but sincere praise. "She was one of the most amiable and worthy people in Paris," he declares, and such praise from Tallemant may be considered praise indeed. Her cousin Bussy, seeking carefully for defects, writes that, "For a woman of quality her character was a little too playful and sprightly," which may have been a fault in a *grande dame*, but it unquestionably added an ingredient of perennial charm to the famous *Letters* by which her memory lives.

To correct this fault, which was probably the result of having missed a mother's training, for it is not generally men who teach the "prunes and prisms" of life, she could not have gone to a better school than the *ruelle* of Madame de Rambouillet. Here she found the insensible correction by example which her quick, sensitive mind would not be long in applying. In this brilliant society, the final polish was added to her natural wit and cultivated intelligence, and the result was such a combination of graces of heart and mind and character as is rarely to be seen. We get one little glimpse of her exquisite personal charm at this period, in an epigram, made by the Abbé Montreuil, "On seeing Madame de Sévigné play Blind Man's Buff":

> " De toutes les façons vous avez droit de plaire,
> Mais surtout vous savez nous charmer en ce jour :
> Voyant vos yeux bandés, on vous prend pour l'Amour ;
> Les voyant découverts, on vous prend pour sa mère."

CHAPTER V

The dissipated young Marquis de Sévigné openly neglects his wife—The birth of Charles de Sévigné—Madame de Sévigné has many admirers—The Comte de Lude, Segrais, the Abbé de Montreuil, the Comte de Bussy-Rabutin—A daring abduction

BESIDES being a frequent visitor at the Hôtel de Rambouillet, Madame de Sévigné had many visitors at her own *ruelle,* and it was not long before the brilliant and charming young Marquise, so full of unspoiled, fresh delight in life, gathered round her a group of friends as gay and vivacious as herself. After her secluded girlhood in the country as the ward of an abbé, it was only human and natural that, with her joyous, pleasure-loving nature, she should desire to join in every new diversion, to enjoy each novel entertainment that Paris had to offer. Her husband, more eager in the pursuit of pleasure than herself, and lacking the good sense and inherent virtue which was her safeguard among the pitfalls of that lax society, was soon drawn into a whirl of vice and dissipation, and, without misgiving or scruple, thoughtlessly left her to her own occupations and engagements.

In France, at this period, ladies rarely drove or walked out alone. Sometimes they were accompanied by a companion, who was one of the many poor gentlewomen for whom, in those early days of society, the day-star of women's higher education had not yet dawned. Frequently, however, two or three ladies would pay their visits together, and one of Madame de Sévigné's intimates at this period, with whom she visited the Duchesse de Chevreuse, the Duchesse de Châtillon, the Marquise de Rambouillet, and other mutual friends, was the Comtesse de Fiesque. This little lady was so frivolous, so light of head and heart, that the witty Madame de Cornuel in after years said of her that "she never grew any older because she was preserved in folly," and, in these veritable days of her youth, she was a quite irresponsible madcap, and not the wisest friend the Marquise could have chosen.

As one of the distinguished *précieuses*, Madame de Sévigné soon attracted a little court of gallants, *un mille honnêtes gens*, as one chronicler puts it, with the exaggeration that must be allowed for in most chronicles. These, after the fashion of the time, had no objection to posing as the devoted gallant of a pretty woman, and at the Foire Saint-Germain, along the Cours-la-Reine, or in the fashionable promenade of the Luxembourg Gardens, would gather round the lady whose society was most pleasing to them, and, hat in hand at her carriage door, or riding beside her on the promenade, would advertise to their world which lady they honoured by their preference.

The Foire Saint-Germain was an institution, a feature of Parisian life which emphasises, as much as most things, the difference between the society of that period and the society of to-day. La Grande Mademoiselle, when she was exiled to Saint-Fargeau for her conspicuous share in the Fronde, declared that of all the pleasures of Paris she most regretted the Foire Saint-Germain. The Foire began at Epiphany and ended at Shrovetide, and for the two months it lasted the fashionable world of Paris went there almost every evening to find amusement. All the rarities that could be procured were on sale; valuable and dainty laces, choice perfumes, Spanish gloves, faience, pictures, pocket looking-glasses, apricot paste, bon-bon boxes, and other costly articles were to be bought at the Foire; and it was the custom—a custom at which the poorer gallants occasionally grumbled ruefully in private—for gentlemen who accompanied a lady to the Foire to buy her any trifle she most desired as a "fairing." But then the trifles of the Foire were so expensive! A set of lace collar and cuffs, English point it is true, cost six louis, and the other bagatelles were proportionately dear. There were shows, of course; lions, performing dogs, two-headed wonders; and Madame de Sévigné mentions having been to the Foire to see a "Monster Woman"; raffling was carried on at almost every shop, and the gambling, dancing, and drinking saloons were always well attended. There was, too, the excitement of going in masks and dominos when the opera or play was over. It would scarcely have been *convenable* for the Marquises, Comtes, and Ducs, and their ladies, to have rubbed elbows with the Parisian crowd in usual recognisable garb; so the liveries of their servants and carriages were of a uniform, non-committal grey, no distinctive heraldic bearings were in evidence, and from behind the disguise of the *loup* or black velvet mask — a fashion brought from Italy — ladies and their gallants might look on, and join in the diversions of the multitude, or prosecute intrigues, without the least fear of detection.

The Cours-la-Reine was a meeting-ground of a totally different character. The name, affixed to the wall of a street to-day, even though some avenues of trees still remain, gives very little suggestion of this superb promenade, which, bounded by the meadows and woods of the Champs Elysées on one side and the Seine on the other, extended from the heart of Paris to the village of Chaillot. It consisted of four fine avenues of trees, planted some years before by Marie de Medici, with a grand circular sweep in the centre, and a superb gateway at each end. Day after day — from *Toussaint*, when the winter Parisian season began, to the *belle saison* commencing in May or June, when the Court went to Fontainebleau and most of the wealthy inhabitants of Paris retired to their country houses — all the fashionable world of Paris drove daily along the Cours after the midday dinner till supper, to see and to be seen. No grey liveries were visible here; the carriages were generally rather small and open, lined with velvet and silk of brilliant hues, gilded and decorated with armorial bearings or fantastic devices; and the ladies, as was natural, donned their most elegant bonnets and becoming costumes. The gentlemen sometimes drove in carriages also, or rode on horses with gay trappings; and with their embroidered costumes, their plumed hats, their long curls worn in graceful Cavalier fashion, they gave a gallant touch of vivacity and movement to the brilliant scene as they rode by the side of this or that lady, or left her to greet a new-comer. What a scene of grace and elegance, of animated life and colour, was this gay procession! Here was the bold and handsome Duc de Beaufort, who was the darling of the Parisian fishwives, and, said Cardinal de Retz, "thought and spoke like them!"

Here was the Prince de Marsillac, later to be known as the Duc de la Rochefoucauld, and to be chiefly remembered by his bitter *Maximes*, conspicuously attentive to the lovely young Duchesse de Longueville; there was Gondi, the Coadjutor, giving no hint of the ambitions which were seething in his bold and clever brain, and which were presently to come to such terrible fruition; the Prince de Conti, deformed, but with a handsome head, a witty and *spirituel* mind; that sparkling brunette the Duchesse de Châtillon, and the scheming Duchesse de Chevreuse—all so soon to be linked together in the intrigues of the Fronde. The carriage of Gaston d'Orléans appears, and all traffic stops, for this handsome, treacherous prince is Monsieur, the uncle of the boy-king. But Gaston has gracious manners; he is, besides, terribly afraid of a crush, and he calls out in some agitation, "Pray do not stop, gentlemen; keep on, keep on!" and the carriages move on slowly again, and badinage and conversation is renewed. Or the Grande Mademoiselle, his tall, pretty daughter appears, and thoroughly enjoys the movement of deference and admiration her coming produces, while she bows with the condescending grace and royal air which makes her one of the most popular members of the reigning family.

Among the gallants who paid frequent court to the young Marquise de Sévigné was the Comte de Lude, a handsome, fashionable young *élégant* in whose attentions she found a most seductive flattery. He was a good dancer, a wit who could pay back her own clever speeches in the same light coin, who could whisper dainty nothings in the most charming fashion in the world, who had, in fact, every art of society, and, in addition, one that must have been peculiarly his own—he could melt into tears quite naturally when he was wooing the lady of the hour! Madame de Sévigné had a perfectly friendly and frank liking for this fascinating cavalier, and years later, when he was a Duke, and Grand Master of Artillery, her daughter, who had heard much of the Duc de Lude, told her laughingly one day, that "her pen was always cut to write wonders of the Grand Master." Madame de Sévigné cheerfully admitted the soft suggestion, and once, when talking of chocolate, she writes gaily: "The Grand Master, who used to live upon it, has become its declared enemy; judge, then, whether I can be its friend!"

There was the Comte de Vassé, too, one of her husband's friends, who had already made some noise in the polite world of Paris by a gallant adventure which ended in a notorious duel. But Madame de Sévigné's perfect rectitude of conduct was proof against the temptations that beset her on all sides at this perilous period of her life, when, in the early twenties, new to Parisian ways, and extraordinarily attractive, she was left so much alone by her husband among a society that boasted openly of its conquests.

Segrais, the poet, who was a gentleman in the household of Mademoiselle, in addressing some verses to her, finishes with this testimony: "But what have I said? Do I not know that with you one loses all and gains nothing!"

The friend of her girlhood at Livry, the hunchback Saint-Pavin, sometimes met her at the Hôtel de Rambouillet, or on Fridays in summer, when she always drove from Paris to see the Bien-Bon, she would meet him at the Abbaye. So charming was this weekly reunion of her new friends from Paris with those old and valued friends of her girlhood, that Saint-Pavin, with his ever-ready pen, once wrote a prayer in ten lines, which may be compressed into three: "Lord, of all the gifts and blessings which Thou hast bestowed upon me, I entreat Thee to multiply the Fridays, and I will willingly forego all the rest."

Another gay and witty companion was the young Abbé de Montreuil, who was always showing his white teeth in laughter, and whose title of abbé brought him a satisfactory income for which he performed no duties. An abbé was the most privileged and irresponsible of beings: he had all the advantages of belonging to the Church, which sometimes included a fine revenue, with none of the drawbacks of being a priest. We see by one of the Abbé de Montreuil's letters to the Marquise how pleasantly familiar was his intercourse with her; we learn incidentally, also, that it was about this time that her husband was made Lieutenant de Roi de Fougères, a small town in Brittany, not far from Les Rochers, with a grand old castle of which there are only the dilapidated remains to-day.

"As your merit will not allow you to remain long in any place without its being known," writes the Abbé, "it is reported that you are in Paris. I do not know how to believe it; it is one of those things that I most earnestly desire, and therefore it cannot be true. I send, however, to know if it is true, so that, if such be the case, I may no longer be ill. This will not be the first miracle you have performed; in your illustrious race they are performed from mother to son. You know that Madame de Chantal was greatly given to them, and all the honest people who see and hear you, agree that Monsieur her son, who was your father, performed a great miracle. I beg you then, if you have returned, not to keep the news of it from me, so that I may have the pleasure of being quite well and coming to see you. It is a favour which I believe I deserve as much as formerly, since I am as giddy and wild as ever, and still say things as much out of place. I am forgetting that if I am not changed you may be, and that, instead of the monosyllabic letter which I received from you last year, in which there was only 'yes,' you may send me one of the same length in which there will be only 'no.' . . . I am, with all the seriousness and respect of which I am capable (the first is not great, the second is much),—Your very humble servant,

"DE MONTREUIL

"*P.S.*—I have forgotten to put *Madame* in my letter, and as you are now Lieutenante de Roi de Fougères it is a great omission. Here are three then, distribute them as you wish: Madame, Madame, Madame."

But of all the men who crowded round the witty young Marquise, eager for her smiles, her gay speeches, her trifling marks of favour, no one was more dangerous than her cousin Roger, the Comte de Bussy. There was a singular affinity between these two gifted people, but it was much more an affinity of intellect than of mind or heart. The one was incapable of a mean or dishonourable action, was loyal and loving to her friends, with a fine moral discrimination between right and wrong; while Bussy showed himself lacking in every one of these qualities. But neither time nor adversity had yet tested his character and publicly proved his baseness, when he was

THE BIRTH OF CHARLES DE SÉVIGNÉ

coolly and with definite purpose striving to win the affections of his beautiful cousin. To her eyes, as to the eyes of the world, he appeared a handsome soldier, accomplished, witty, brave, even though Maréchal Turenne cruelly said that "Bussy was the best officer in the army—for writing *chansons*." He had been in the King's service from the age of sixteen, and, by the time he was twenty was a colonel, commanding his father's regiment. His personal advantages, too, were considerable, and could not fail to have some influence with a woman who was peculiarly susceptible to the power of beauty; but his greatest advantage was the opportunity of seeing her privately in her own home, with all the privileges of a near relative. She was proud, too, of her cousin, with a sisterly pride, because he was of her blood, her nearest relative on her father's side; she makes frequent mention of the Rabutins, and we easily perceive that, besides having a natural delight in her noble race, she recognises that it is from the Rabutins that both she and her cousin inherit that strain of mingled wit, gaiety, and irresponsible wildness, which she calls *Rabutinage.*

One of her earliest known letters to her cousin is dated 1648, from Les Rochers, shortly after the birth of her son Charles de Sévigné. It is much too frank to be quoted to-day, for in France as in England, two centuries and more ago, it was customary to be quite outspoken on the elemental subjects of life; indeed, Madame de Sévigné in after years discussed with her daughter subjects that few people would think of writing in a letter to-day, for the Marquise held the opinion that everything might be a subject for conversation so long as it was treated in the right way.

After giving Bussy the news of the birth of her son, and scolding him for not writing before, she ends thus—

". . . But enough of concealing my tenderness, my dear cousin, nature is more powerful than policy. I had intended to scold you for your laziness from the beginning of my letter to the end, but it is too great an effort, and I am obliged to tell you that M. de Sévigné and I love you well, and often speak of the pleasure we should have in being with you."

In answering this letter Bussy, tells his cousin, "I envy M. de Sévigné more than any man in the world," with a good deal more in the light, gallant, somewhat free strain in which at that time, and indeed till Madame de Sévigné found means of stopping it, the Comte always wrote to her.

While Madame de Sévigné was spending the summer at Les Rochers with her husband and two baby children, her cousin Bussy was engaged in a most daring and scandalous enterprise, which gives a faint indication of the insolent power and audacity of the nobles of seventeenth-century France, which, notwithstanding all Richelieu's efforts, had been as yet only scotched, not destroyed. It was not till Louis XIV came to the full power of his manhood that, by his extraordinary force of will and his unequalled egoism, he made himself the sun and centre of the social system of France, round which the nobles revolved and looked for recognition and life, knowing well that any attempt at the old feudal lawlessness and independence would be promptly crushed.

The Comte de Bussy, who had married just a year before Madame de Sévigné, lost his wife in 1646. After two years of widowhood he was now looking out for a second wife who should advance his fortunes. His paternal estates were impoverished, and the gay life he led, with high play, and all the other expenses incidental to his rank as a young cavalry officer of noble birth, did nothing to improve his prospects. But Bussy was exacting. His handsome person, distinguished name, and long ancestry were considered — by him! — a fair exchange for beauty, wealth, and youth, and if possible good birth also. But as even an impoverished noble cannot have everything, he was willing to forego this latter, perhaps because he knew that other possessors of noble names would not barter them for empty titles *sans* wealth and lands.

He frequently talked over these matters with his uncle, Hughes de Rabutin, the Grand Prieur du Temple, with whom he usually stayed when he came to Paris, and it chanced that while he was staying with the Grand Prieur at his country house near Sens, he heard of a lady who seemed by report to fulfil to a marvel the chief conditions he demanded.

The affair was absurdly romantic, but Bussy, who tells the shameful story himself, appeared to look on it as a commonplace matter. The lands adjoining those of the Grand Prieur belonged to a wealthy bourgeois named Le Bocage, and, as a near neighbour, Bussy became friendly with the old man, who, knowing that he was looking for a rich young wife, told him one day that he had heard of a widow, beautiful, young, of a pious and angelic sweetness, and, most important qualification, worth several millions! He did not know the young lady himself, said Le Bocage, but a friend of his, Père Clément, was her confessor, in whom she placed considerable confidence, and he thought that by his means a marriage could be brought about.

Père Clément was consulted, and readily consented to do his best in the affair. He was, in fact, a worthless priest who had no other object than to extort money from Bussy, and no stage-villain could more effectively have played his part. As a preliminary, he told Bussy at what hour he would be able to see the pretty widow in church; and Bussy, who saw her twice, thought her superlatively lovely. He neither spoke to her, nor even approached her; but Père Clément assured him that the lady was pleased with his appearance, but that she could do nothing without the consent of her relatives.

Every word of this was fabrication. The young Madame de Miramion, so far from thinking of Bussy as a possible husband, had only an overwhelming desire to devote herself to the service of God. She had been married at sixteen to Jean de Beauharnais, Seigneur de Miramion, a handsome, devoted young husband, who lived but six months after their marriage. Heartbroken at his death, the young girl would fain have buried her grief in the cloister, had it not been for the frail baby daughter who was born some time after its father's death. The first two years of her widowhood she had spent in the most austere retirement, dividing her days between the altar and the cradle; and now, at the age of nineteen, her friends were hoping to bring about a marriage between her and M. Caumartin, although her supreme desire still was to become a *religieuse*, a desire that nothing prevented her from fulfilling but maternal duty and tenderness.

But of all this Bussy knew nothing, save the garbled and false accounts which Père Clément periodically gave him. This latter was always demanding money, and, in all, Bussy paid him about two thousand crowns for his services. After much circumlocution, and a tissue of falsehoods, the priest assured Bussy that the relatives would never consent to Madame de Miramion's marriage with him, but that the widow herself was quite willing, and the only alternative was to carry her off by force!

Bussy was not at all startled by the proposal. It may possibly have been his own, but in any case he felt confident that the young lady would be delighted to become the Comtesse de Bussy, and be fully compensated for any inconvenience the abduction might cause her by the privilege of being presented at Court, where she had hitherto not been admitted.

A fact that throws in higher light the social disorder of the period, is that the Prince de Condé, in whose army Bussy held his commission, and to whom he confided the scandalous affair, promised the Comte his protection, and even offered to help by giving him a mission in Paris, and to place him in command of Bellegarde, one of his strongholds in Burgundy, where he might retire after the abduction! Backed as he was by this powerful prince, Bussy felt fresh confidence, and was reckless as to consequences. He laid his plans with all the forethought of which his clever, unscrupulous mind was capable, and arranged everything to ensure success. By the aid of spies he learned that Madame de Miramion was staying at Issy with her late husband's grandfather, and that on the 7th of August she intended to visit the convent at Mont Valérien for the purposes of devotion.

Bussy posted four relays of horses along the road from Saint-Cloud to the Chateau de Launay, belonging to the Grand Prieur, about twenty-five leagues distant, where he had gathered a band of armed gentlemen and retainers to help him in case of trouble. Near Paris another strong escort of armed men, among whom was his brother Christophe de Rabutin, awaited the passing of Madame de Miramion's carriage. The young widow, thinking only of her devotions, left Issy at seven o'clock in the morning, accompanied by her mother-in-law and some of her waiting-women.

Just as the carriage had crossed the bridge on the way from Saint-Cloud to Mont Valérien, it was suddenly stopped by two cavaliers, who presented themselves at the door to lower the apron, or leather curtains, which shut them in. Madame de Miramion, thinking they were robbers, tried to repulse them by striking at them, and calling " Help ! Help ! " with all her strength. Her cries and efforts were alike useless. One of the gentlemen, finding they could not lower the apron, drew his sword to cut the strings, and the young widow, with frantic courage, tried to snatch away his weapon as a defence, only succeeding, however, in cutting her hands and covering them with blood.

Resistance was useless. Bussy had six horses harnessed to Madame Miramion's carriage, and the cavalcade trotted off, armed men on each side of the carriage door guarding the helpless women within. When they stopped at inns for fresh horses, Madame de Miramion implored people to help her, but her hands covered with blood, the disorder of her appearance after her struggles to get free, and her mental agony, gave her such a wild, distraught look, that when Bussy and his gentlemen assured the people that it was a mad woman whom they were taking away to put under restraint, they willingly believed them.

At length they reached the Chateau de Launay, and at the sight of the two hundred armed men awaiting them in the sombre courtyard the young widow was almost frantic with terror. She utterly refused to leave her carriage, to eat, or to have her maid taken from her. Fortunately one of the gentlemen, a Chevalier of Malta, touched by her distress and helplessness, assured her of his desire to serve her, and, gaining her confidence in a slight degree, induced her to enter the chateau.

Then Bussy came to see her, but of him she felt the utmost horror and loathing. He talked of his devotion, and mentioned marriage, but she swore a solemn oath that no power on earth should induce her to become his wife. This, to Bussy, was a serious matter. Had the affair been successful, he would have gained his fair widow and her millions ; the matter would have caused some gossip, but he would have been a hero who had carried off his bride for love. But now, instead of being a hero, people would not hesitate to call him a scoundrel—there is such a wide gulf between failure and success ! To add to his concern, news was brought to the chateau that Rubelle, the brother of Madame de Miramion, was on his way to the castle with an armed force of six hundred men.

He quickly decided to send her away to the town, and the Chevalier of Malta accompanied her carriage, but even he did not think it prudent to enter Sens. Her brother, M. de Rubelle, soon discovered her at an inn, but the poor young widow was so exhausted by the excitements and terrors of her extraordinary adventure, that she fell dangerously ill, and had to be removed to Paris for medical advice. Her life was in the greatest danger, and the sacraments were even administered to her; but fortunately for Bussy she recovered, though only after a long and painful convalescence; when, with a magnanimity that the Comte did not deserve, she begged her friends to deal leniently with him on condition that he should never attempt to see her again.

CHAPTER VI

A visit to the Bishop of Châlons—The Marquis and his wife return to Paris—The beginnings of the Fronde—The flight of the Court to Saint-Germain—Paris besieged by the Queen—"Mazarins" and "Frondeurs"—The Duchesse de Longueville at the Hôtel de Ville

THE family and friends of Madame de Miramion were naturally greatly incensed at the Comte de Bussy's audacious conduct, and had it not been for the powerful intercession of his patron, the Great Condé, things would not have gone very well with him. While it was still doubtful whether he would be pursued by the law, he went to visit his uncle, Jacques de Neuchèze, the Bishop of Chalon, where the Marquis and Marquise de Sévigné were spending the autumn with their children. This bishop, uncle to both the cousins, had, it will be remembered, officiated at the marriage of Madame de Sévigné; he was also godfather to her daughter, and he now gave a cordial welcome to his young relatives at his beautiful old Abbey of Ferrières on the banks of the Loing. Here the days passed pleasantly enough, and we know that they had excellent entertainment, for Bussy declared that Crochet, the Bishop's cook, made such good soups that they gave him a distaste for all others. The Comte, doubtless, was glad to escape for a while from Paris, to avoid the mockery of his friends at his failure, and the scorn of those who were disgusted at his conduct. It was delightful, too, to be with his young cousins, both as gay and witty as himself, and who, whatever they may have thought of his disgraceful enterprise, were too loyal to their relative to say much on the subject. But he had hardly been with them a week when a letter from his mother recalled him to Paris, urging him to come at once to settle some business in connection with the abduction of Madame de Miramion. Bussy left this pleasant company most unwillingly, only to find that his recall had been quite unnecessary. Some time after he wrote to both his cousins, who were still at Ferrières : " If you do not soon return to Paris I shall come to find you, even though my affairs here will not be settled till after Christmas." It was then the 15th of November 1648, and they must have come back to Paris very shortly after this, for on the 11th of December Madame de Sévigné was at the Parlement in the " Lantern," with her relative the celebrated lawyer Olivier d'Ormesson, listening to a case in which they were both interested, when the *députés des enquêtes* came in a body into the Grand Chamber and demanded a General Assembly.

This scene was probably Madame de Sévigné's first actual experience of the Fronde, the "Ladies' War," as it has been lightly called in derision, but which, nevertheless, for four long years was to divide France into violently opposed factions, to cause bitter family dissensions, and to bring untold misery and bloodshed throughout the kingdom. While Madame de Sévigné had been staying at the peaceful old Abbey of Ferrières in the autumn of 1648, the Fronde had commenced with the one or two dramatic little "curtain-raisers," so to speak, by which the long and bloody drama of the civil war was ushered in.

Since the death of Louis XIII in 1643, the affairs of the State had prospered marvellously. It was "the good regency when court and town thought of nothing but pleasure and love," wrote Saint Evremond. "The Queen is so good," was a phrase on everyone's lips, and the handsome little King, whenever he appeared in public, was idolised by the people. To add to the general sense of security and triumph, the Great Condé, even before his father's death, while he was yet only the Duc d'Enghien, had gained for France such astounding victories that they could only be compared with those of the ancient world. But, underlying all this apparent prosperity, there was a growing discontent among the masses. The wars, though they added glory to the name of France, drained the nation of men and resources. Paris was filled with disabled soldiers, who, with no provision made for their needs, and maddened by their misery and want, helped to foster disaffection among the people. Revolt was in the air of Europe. Cromwell's troops were every day more victorious in England;

DISAFFECTION IN PARIS

Charles I was in prison, and his Queen and her two sons had been hospitably received by their royal relatives in Paris; and the presence of these victims of the Revolution in England probably had a share in turning the thoughts of the Parisians towards rebellion.

The treasury of France was empty. Mazarin, the humble, smooth-tongued Italian, "who reverenced no virtue and hated no vice," who ruled the haughty Anne of Austria by his lightest word, had bribed, quite openly, with honours and emoluments, people of all sorts and conditions who had joined his party, and had spent in advance four years' income of the treasury of France. He had contrived, also, at the same time, to amass an enormous and shameful private fortune during the few years he had been minister in fact, though not in name. The natural result of this policy was a frequent and oppressive taxation, which closely affected all classes; and when, in 1648, fresh duties were imposed on the supplies entering Paris, Parlement assembled, under its venerable First President Matthew Molé, and refused to register the new decrees. It determined also to check this growing abuse of excessive taxation, and made an order, called *Arrêt d'Union*, which summoned its members to the Grand Council Chamber for the purpose of deliberating on State affairs, and of reforming the Constitution.

Mazarin was alarmed at such unheard-of assertion on the part of Parlement, which by this action went far beyond its privileges. The Court party professed a boundless contempt for "those square-capped devils" the men of the law, and Mazarin forbade them to assemble. But these were men of intelligence and education who had a real grievance, and who were determined, if possible, to have it redressed. Matthew Molé, Blancmesnil, Charton, and Broussel held meetings, harangued and argued, and the latter "talked like a Roman of the liberties and rights of the people."

Anne of Austria was furious at this dissatisfaction among the men of the long robe. At every fresh act of assertion on the part of Parlement she became more angry, more eager to punish them for daring to oppose her will. In August the arrest of Broussel had been followed by the famous Jour des

Barricades, and disaffection had been simmering all through the autumn. The popular hatred of Mazarin was increasing daily; Parlement was growing more arrogant, more insistent in its demands; and the Queen Regent, more haughty at each encroachment on royal prerogatives, more furious at every fresh insult to Mazarin—who, it was commonly believed, was her lover or her husband—was maturing a plan of punishment which should appal the good people of Paris, and soon reduce them to abject obedience. Few, very few, were in the secret. On the Eve of the Epiphany, while her confidential ministers were making ready for the great *coup*, Anne talked and laughed among her ladies, as usual; and one of them, Madame de Motteville, gives us a charming little picture of how this Twelfth-night of 1649 was kept at the Court of France.

"On the 5th of January, the Eve of the Epiphany, the evening so famous that it will be talked of for ages to come, I went to the Queen, with whom I was accustomed to pass the greater part of my life. I found her in her little room, tranquilly watching the King playing cards, and leaning carelessly against the corner of the table as if she were thinking of nothing but of what she was looking at. . . . To amuse the King, the Queen cut up a cake, and as my sister, Madame de Brègy, and I were the only ladies present, she did us the honour of making us share it with the King and herself. We made her the Twelfth-night Queen, because the bean was found in the Virgin's slice, and to make merry she sent for a bottle of hippocras, which we drank before her; and having no other purpose than to amuse ourselves, we forced the Queen to drink a little also. Then, wishing to fulfil the obligations which the extravagant follies of the day demanded, we cried out 'The Queen drinks!' We supped as usual in her dressing-room, and made good cheer without the slightest uneasiness."

Shortly after, the Queen retired, and apparently everything went on at the Palace as usual. But at three o'clock on that cold January morning the King, and the little Monsieur his brother, were awakened, hastily dressed, and taken to the carriage which awaited them at the garden gate of the Palais Royal, where the Queen joined them. They drove to the Cours-la-Reine, which was the rendezvous for those in the secret, and surely that magnificent promenade never witnessed a stranger sight than the assembling, in the weird, chilly moonlight of a winter morning, of the Princes of the Blood, the Court officials, the ladies and gentlemen of the Court, all, in fact, who were of any importance in the political party of the Queen's adherents. One by one carriages drove up with occupants who were more or less sleepy, more or less annoyed that the rendezvous should be at such an unseasonable hour. There was Gaston d'Orléans, with Madame his second wife and her baby daughters—the former much troubled at such an unheard-of expedition; La Grande Mademoiselle, Gaston's eldest and imperious daughter, not very pleased at having to get up at such a cold and early hour; and the dowager Princesse de Condé, who only at the last moment had been wakened by her son the Prince de Condé, and consequently was angry and annoyed at not having been told the secret sooner. There was, however, no time to scold, so, taking her daughter-in-law and the little Duc d'Enghien, then five years old, she also drove to the Cours-la-Reine. All the Princes of the Blood and their families were present save one member, the Duchesse de Longueville. But no one at this juncture thought her absence ominous. When she had been urged to leave the town with the Queen and Court, she had sent back a plausible message that the state of her health would not allow her to bear the fatigue of travelling; she was confident, however, that the good citizens of Paris would do her no harm.

The royal cavalcade started on its way to Saint-Germain-en-Laye, and reached there about five o'clock in the morning. Everyone was cold, sleepy, and supremely uncomfortable in the great palace, which was almost bare of furniture. Cardinal Mazarin had sent two or three small beds from Paris a few days previously, and these were made ready for the Queen, the King, the little Monsieur, and Cardinal Mazarin. La Grande Mademoiselle was fortunate; she slept on a mattress in an attic with no glass to the windows; but the Duchesse d'Orléans, the Princesse de Condé, and most of the others of the party, were thankful for a heap of straw to lie on. Even this presently became so scarce and precious that none was to be had at any price.

5

"I will starve Paris into submission," the Queen declared triumphantly. And the Great Condé, well versed in the tactics of war, assured her that it could be besieged and taken in a fortnight.

Paris, waking up to find itself bereft of Queen, King, and Court, was for a short time in a panic of alarm. But the Coadjutor of Paris, Madame de Sévigné's relative by marriage, now came into prominence as the leader of the Frondeurs, and soon reassured his flock. Parlement took counsel with the Coadjutor, the Duc de Beaufort, and other leading Frondeurs, and, as a first step, levied a tax on all who could pay it, and in this way collected an immense sum of money for provisions and arms. The Queen, however, sent out a decree forbidding all villages round Paris to carry provisions of any kind into the city by land or water, intending to blockade Paris by river as well as by road; but as the farmers of the surrounding villages obtained such good prices for their produce in Paris, the besieged town experienced no difficulty on that point.

Such a general and disastrous upheaval could not fail to affect every person in Paris, and it became a necessity for each one to declare for one party or the other, to announce himself as a "Mazarin" or a "Frondeur." The hatred of the multitude for Mazarin had grown to such a point, that all their grievances were identified with him, and the whole Court party was vilified under his name; while the Frondeurs took their title from a group of idle youths and loafers who hung about the confines of the town, flinging stones at each other or at peaceable passers-by. *Fronder* means literally "to fling," or "to censure," and when the word was used by one of the Parlement it was taken up immediately by their party, and used as a catchword with the customary popular frenzy; and gloves, hats, ribbons, and canes, to be quite fashionable, were all presently labelled in the shop windows *à la Fronde*.

Madame de Sévigné and her husband were naturally on the side of the Frondeurs. The Coadjutor of Paris, of the powerful de Retz family, was the unscrupulous, intriguing soul of the Fronde, and as he was the head of their house, they, as a matter of course, belonged to his party. At this period the strife centred round the lovely Duchesse de Longueville, who for the sake of the Prince de Marsillac, son of the Duc de la Rochefoucauld, broke with her family, and contributed by her powerful influence to keep alive the flame of civil war. Her sway over her own family and friends was so great, that, as Madame de Motteville said, " her approval was looked on as the greatest blessing."

Three days after the Queen and Court had left the capital, the Duchesse sent a message to her husband, and to her younger brother the Prince de Conti, asking them both to join her in Paris. These two men were completely under the dominion of this lovely and clever woman, and had no thought but to obey her; knowing, however, that they would be followed by the execrations of the whole Court for deserting the Queen, they secretly left Saint-Germain in the evening, and reached the gates of Paris at midnight. Here they were met by a torchlight procession, at the head of which were the Coadjutor and the Duc de Beaufort, while the greater part of Paris shouted itself hoarse in welcoming a Prince of the Blood among their leaders.

The Parisians, however, found it almost too difficult to believe that a prince and princess were actually identifying themselves with the popular interest; it was unnatural; such good news could not be true, and they suspected an intrigue by which they would be betrayed. It was therefore necessary to gain their entire confidence, and the leaders soon devised a plan which appealed with immense force to the popular imagination, and assured the good citizens that these royal personages were in sympathy with the Frondeurs. The Duc de Longueville went to Parlement and told those who had assembled there that Madame his wife would, with Madame de Bouillon, take up her residence at the Hôtel de Ville! Such condescension was unheard-of! It brought tears to the eyes of the *citoyennes*, and *vivas* of delight from their husbands. Years after, when the Coadjutor (then Cardinal de Retz) was writing his memoirs, he gave this little pen-picture of the circumstance, which shows that he was fully aware of the value of the incident as a stroke of policy—

" Imagine, I pray you," he wrote, " these two ladies upon the steps of the Hôtel de Ville, the more beautiful because they appeared to be carelessly dressed, though this was not really the case. Each held in her arms one of her children, who were as beautiful as their mothers. The Grève was crowded with people up to the roofs; all the men gave shouts of joy, and all the women shed tears of tenderness. I threw five hundred pistoles from the windows of the Hôtel de Ville."

The room of the Duchesse de Longueville became the council chamber, as it were, for the leaders of the Fronde. Here came the Frondeur nobles, the Duc de Bouillon, the Duc d'Elbœuf, the Marquis de Noirmoutier, and, to her the most important of all, the Prince de Marsillac. The magistrates and town officials came here also, and the details of the programme of the Fronde party were all discussed and settled only with her approval.

In the midst of all this intrigue Madame de Longueville's youngest child was born on 29th January 1649. The next day she paid a high compliment to Messieurs of the Parlement, which delighted the Parisians. She begged President le Féron, in the name of the Parlement, to act as godfather to her little son in conjunction with the Duchesse de Bouillon; and the baby received the name of Charles-Paris, in honour of his birth-place.

The men of the Sévigné family had their part to play in the Fronde, though it must be confessed that it was not performed with distinction. The Duc de Longueville hastened to his province of Normandy to rouse it to rebellion against the Regent, and the young Marquis de Sévigné joined the expedition. They did not accomplish much in any way, but it was quite a pleasant campaign, and Saint-Evremond, who wrote a delicate satire on the occasion, records that the Marquis de Sévigné had the honour of affording much amusement to the Duc de Longueville by his clever buffoonery.

Renaud de Sévigné, an uncle of the Marquis, was scarcely more fortunate in the matter of military laurels. He was sent to command a regiment raised by the Coadjutor, and, because of his title of Archbishop of Corinth, it was called the "Corinthians." When this regiment was badly beaten by the Royalists, the latter called them in derision the "First of the Corinthians," which amused even the Frondeurs themselves.

MADAME DE SÉVIGNÉ AMONG THE FRONDEURS 69

They were very light-hearted, these Frondeurs and Royalists. Everything was a subject for jest and biting epigram, for *chansons* and witty madrigals. The Coadjutor employed the poet Marigny to use his poetic gift in showering clever insults on the enemy, anonymously of course. His muse, one is inclined to think, must have been too hard-worked at this period, or he would never have sent such wretched rhymes to Madame de Sévigné as a New Year's greeting—

> "Adorable et belle marquise,
> Plus belle mille fois qu'un satin blanc tout neuf;
> Au premier jour de l'an mil six cent quarante-neuf,
> Je vous présenterais de bon cœur ma franchise. . . ."

However, since they were sent with such good intentions, she probably did not criticise them very severely.

Madame de Sévigné was among the Frondeurs who paid court to the Duchesse de Longueville, and joined in the gaieties that went on in Paris while each side was preparing for war. The Comte de Bussy was in the army of the Prince de Condé, commanding a company of light horse, just outside Paris on the plain of Saint-Denis. In February he wrote the following letter to his cousin—

"I have long hesitated to write to you, not knowing whether you had become my enemy, or whether you were still my good cousin; whether to send you a lackey or a trumpeter. But having remembered once hearing you blame the brutality of Horace for having said to his brother-in-law that he would no longer recognise him after war had been declared between their republics, I believed that the interests of your party would not prevent you from reading my letters; and as for me, except in what concerns the service of the King my master, I am your very humble servant.

"Do not think, my dear cousin, that this is the end of my letter; I wish to say a few words to you concerning our war.

"I find that keeping guard is very cold work. It is true that wood costs nothing here, and that we can live well at a cheap rate. With all that, it is a most wearisome business, and without the hope that you would fall to my share at the sack of Paris I should be tempted to desert; but that prospect gives me patience.

"I send my servant for news of you, and to bring from Paris my carriage horses, in the name of our uncle the Grand Prieur. Adieu, my dear cousin."

Bussy, however, was not destined to see his carriage horses again. Finding that the efforts of his servant were useless, he begged Madame de Sévigné to use her influence in having them sent to him; and at the end of his letter he says, "If Cardinal Mazarin had a cousin as charming as you in Paris, I am very much deceived if he would not make peace at all costs; and I would do the same, for upon my faith I love you well. Adieu."

Madame de Sévigné did her best to get Bussy's carriage horses sent to him, but the Frondeurs knew too well to whom they belonged, and would not give them up. The Comte de Bussy, making the best of his loss to his cousin, assured her that he was consoled for the loss of his horses by the friendship she showed in trying to have them sent to him.

From a letter written by Madame de Sévigné in the beginning of the war, to Lenet, the friend who had sent her the rhyming letter to Les Rochers in conjunction with Bussy, the same Lenet with whom she laughed so much in her youthful days, we learn what the Marquise thought of the war, though at this period its miseries and horrors had barely begun—

"PARIS, *March* 25, 1649

"MONSIEUR,—You must permit me to wish for peace, for, with your permission, I think an hour's conversation is worth fifty letters. When you come here, and I have the honour of seeing you, I shall compel you to agree with me that war is a foolish thing. I passionately desire it to end, and to remain in your good graces, which I hold in particular esteem, and am with truth, Monsieur, your very humble and obedient servant,

"M. DE RABUTIN-CHANTAL"

Notwithstanding her passionate desire, and that of many thousands more, the war was far from its end, and before that longed-for event, Madame de Sévigné was to experience a private grief and affliction that for the time caused her to regard the war as of quite secondary importance.

CHAPTER VII

The "Princes' Fronde"—The Sévignés give a supper-party to the Duchesse de Chevreuse—The *appartement* of the crippled poet Scarron—The Marquis de Sévigné and Ninon' de l'Enclos—An intercepted letter—The Marquis conducts his wife to the solitude of Les Rochers—The diamond earrings—The Marquis de Sévigné is killed in a duel

"CAMP OF MONTROND, *July* 2, 1650

"I HAVE at last declared myself for Monsieur le Prince, and I may say to you, my fair cousin, that it has not been without great reluctance, for, against my King, I am serving a Prince who does not care for me. It is true the position he is in fills me with pity. I shall therefore serve him while he is in prison as if he loved me, and if ever he comes out, I shall return him my lieutenancy and leave him at once.

"What do you say to such sentiments, Madame? Do you not think them grand and noble?

"Let us write often to each other, the Cardinal will know nothing of it; and at the worst, if he sends you a *lettre de cachet*, it is a fine thing for a woman of twenty to be mixed up in affairs of state. The celebrated Madame de Chevreuse did not begin earlier. As for myself, I declare to you, my charming cousin, that I would willingly cause you to commit a crime, no matter what.

"When I think that last year we were on different sides, and are so still, though we have both changed, I fancy that we are playing at prisoner's base. However, your side is always the best, for you never leave Paris, while I go from Saint-Denis to Montrond, and I am afraid I shall end by going from Montrond to the devil. . . ."

From this entirely characteristic letter of the Comte de Bussy, written a month after his second marriage, we gather what an amazing change had occurred in the affairs of the Fronde in one short year. In its beginning, Anne of Austria had besieged Paris, hoping thus to reduce her subjects to obedience, and the Prince de Condé had been her most loyal and trusted commander. The Frondeurs, whether men of the robe, bourgeoisie, or *canaille*, were resisting the Queen because they resented the crushing taxes, and hoped to be able to stipulate for a less oppressive rule. But the nobles were not united by this single aim; almost everyone, in fact, was occupied with his own pet ambition, from the Prince de Marsillac, who, quite unfairly, during his father's lifetime demanded the *honneurs du Louvre*, to the Coadjutor, who was scheming for a cardinal's hat.

In this network of intrigue, cohesion was impossible, but when the Queen Regent and Court returned to Paris everyone hoped that affairs would be amicably settled. The Prince de Condé, however, gave great offence to the Queen by his arrogant behaviour, and as a punishment she caused him and his brother the Prince de Conti, with their brother-in-law the Duc de Longueville, to be conducted to Vincennes as prisoners of state.

A thunder-bolt from heaven would not have seemed more terrifying to all classes in France. The Princes of the Blood in prison! Their sacred persons brought under the law like mere nobles! It was incredible! inconceivable! but it was nevertheless true, and the whole aspect of the Fronde changed as by magic. It was now the "Princes' Fronde." The Coadjutor and his party executed a *volte-face*, and were supporting the Queen and upholding her authority in Paris; while the provinces, hating Mazarin rather than Anne of Austria, were making war on the Crown on behalf of the Princes, urged to rebellion by the Duchesse de Longueville and the Princesse de Condé. The poor dowager Princesse, broken-hearted at the indignity put upon her sons, did not long survive their disgrace. While her sons were in prison, and her daughter Anne, the beautiful Duchesse, was in active rebellion against the Queen, she died in bitter loneliness, without one of those children whom she had loved so well, to soothe her last sad hours.

Madame de Sévigné and her husband were now both in Paris, and, following the lead of their relative the Coadjutor, supported the royal cause, though it must not be supposed that there was anything approaching unity of purpose or action among the Queen's adherents. This party was split up into several factions, most of which were governed by the intrigues of the Duchesse de Montbazon, who entirely ruled the actions of the Duc de Beaufort; the Duchesse de Chevreuse, who dictated to Gondi; and the Duchesse de Châtillon, who was the confidential friend of the Prince de Condé. The Fronde, indeed, now justified its name of "The Ladies' War."

Amid all this inconceivable confusion and bewildering intrigue, the gaieties of Parisian life went on as usual, with a licence and gay freedom that had been unknown in the days of the "good Regency," the time of the *précieuses*, and the receptions of the Hôtel de Rambouillet. Madame de Sévigné and her husband, though neither was mixed up in political intrigue, were, nevertheless, brought frequently into contact with the Coadjutor's party, and in July 1650 they gave a supper to the Duchesse de Chevreuse, Gondi's clever and powerful ally, one of the most notorious women of her day. Loret has recorded it in his curious chronicle, the Rhyming Gazette, a diary in rhyme that he kept for Mademoiselle de Longueville, the stepdaughter of the Duchess.

"There is a good deal of talk here," wrote Loret in easy doggerel, "of a fine collation that Sévigné gave to the Duchesse de Chevreuse four or five days ago, after their return from driving along the Cours-la-Reine. The supper-room was well lighted with candles, there were several pretty ladies and a good number of gallants. It was a merry party. They ate ortolans, they sang drinking songs; they argued excitedly, 'no'—'yes'—'no'—'we shall see' was repeated a hundred times, and it is said they applauded the Fronde. Someone spilt soup; a silver dish was stolen, and—I know nothing more about it!"

This rather wild supper-party was, however, a simple affair in comparison with some of the excesses of the Fronde. All society was disorganised; Parisians breathed intrigue and lived in an atmosphere of masquerade and disguises. The house of the crippled poet Scarron was at this period one of the chief rendezvous for the licentious and aggressive spirits of the Fronde. All those who hated Mazarin were sure of hearing him vilified at Scarron's *appartement* in the Marais. The general hatred of the minister was here concentrated into witty lampoons, epigrams, and insulting street songs which sooner or later found their way to the Pont Neuf, and were repeated with delight by the Parisian mob.

The satyr-like host of the house in the Marais was one of the "lions" of Paris. He was so terribly crippled that he could not walk; so poor, that he hardly knew where to find daily bread; but so devoted to art, that in his greatest poverty, during the Fronde, he ordered a picture from Nicolas Poussin—a Bacchic subject of course! So witty that everyone—except his victims—enjoyed the sinister sneers, the biting jests, the wounding epigrams, that he dispensed so freely. He complains that visitors came to see him "as if he were a lion at a fair," but he probably did not object to this notoriety. His guests were among the most distinguished men in Paris; Gondi the Coadjutor, the Duc de Lesdiguières, the Comte de Fiesque, the President de Pommereul, and among many others came the young Marquis de Sévigné. Few ladies would visit at his house; his lack of even ordinary moral sentiments was too well-known, but he was such a witty talker that he was frequently carried to the houses of the ladies whose husbands visited him. Ninon de l'Enclos, however, who, like himself, scorned all social conventions, was sometimes a guest at his gay and licentious suppers, and it was here that she probably often met the young Marquis de Sévigné.

The Marquise, it need hardly be said, was not of the number who sought the acquaintance of Scarron, though, later, he begged her to go and see him. She learned, however, to her sorrow and annoyance, of the irregular life her husband was leading. Bussy, ever since their marriage, had tried to persuade both husband and wife that he was the entirely devoted friend of each. As he was a near relative, some eight years older than herself, a clever and polished man of the world, with a deferential manner to women, and a persuasive tongue, the Marquise doubtless looked upon him as a friend on whom she could rely for safe guidance. Whenever he was in Paris during the intervals of warfare, she begged him to use his influence with her husband to keep him, if possible, from the low and vicious acquaintances who were continually causing her annoyance as well as grief, for his irregularities were no secret to the society in which they lived.

Bussy declares in his memoirs that he did influence the young Marquis for some time, and that through him he broke with some of his vulgar associates; and he evidently was entirely in his confidence, for one afternoon, during the drive along the Cours-la-Reine, the Marquis came into Bussy's carriage, and confided to him with fatuous delight that he was the accepted lover of Ninon. Ninon! Who in Paris at that period had not seen or heard of Ninon? Anne de l'Enclos—Ninon is merely a charming diminutive of the sober Anne—had been left an orphan at fifteen, and having a sufficient fortune for her needs she had elected to live her life without any respect to convention or morality. She was of good family, which gave her a certain standing, though she soon lost her place in society by her openly immoral life. But to the day of her death, at the age of ninety, she had her own peculiar place in Paris. The beautiful and dangerous courtesan was even more witty than beautiful; and her openly avowed sentiments of free-thought aroused more horror than her notorious life. Ninon scoffed at the *précieuses*, and her wit was eagerly repeated in society. A man once complained to her that his daughter had no memory.

"Be thankful, Monsieur," said Ninon, "for then she cannot quote."

Her conversation was so gay, so witty and brilliant, that people came in crowds to her evenings; and though she drank nothing intoxicating, her guests used to say that the soup got into her head as if it had been wine.

More than once Ninon was in danger of being exiled by the stern Anne of Austria, who, as far as she could, kept a check on licence and immorality, but each time she was saved, either by a witty *mot* of her own, or by the intervention of powerful friends. On one such occasion, when Ninon was in disgrace, the Prince de Condé, once her lover and always her friend, meeting her among a great crowd of people, lifted his hat and stood for some minutes talking at her carriage door. This deference from a Prince of the Blood saved Ninon, and there was no more talk of exile!

Ninon had a singular and fatal attraction for the men of the Sévigné family. Madame de Sévigné's husband was the first victim of her fascination, and in due time his son followed in his unworthy father's footsteps; and many years later, when Ninon in her old age was still one of the attractions of Paris to fashionable and gilded youth, her grandson, the young Marquis de Grignan, took pleasure in seeking her company. Strangely enough, when the Queen of Sweden came to Paris, and passed free comments on all she saw and heard, she declared that the two most interesting women she had met were Madame de Sévigné and Ninon de l'Enclos; all of which seems to suggest some similarity in their gaiety of mind, their frankness and *joie de vivre*, in spite of their total dissimilarity of morals.

Bussy had no sooner heard the news which the Marquis de Sévigné had been so eager to give him, than he hastened to tell his cousin. Madame de Sévigné coloured with anger and annoyance when she heard the humiliating truth, and when Bussy advised her to say nothing about it she saw no wisdom in his counsel.

"You must be mad to give me such advice, or else you think that I am mad," said the indignant young Marquise.

"You will certainly be foolish if you do not follow his example," insinuated Bussy. "Revenge yourself, my pretty cousin, and I will share your vengeance, for your interests are as dear to me as my own."

But Madame de Sévigné was not to be led away by such specious reasoning.

"That is all very well, Monsieur le Comte," she said laughingly, "but my annoyance is not great enough for that."

The unscrupulous Bussy writes with an absolute lack of shame of the scandalous part he played between the weak young Marquis and his wife. The next day, when the Comte met Sévigné again at the Cours-la-Reine, the latter at once came into his carriage.

"I think you must have mentioned to your cousin what I told you yesterday," he began, "because she has hinted something of it to me."

"I have not said a word of it, Monsieur," declared the false de Bussy, "but as she is very clever, and has said a good deal on the subject of jealousy, she may have chanced to hit on the truth."

The foolish young Sévigné, full of his new affair, was easily satisfied on the point of his wife's jealousy, and told the Comte that he was going to Saint-Cloud that evening, where the Marquis de Vassé was giving a grand fête to Ninon, and that he should not return to Paris before the next day.

Bussy warned Sévigné that such openly scandalous conduct would drive his wife to despair, and that, however prudent and virtuous she might be, she would seek revenge if he persisted in his shameful courses. Then, taking leave of the Marquis and driving home, he at once wrote the following subtle and pernicious counsel to his young cousin—

"I was not wrong yesterday, Madame, in suspecting your prudence. You have repeated to your husband what I told you. You can see quite well that it is not for my own interest that I reproach you, for all that would happen to me would be to lose his friendship; but for you, Madame, there is much more to fear. I have, however, been fortunate enough to allay his suspicions. For the rest, Madame, he is so persuaded that he cannot be a man of the world without being always in love, that I despair of your ever being satisfied if you aspire to be the only one loved by him. But this need not alarm you, Madame; as I have begun to serve you, I will not forsake you at this juncture. You are aware that jealousy has sometimes more power to retain a heart than charms or worth; I therefore advise you to make your husband jealous, my pretty cousin, and for that purpose I offer myself to you. If I bring him back by this means I have enough affection for you to return to my first part of being your agent with him, and I will sacrifice myself again to make you happy. And if you must lose him, love me, my cousin, and I will help you to take your revenge by loving you all your life."

Bussy sent this letter early in the morning to Madame de Sévigné's house by a page, who, learning that she was asleep, waited about till he could give the letter into her own hands, as he had been ordered. Shortly after, the Marquis de Sévigné arrived home from Saint-Cloud, and, finding the page with a letter from the Comte de Bussy to Madame de Sévigné, he took it from the lad, and, after reading it, told him he might return to his master as there was no answer. When the Comte de Bussy heard who had read the letter, he declares that he felt fit to kill the page, and did not sleep the whole night for thinking of the danger to which he had exposed his cousin; and since one knows the character of the Comte, we may guess that some fear of the annoyance it might bring to himself may also have contributed its share to his sleepless night.

The weak young Marquis, however, took no very decided action. He merely forbade his wife to see the Comte de Bussy again; and with her usual charm and sweetness she wrote to her cousin, telling him to have a little patience and the affair would soon be forgotten. But the intercepted letter probably had its influence, for Sévigné thought that if his wife were away from Paris he might continue his dissipated life with more freedom than if she were at hand to hear of his dishonourable doings; and shortly after this he took the Marquise and her two young children to Les Rochers, and leaving them there with callous unconcern, he returned to Paris, flinging himself anew without the least restraint into his evil courses.

It is not surprising that such a life required more money than he possessed. Though they had been married hardly more than six years, Madame de Sévigné, in self-protection, had already had a separation of property, probably by the advice of the good Abbé de Livry. But when her husband plunged daily deeper into the slough of dishonour and debt, Madame de Sévigné, like the true woman that she was, forgave his flagrant sins against her, and came to his help with fifty thousand crowns. What the good thrifty Abbé, who so well knew the value of money, said on the occasion has not been recorded, but Ménage, who cordially disliked the selfish young Marquis for so openly neglecting his charming wife, used his privilege of being tutor and scolded her sharply for her weakness.

"Madame," he said severely, "a prudent woman would never throw away such sums upon a husband!" But Madame de Sévigné was never prudent where she loved.

After the Marquis de Sévigné had left his wife in the gloomy solitude of Les Rochers, he threw himself with less restraint than before into the pleasures of Paris. Ninon, to whom "three months was an eternity," soon tired of him; but instead of joining his wife in Brittany, and endeavouring to retrieve the fortune he had so nearly ruined, he now made himself conspicuous as the slave of a worthless woman who had already been the talk of polite Paris because of what were termed her "galantries."

Though this Madame de Gondran was undoubtedly a beautiful and attractive woman, Tallemant, in writing of Sévigné's infatuation, adds, "For my part, I should have liked his wife better." Bussy, too, with the frankness of a friend and cousin, pointed out to the Marquis that Madame de Sévigné was so charming that if she were not his wife he would certainly desire her for his mistress.

"Very possibly I might," assented Sévigné, but the admission did not make him a whit more faithful.

Strangely enough, his intimates and acquaintances could all perceive the rare charm and beauty of his young wife; everyone admitted it except the foolish, dissipated young Marquis, who thought it *bon ton* to neglect her. He now became so infatuated with Madame de Gondran—"Lolo," as her intimates called her—that he could refuse her nothing, and he carried his complacency to such an absurd point that for a while all the gossips of his circle were set talking in amazed indignation.

Mademoiselle de Chevreuse owned a pair of exquisite earrings, and these, no less, Madame de Gondran desired to wear at a ball during the Carnival. It was a little difficult for a woman of Madame de Gondran's rank, to say nothing of her lack of character, to borrow earrings belonging to the daughter of a duchess; but capricious beauty never believes that anything it desires is impossible, and Madame de Gondran contrived to make the Marquis de Sévigné believe it also. With a headlong determination to gratify Madame, he went boldly to Mademoiselle de Chevreuse and begged her to lend her earrings—not to Madame de Gondran, *that* request he knew would have been useless! but to Mademoiselle de la Vergne, his wife's intimate friend, whose mother had quite recently married his uncle, the Chevalier Renaud de Sévigné.

Mademoiselle de Chevreuse lent them willingly, and that same evening the bourgeoise wore them with complacent vanity at a ball. The earrings were immediately recognised, and several of the guests spoke of their amazement at seeing them worn by Madame de Gondran, hardly, indeed, believing the evidence of their own eyesight, and openly curious as to how she could possibly have obtained them.

The Marquis de Sévigné knew that someone would be certain to tell Mademoiselle de Chevreuse who had worn her jewels, and, fearing to be found out in his disgraceful falsehood, he went to Mademoiselle de la Vergne. To her he confessed the whole shameful truth, and throwing himself on her mercy, he begged her to help him out of the tangle into which he had drawn himself. Mademoiselle de la Vergne, who afterwards became the celebrated Madame de la Fayette, was then a charming and gentle girl of about nineteen, and, taking pity on the Marquis, promised to do her best. She went to Mademoiselle de Chevreuse and thanked her for the jewels; then, to save her friend's worthless husband, added the falsehood that she had lent them to Madame de Gondran!

The Marquis de Sévigné procured invitations for the Gondrans to all kinds of entertainments, where on their own merits they would never have been admitted, and, in consequence, their vanity increased daily. They began to speak with the utmost disdain of their old friends and relatives, and affected to know only the most charming people of the Court. It was inevitable that such absurd pretensions should meet with ridicule, and one evening, at her own house, the Abbé de Romilly grossly insulted Madame de Gondran while in the company of her husband. That good, easy man apparently dared not notice an insult to his wife from a person of superior rank, and a man named Lacger, who saw the curious scene, industriously spread the report of it.

When the Marquis de Sévigné heard of it he was furious, and made no secret of his intention of caning Lacger before a numerous company. Lacger, warned in time, did not appear, and Dame Rumour, disappointed of the actual duel which would assuredly have followed, invented one entirely on her own account, and, with her usual careful attention to detail, added that the Marquis had been badly beaten and was dangerously wounded by a sword-thrust.

This entirely fabricated story found its way to the provinces, and Madame de Sévigné, in alarm for her faithless husband, wrote him a letter full of tender reproaches, breathing a deep anxiety about his health. The Marquis never replied to this letter; for the next few days, far from thinking about his devoted young wife, his whole thought and attention were absorbed by an "affair of honour," the indirect result of his quarrel with Lacger. This young man, in great anger at Sévigné's threats, determined to be revenged without risking his own person. Knowing that the Chevalier d'Albret, another of Madame de Gondran's admirers, had for some time been refused admittance to her house, he spread the report that Sévigné had been scoffing at his discomfiture, not only with Madame de Gondran, but in the hearing of other people also. The Chevalier, determined to know the truth of the story, sent his friend the Marquis de Soyecour to Sévigné to ask whether he had been talking about him in the manner mentioned by Lacger.

Sévigné replied at once that he had never said a word to the disadvantage of the Chevalier d'Albret; then, not wishing to be suspected of trying to conciliate a rival, he added haughtily "that he had only said this in the cause of truth and not to justify himself, for that he never did except with a sword in his hand!"

There was only one possible answer to this, and probably both young men—the one hotly jealous of his rival, the other burning to avenge the insult to Madame de Gondran on someone—were more than willing to fight. A meeting was arranged, and at midday on Wednesday, 4th of February 1651, they drove, attended by their seconds, to a spot behind the convent of Picpus, a short distance from Paris.

Every detail was carried out with the punctilio such occasions demanded. The Marquis de Sévigné, who had chosen swords, bowed to the Chevalier, saying that he was his servant, and again declared that he had not said the words which had been falsely reported. The young men then embraced.

"But," said the Chevalier, "we must fight all the same." "Certainly," agreed Sévigné; adding that he had not come out there merely to return without having done anything.

Did a glimmer of their folly in fighting—indirectly—for such a worthless woman pierce for a moment their hot and foolish young heads? Even supposing that such wisdom had illumined them for a brief space, the laws of "honour" (and honour meant neither truth, chastity, honesty, faith, nor any other virtue save that of courage; but in that respect, as Madame de Sévigné wrote years after, a man's reputation was more delicate than a woman's) would have forbidden them to do anything but fight; and fight they did in grim earnest. After a few minutes' practised sword-play Sévigné received a thrust in the body, and he fell. He was taken from the ground to a carriage, and conveyed at once to Paris, where the surgeons pronounced that he was mortally wounded. His wild and foolish companions of pleasure came to see him; Gondran, the complacent and ridiculous bourgeois, wept bitter tears at the thought of losing his aristocratic friend the Marquis; and of Sévigné himself there is not a word recorded to indicate that even at that late hour he regretted his misspent life, or repented of the wrongs he had inflicted on the Marquise. His one futile refrain was the regret that he had to leave this pleasant world at the early age of thirty-two.

CHAPTER VIII

Madame de Sévigné's widowhood at Les Rochers—She returns to Paris and gradually re-enters Parisian society—Rival suitors—The quarrel between the Duc de Rohan and the Marquis de Tonquedec in her *ruelle*—A haughty Duchess—The battle of Saint-Antoine

MADAME DE SÉVIGNÉ had just passed her twenty-fifth birthday when the sad news of her husband's death reached her among the sombre woods of Les Rochers, and who can say what dark hours of desolation and anguish were spent by the young widow in her lonely chateau, where, so few years before, she had enjoyed a brief bright period of happiness as a bride? Few mourned the Marquis save his young wife; he had been a selfish egoist, seeking nothing but his own vicious pleasure; he had wasted his own fortune and part of his wife's also by his reckless dissipation; he had heaped humiliation on the Marquise, and it is scarcely surprising that the cynical Bussy found it difficult to believe that Madame de Sévigné's sorrow for her husband could be genuine.

But no one save this cynic doubted the reality and entire sincerity of Madame de Sévigné's grief. We know from her letters what a sensitive and impressionable heart and mind were hers; how keenly alive to pleasure, how readily touched by sorrow; and, notwithstanding the humiliations her husband had caused her to suffer, in spite even of the crowning outrage of the manner of his death, she was overwhelmed with grief at her loss. Even her pride was dominated by love and yearning sorrow. Tallemant tells the story, that the Marquise, who had neither a lock of hair nor a portrait of her husband, putting aside all wifely anger and just resentment, went to Madame de Gondran, who at once gave her what she required; while Madame de Sévigné, on her side, returned to the bourgeoise all the shameful letters she had written to the Marquis. This may or may not have been true, there is only an inveterate gossip's word for it, but it is quite conceivable that in the abandonment of her grief the young widow may have acted in a manner she would not have thought permissible in calmer hours.

We have, too, a record of her emotion when, two years after her husband's death, she saw Soyecour, who had taken part in the affair that led to the duel. Tallemant saw her turn pale and almost faint at the sight of this man; and the first time she saw the Chevalier d'Albret, the man who had killed her husband, she lost consciousness entirely. Once, too, when walking among the beautiful allées on the heights of Saint-Cloud, she caught sight of Lacger, and turning to her friends, she said in a low voice—

"There is the man I hate more than anyone in the world, because of the misfortunes he has brought upon me."

The two officers who were walking beside her immediately offered to thrash him in her presence, but the Marquise, who shrunk from such notoriety, refused their kind but embarrassing offer by saying tactfully—

"Pray take care; he is with several of my relatives whom you would not wish to offend, I am sure." And she turned with the officers into another allée of the park to avoid meeting Lacger.

Many years after, she chanced to write to her cousin Bussy that she could scarcely tell one year from another, because they were so mingled in her memory that only one or two were worth remembering.

"I should like to know," wrote the malicious Bussy, "which are the two years you consider worth remembering. If it were anyone else I should say that they were the years when you were married and when you became a widow."

The Marquise glided lightly over this impertinence. "I had only retained the dates of my birth and of my marriage," she replied; "but without increasing the number I will forget the year when I was born, which saddens me [she was then sixty], and I will put in its stead that of my widowhood, and the commencement of an existence which has been sufficiently pleasant and happy, without triumphs, and without distinction;

CHRISTOPHE DE COULANGES, ABBÉ DE LIVRY

but it will finish in a more Christian manner than if it had been disturbed by great events, and that truly is the chief thing."

All the spring, summer, and autumn of that sad year of 1651 the Marquise spent on her estate at Les Rochers with her two little children and her good uncle the Abbé de Coulanges, who immediately set himself to work to repair the shameful inroads that the late Marquis had made in his niece's and her children's fortune. Gradually all debts were paid, and by the virtue of that "holy economy" which the Abbé revered and daily instilled into his niece, her estates were brought again into good order, though only at his death did the Marquise reveal what a perilous state her affairs had been in at this period. "He extricated me from the abyss into which I was plunged at the death of M. de Sévigné; he gained my lawsuits, improved my estates, paid my debts, and made my son's estate the prettiest and most agreeable place possible," she tells her cousin, the Comte de Bussy, at the Abbé's death in 1687.

After nine or ten months of solitude and inevitable regrets for what might have been, Madame de Sévigné returned to Paris in the November of 1651. Loret, who recorded all events of importance in the polite world of Paris, noted the fact in his society chronicle—

> "Sévigné, veuve, jeune et belle,
> Comme une chaste tourterelle
> Ayant d'un cœur triste et marri
> Lamenté monsieur son mari
> Est de retour de la campagne,
> C'est-à-dire de la Bretagne;
> Et, malgré ses sombres atours
> Qui semblent ternir ses beaux jours,
> Vient augmenter dans nos ruelles
> L'agréable nombre des belles."

It is probable that the young widow, whose year of mourning was not yet complete, in the first few months of her return saw only her relatives and most intimate friends. There was her mother's sister, Henriette de Coulanges, Marquise de la Trousse, who was also a widow. She was frequently with her niece; indeed, she seems at this time to have been a companion and chaperone to the young Marquise, who was much too charming and attractive to live alone, even if etiquette had permitted it.

Another relative by marriage was Madame Renaud de Sévigné, at whose house she frequently saw the pretty and clever young Mademoiselle de la Vergne, her aunt's daughter by her first marriage; the young girl who, greatly against her will, had been mixed up in the affair of the diamond earrings. A lifelong friendship commenced between the Marquise de Sévigné and Mademoiselle de la Vergne, who, a few years later, as Madame de la Fayette, became one of the celebrated women of her time. There was a difference of eight years between the two friends, but the younger, by her grave philosophical character, her rather sombre outlook on life, and, in later years, by her illhealth, seemed fully as old as the Marquise de Sévigné, who by her gaiety, magnificent health, and joyous delight in life, kept her youth for an unusually long period.

It is pleasant, too, to find that the beautiful young widow, in the midst of the many perils of that unscrupulous society, was carefully guarded by her uncles the de Coulanges. Bussy sneers lightly at them for being jealous of her reputation; but the Comte, whose professions of affection for her were, at this time especially, greatly in evidence, could never have been accused of such a virtue.

When Madame de Sévigné again appeared in society, there was no lack of pleasant houses at which to visit. In these last months of the Fronde all classes of Paris were seeking amusement with a feverish gaiety, on the eve of they knew not what. La Grande Mademoiselle held her little court at the Tuilleries, and two or three nights in the week there was a comedy, a band of twenty-four violins to make music, and afterwards a supper and a ball. Indeed, the entertainments at Mademoiselle's were the chief of those in Paris. Anne of Austria gave no fêtes, or balls, or comedies; she was indolent by nature, much absorbed by her devotional exercises, and had probably little taste left for amusement among all the intrigues of the Fronde, which, however amusing they might be to the gay conspirators, were serious enough for her and her son, whose kingdom was at stake. Besides the charming entertainments at the Tuilleries, other heroines of the Fronde were constantly providing balls, suppers, fêtes, plays, at which not a few of the political intrigues were developed. The Duchesse de Châtillon, the daughter of

Bouteville de Montmorency, whose friendship had been so fatal to Madame de Sévigné's father, had grown up to be a triumphant beauty, who dominated a little circle of which she was the brilliant directress. The Prince de Condé was her abject slave, while she played the political cards entirely in his interests. The Duchesse de Chevreuse, another prominent Frondeuse, had her evenings too; and the Comtesse de Fiesque, the gay, irresponsible trifler, was attached to the court of La Grande Mademoiselle, and generally, on those evenings when the royal lady did not receive, gave some diversion or entertainment at her house. All these were the heroines of the Fronde, and, strangely enough, though Madame de Sévigné had no taste for intrigue—indeed, she was too frank and outspoken for the subtle rôle of *intrigante*—they were all her intimate friends. We gather that she was warmly welcomed in this society, for this was the most triumphant, and at the same time the most perilous period of her life. Her beauty was at its finest flowering point; her wit had been polished and her manners formed in the exacting school of the Hôtel de Rambouillet, and by five years of the best Parisian society; while her freedom of speech, which was the only fault that even Tallemant could find, must have been benefited by the softening and refining influence of grief and adversity. A circle of admirers gathered round her whenever she appeared, all eager for her preference; and some, we cannot doubt, hoping to be accepted as the successor of the late Marquis. All, however, among these gallants had not such honourable intentions, and she, well knowing her world, and realising her lonely situation with no father, husband, or brother to defend her, was probably the more determined to protect herself by her prudent and careful conduct.

But they were the troublous times of civil war. Party feeling ran high, the least social offence was magnified into an insult, and it is perhaps not surprising that there should be ill-blood among the hot-headed young gallants who strove for the first place in Madame de Sévigné's regard. A little more than a year after her husband's death, she found, to her intense annoyance, that an incident which occurred at her house, and of which she was the heroine, became the subject of conversation in all the *ruelles* of Paris.

Among the men who at this time were paying her the most marked homage was the Duc de Rohan, who had, not long before, by his handsome person, his graceful figure, his skill as a dancer, and similar qualities, won the heart of the haughtiest heiress in France, Mademoiselle de Rohan. This lady, who might have married a prince or a duke, would have none other than the handsome Chabot, a simple and obscure gentleman who brought her neither wealth nor titles. Her mother violently opposed this choice, but the pious Queen promised to give Chabot the name and dukedom of the Rohans, on condition that the children of the marriage should be brought up in the Roman Catholic faith. The bargain was gladly made, and Chabot rose with a bound from his modest condition as a mere gentleman, to every privilege belonging to a duke and peer of France. He was greatly attracted by Madame de Sévigné, and was a frequent visitor at her *ruelle*; though we may be quite certain that the Marquise, who, said her cousin Bussy, "was too jealous of her own honour," gave him no more than the pleasant welcome that was ordinarily given to gentlemen in the *ruelles* of the ladies of their acquaintance. Conrart, the first Perpetual Secretary of the Academy, gives such a quaint picture of the manners of the time in his piquant recital, that no mere paraphrase could do the incident justice. Tonquedec, it may be mentioned, was a neighbour and friend of Madame de Sévigné in Brittany.

"A gentleman of Brittany," writes Conrart, "named the Marquis de Tonquedec, related to the young Madame de Rohan, was attached [by feudal service] to the Duc de Rohan, and had promised to raise a regiment for him in the party of the Princes, but instead of doing this he joined the party of Cardinal Mazarin. After this the Duc de Rohan complained of him and would receive him no longer.

"On the 18th of June, Tonquedec was at the house of the widow of the Marquis de Sévigné when the Duc de Rohan arrived there. Tonquedec, who was in an arm-chair at the head of the bed in the *ruelle*, rose slightly, lifted his hat, and sat down again before the Duke had taken a seat, and without offering him his place. The Duke did not, however, show any resentment at this, but as he was leaving, he said to the Marquise de Sévigné that if it had not been her house he would have taught Tonquedec the duty and respect he owed him. The Marquise said to the Duc de Rohan that she was very sorry indeed that Tonquedec had been so impertinent at her house, and that she would beg him not to come again, for which the Duc de Rohan thanked her and went away. The following Thursday the Duc de Rohan passed Madame de Sévigné's house, and seeing the carriage of the Comte de Lude outside, he asked the coachman if his master was there. The man said no, it was M. de Tonquedec, to whom his master had lent his carriage. The Duke was attended by several gentlemen, whom he left below while he went upstairs to the *ruelle* of the Marquise de Sévigné. When the Marquise saw him she was very confused, and the Duc de Rohan, after having saluted her, turned to Tonquedec, and said—

"'I have been told that you boasted of having defied me in this house, and I have come to-day to teach you the respect you owe me.'

"'Monsieur,' retorted Tonquedec, 'I always pay you more respect than you deserve.'

"'You do not know your duty,' repeated the Duke, 'and I shall have to show you what it is.'

"Upon this, the Marquise de Sévigné, who was alone, and who well knew to what such words would lead, begged Tonquedec over and over again that he would leave the house at once.

"'Madame,' said the Duc de Rohan, 'do you really wish him to go?'

"'Certainly, Monsieur,' she replied.

"'It is only right that you should be obeyed,' answered the Duke, and with these words he turned Tonquedec out of the house."

This, said Conrart, was the Duc de Rohan's version of the affair, but that of Madame de Sévigné was somewhat different. In the first place, she denied that she had ever promised not to receive Tonquedec at her house again. Indeed, on this point she greatly offended the Duchesse de Rohan. After the first visit of de Rohan, on the 18th of June, Madame de Sévigné, who all through her life was particular in the observance of small, as well as important, social duties (and who continually scolded her daughter for the neglect of them), paid a visit to the Duchesse de Rohan in the Place Royale, to say how sorry she was that the affair should have occurred at her house. The haughty Duchesse received her with marked coldness, which perhaps was hardly surprising when the homage that her husband, whom she passionately loved, was paying Madame de Sévigné was just then the most freely discussed topic in Paris! Then the Marquise, anxious to make peace, mentioned the affair to Mademoiselle de Chabot, the sister of de Rohan, who replied that if she wished the Duchesse to be satisfied with her conduct, it was necessary that she should refuse to see Tonquedec again. "This," remarked Conrart, "was thought very imperious," and Madame de Sévigné had no intention of discarding an old friend for such insufficient reasons.

It was generally believed in society that it was the proud Duchesse de Rohan who was so determined that Tonquedec should be humiliated by the Duke. When the latter told his wife of the manner in which Tonquedec had almost ignored his presence, and had kept the seat of honour in the Marquise de Sévigné's *ruelle* without offering it to him, his feudal lord, the Duchesse had exclaimed that "the affront was too great to endure!"

It was because of her anger that the Duke had paid the second visit, knowing that Tonquedec was there, and had then "reprimanded him as if he had been his valet."

Nor was Madame de Sévigné alone, as the Duc de Rohan had said, for her aunt, the Marquise de la Trousse, was in the *ruelle*, and Marigny the poet was there also, and when the Duc de Rohan spoke so insultingly to Tonquedec, they both implored the latter to leave the house at once, knowing that in the heat of passion a duel on the spot might be the result if he stayed.

All this caused much gossip in Paris, and everyone, "especially the ladies," said Conrart, "blamed the behaviour of the Duke in the presence of the Marquise de Sévigné." Even Loret, who of course gave the piquant incident a place in his chronicle, deplored that it should have happened *dans un lieu de respect*, and the general feeling was against the de Rohans. Madame de Sévigné had no near relative to call out the Duke; even Bussy was with his regiment in Nivernais, but the Chevalier Renaud de Sévigné, the nearest of her late husband's kin, challenged the Duc de Rohan, while Tonquedec demanded satisfaction on his own account; and the Comte de Vassé, the Comte de Lude, Chavagnac, and others among her friends, were all anxious that the insult to the Marquise should be answered for.

But the watchful Duchesse, passionately devoted to her husband, was determined that no meeting of the kind should take place. Knowing what would be the inevitable result of her husband's arrogant conduct, she never allowed him to go out without a guard of men, and Loret recorded that "the Duke was held back, though he frantically desired to fight." But unkind rumour said that it was not necessary to hold him very tightly!

Conrart finishes his recital of the incident with this terse comment: "The true cause of the misunderstanding between the Duc de Rohan and de Tonquedec was that they were both in love with Madame de Sévigné."

But the attention of Paris was soon directed to other, more serious matters than this nobleman's quarrel. The Fronde, after nearly four years of the turmoil and bloodshed of civil war throughout France, was now drawing near to its end. Paris was brilliant with the colour and commotion that differing parties brought in their train. The followers of Condé wore scarves of the *couleur isabelle* or dove colour; red was the badge carried by the soldiers of the brigand king the Duc de Lorraine, who, when those intriguing ladies the Duchesses de Montbazon and de Châtillon asked him what part he intended to take in the Fronde, gallantly took the hand of each, and replied, "Let us call the violins, and dance, Mesdames; that is the way one negotiates with ladies!" The adherents of Gaston d'Orléans wore blue; and, to the lasting shame of the House of Condé, there were many Spaniards flaunting their yellow scarves, a continual reminder of the treason of those who had sought a Spanish alliance against their own King.

Paris, weary of war, was desiring peace above all other things, and in desperation decided to appeal to its venerated saint, "Madame Sainte-Geneviève." This was, of course, to satisfy the demands of the people; for even in that day there were many among the educated and upper classes who openly scoffed at it as superstition.

La Grande Mademoiselle mocks gaily at the custom in her memoirs, and Madame de Sévigné's attitude towards it may be guessed from the jesting account of the procession she long afterwards gave to her daughter.

"I have been with Madame de Vins, the Abbé Arnauld, and d'Hacqueville to see the procession of Sainte-Geneviève. Do you know that this procession is considered a very fine sight? It is composed of all the different religious Orders [of the mendicant friars—the Cordeliers, the Jacobins, the Augustins, and the Carmelites], all the parish priests, and all the canons of Notre Dame, preceded by the Archbishop of Paris, who goes on foot, giving his benediction right and left till he comes to the cathedral. I should have said to the left only, for the Abbé de Sainte-Geneviève walks barefooted on the right, preceded by one hundred and fifty friars who are barefooted also. The cross and mitre are borne before him, as before the Archbishop, and he bestows his benediction in the same manner, but modestly and with much devotion, fasting, and with an air of penitence which shows that he is to say mass at Notre Dame. The Parlement in red robes, and the chief companies, follow the shrine of the saint, which glitters with jewels, and is carried by twenty men robed in white and barefooted. The Provost of the merchants and four councillors are left as hostages at the Church of Sainte-Geneviève for the return of this precious treasure."

The procession was carried on the 13th of June, and on the 1st of July the decisive and disastrous battle of Saint-Antoine was fought just outside Paris, that extraordinary conflict between the two greatest French heroes of their century, the famous Turenne and the equally famous Condé. King, Queen, and Court watched the struggle from Charenton on one side, while the townspeople, crowding on to the roofs, watched with eager, fascinated eyes from the other bank. Condé, hotly pursued by Turenne in the rear, and faced by the closed gates of Paris, seemed doomed to ignominious death and defeat before the eyes of the Parisians, who had once adored him for his military genius. Then Mademoiselle, her heart touched by the hero's distress, insisted on the opening of the Porte Saint-Antoine, and had the cannon of the Bastille turned on Turenne's army. Condé was saved, and it was practically the end of the Fronde, of which Mademoiselle was declared the "Heroine," a proud title for which she was yet to pay an extravagant price—a dreary exile of six years!

CHAPTER IX

The Comte de Bussy pays court to the Marquise—He gives a fête in her honour in the Temple Gardens—Madame de Sévigné at the height of her charm and popularity—A period of temptation—Dangerous gallants—The Prince de Conti—Nicolas Foucquet

THE Comte de Bussy in his scandalous memoirs boasts that he was the first to speak of love to Madame de Sévigné after her husband's death, but we have seen that the young widow was surrounded by many admirers as soon as her year of mourning was completed, and as Bussy was only able to leave his regiment for a short visit to Paris in the October of 1652, he must have been deceived by his vanity on this point.

In the following February, however, he came again to Paris, and stayed there till the autumn. Then, there is no doubt, he paid the most assiduous attention to his charming cousin, who, besides being one of the most attractive women in Parisian society, was doubly desirable to a man of Bussy's character, because of the many distinguished men who were constantly seeking her.

Bussy himself lacked neither distinction nor charm. He, too, was of that strangely seductive Rabutin blood, and had not yet proved what a base alloy was lurking in his character. To outward seeming he was a brave soldier, a polished courtier, a witty and handsome man, who never forgot that he was of the nobility; who, however little he might esteem women, always paid them the most courteous homage in speech and manner. But though, as the cousin of the Marquise, he had the advantage of being able to visit her more frequently, and on more familiar terms than other friends who were not her relatives, the young widow was in no danger from the fascinating Comte. He has written much that was spiteful and malicious about her, but he bore constant witness to the absolute rectitude and virtue of her life; and this from Bussy, who once at least in his anger would so gladly have soiled her good name, has been considered by her biographers as a testimonial indeed.

But with all her undoubted and indisputable virtue, which shines with star-like purity among the astonishing intrigues by which she was surrrounded in her daily society, she was never austere. She met Bussy's amorous speeches, his veiled advances, his most cunning innuendoes, with the same laughing repulses, none the less effectual because they were witty and showed a perfect comprehension of the situation. Bussy records that he got nothing but "the answer of the oracle," and though he still continued his attentions to his cousin, trying his utmost to make her believe that he was desperately in love with her, he transferred some of his affections to Madame de Montglas, who received them with more gratitude than Madame de Sévigné.

Bussy had been staying all that summer of 1653 with his uncle Hughes de Rabutin, the Grand Prieur of the Temple, and just before leaving Paris, to join his regiment in Flanders, he gave a fête in the Temple Gardens, ostensibly to Madame de Sévigné, but in reality to Madame de Montglas; and it was so like Bussy's double-dealing to make each of them believe she was the lady he delighted to honour. And all this time not a word of his wife, who was probably safely away in Burgundy at his estate of Chaseu! Bussy was very well pleased with his fête, and gives an account of it which shows that he at least appreciated it at its full value.

"Some days before I departed," he writes, "I gave to Madame de Sévigné a fête so beautiful and extraordinary, that you will, I am sure, like to have a description of it. First, picture to yourselves the Temple Gardens, which you know well, where there is a grove traversed by two walks. At the point where they meet was a rather large circle of trees, to the branches of which had been fastened a hundred glass chandeliers. On one side of this open space a magnificent theatre was erected, of which the decoration was worthy of the illumination. The light from hundreds of candles, which the leaves of the trees prevented from being diffused, threw such a glow on to that spot, that the sun could not have made it more brilliant, and, from the same cause, the surrounding places were so dark that eyes were useless. The night was beautifully clear and tranquil. The entertainment began with a comedy which the guests found very amusing, and after this the twenty-four violins played some *ritournelles, branles, courantes,* and *petites danses.* The company was more select than numerous; some danced, others looked on, while others wandered away among the allées. This lasted till the break of day, and, as if Heaven had acted in concert with me, the dawn appeared just as the candles flickered out. This fête was such a success that I received many inquiries as to the particulars of it, and to this day it is spoken of with admiration."

Bussy, who was now *mestre de camp général* of light cavalry —a promotion for which he had been negotiating during his stay in Paris—joined Turenne's army not long after this, and though he corresponded with his cousin after his departure, several letters of this period have been lost, for which, he says, he would willingly have paid their weight in gold to anyone who brought them to him.

Madame de Sévigné had not time to miss her cousin amid the gaieties of the Parisian winter season. The Fronde was now happily over, and Paris was settling down to pleasure after the distractions of civil war, precisely as she had sought it when the strife had been at its worst; for does not Paris, under all superficial change, ever remain *au fond* the City of Pleasure? The leading spirits of the Fronde were now in exile. The Cardinal de Retz languished in Vincennes; La Grande Mademoiselle was experiencing the deadly monotony of winter in the provinces, in her dilapidated old Chateau of Saint-Fargeau; her vacillating father, Gaston d'Orléans, was banished to his estate of Blois, and even refused his daughter's visits as often as he dared defy that determined young Princess, fearing lest a too great intimacy with the chief heroine of the Fronde might be considered compromising by the young King. Condé, once the greatest hero in France, was utterly demoralised by the ignominy of his imprisonment. "I went to prison an honest man," he declared, "and came out a criminal." He was now misusing his military genius in making war on the King in the provinces; his army a very Adullam's cave for the disaffected. Those poor provinces! Words cannot paint the sufferings the peasants, farmers, and lesser gentlemen endured after the passing of an army, even though that army was composed of fellow-countrymen! Whole villages were laid waste, and sometimes left a smoking ruin after everything had been seized by the rapacious soldiers; and men and women who resisted or protested were strung up on the nearest trees after the most horrible treatment, or frightfully mutilated as a warning to others. That true saint, Vincent de Paul, went where he could in the wake of this terrible army, binding up wounds, carrying comfort and consolation to stricken hearts, a most faithful and humble "curer" of souls and bodies.

But all these things had no place in the chronicles of Paris. The streak of barbarism in the French character of this and much later periods, showed itself in the absolute insensibility to the wrongs or sufferings of the peasant. A gentleman was always sure of consideration—according to his rank, of course! —but a peasant was of no importance under any circumstances. And while Paris, in the season that followed the battle of Saint-Antoine, was seeking amusement with the same frantic impetuosity that she had sought it during the Fronde, a few, very few, good women of the bourgeoisie—the Presidente Lamoignon and Madame de Miramion were among the foremost—under the direction of Saint Vincent de Paul, carried what help they could to those stricken towns and villages which had suffered from the visit of an army; whether of Condé's men or the King's it hardly mattered, for all the soldiers were poorly and irregularly paid, and almost as indifferent to life as outlaws or barbarians.

The Prince de Conti had made a better bargain for himself than his brother Condé. As payment for his share in the Fronde he had married Anne Martinozzi, one of those attractive Italian nieces of Mazarin who all made such good marriages. This clever young Prince was one of the many men who found an especial charm in Madame de Sévigné's society, and, as will be seen by one of Bussy's letters, deliberately planned to gain a special place in her regard. He was a strange compound of virtues and vices; a man who swiftly passed from excessive devotion to extremes of dissipation. At one time he was intended for the Church, and for a brief period he was the Abbé de Cluny; and Olivier d'Ormesson gives this striking pen-picture of the occasion when, at the Sorbonne, he maintained his first thesis for the degree of licentiate. All the theological faculty of the Sorbonne were present. " M. le Prince de Conti was in an arm-chair on a high daïs opposite the President, under a red velvet canopy, with a table before him. He wore a violet satin cassock with the rochet and *camail*, like a bishop. The Coadjutor (Gondi) presided, and disputed very well, though with great deference; but the young Prince sustained his thesis marvellously well, with much vivacity and spirit, in front of a great number of the Jesuits."

But the Prince de Conti had to relinquish his abbacy when he married, and for a time he threw himself into a whirl of dissipation. In the winter following the Fronde he had met Madame de Sévigné at the Marquise de Montausier's house, and had been greatly attracted by her witty conversation, for he too was clever and *spirituel*, with a gift of persiflage that doubtless harmonised very well with the brilliant gaiety of Madame de Sévigné. Nature, who had been so lavish to him in some ways, had been very severe in others, for with a handsome, well-formed head and face, he had piteously deformed shoulders. We have no record as to what were Madame de Sévigné's impressions concerning him, but we may be quite certain that, whatever his intentions may have been, she looked on him merely as a pleasant and exalted friend of the moment, whose attentions were passing honours to be lightly forgotten.

Another, more dangerous admirer was Nicolas Foucquet, the new Surintendant des Finances, a perilous friend for a young, unprotected woman because of his extraordinary personal charm. He had had an amazing career of unbroken prosperity. At the age of sixteen he was an advocate of Parlement; two years later he was a councillor of the Parlement of Metz; and before he was twenty he held the honourable post of Maître des Requêtes.

During the Fronde this precocious young lawyer had rendered important services to Mazarin, and in Parlement was always one of the most zealous supporters of that unpopular minister. Such devotion and ability did not go unrewarded. Mazarin, who had the born ruler's gift for appraising men, gauged his suppleness of mind, his ability and resource as a negotiator, his energy and power as an administrator, and on the day after the entry of the Cardinal into Paris—back again till death to his old power and supremacy—Foucquet, conjointly with Servien, was made Surintendant des Finances.

In the few short years that followed, the life of Nicolas Foucquet reads like that of the younger son in a fairy-tale who has suddenly become prince, with stores of treasure at command. By his peculiar gift for finance, and his almost miraculous power of inspiring confidence, immense sums of ready money were at his disposal; gold poured through his hands, so to speak, in an inexhaustible stream. The King demanded money, always money, for treaties, ballets, fêtes, rejoicings, masquerades; and Foucquet, by his resource, ability, and unlimited credit, was always able to supply it.

His family, his relatives, his friends, all shared in his marvellous success; courtiers, both men and women, were, figuratively, at his feet, and overwhelmed him with the most delicate, the most flattering marks of their regard, which he in turn paid for with gold or remunerative posts. He had a genuine passion for art; and poets, painters, sculptors, and artists of all the minor arts found in him a modern Mæcenas. He gave magnificent entertainments at his house at Saint-Mandé near Picpus; royalty sat at his table, and came out of curiosity to see his magnificence; in all the kingdom there was no man more generally courted than Nicolas Foucquet. Court ladies of the highest rank gladly accepted his attentions, and his charm was not all that of gold. He was gay, witty, clever, with a delight that was almost a passion, in all the good things of life, and he had apparently no greater happiness than in putting himself and his riches at the service of his friends. La Fontaine, who for some years lived under his protection—for those were the days when literary men did not disdain to pick up the crumbs from great men's tables—declared of Foucquet "that his manner of giving was better than the gift."

Madame de Sévigné frequently met Foucquet in Parisian society after the Fronde. The financier was greatly attracted by this charming, brilliant Marquise, who, unlike so many ladies he met, wanted nothing either for herself or for her friends. Once, when Bussy urged her to beg some favour of the Surintendant, Madame de Sévigné replied almost indignantly, " I would rather ask a favour of any other man in the world than him"; for she knew that only by her absolute independence could she keep him at a safe distance. From a letter, written by Bussy to the Marquise, we gather that she was in the midst of temptation among the gay and corrupt society of Paris, who, if they had ever followed the precepts of the *précieuses*, had certainly forgotten them, or laid them aside as out of fashion. Bussy had accompanied the Prince de Conti to Catalonia, and, while halting for two days at Montpellier, wrote to his cousin a letter which, under its light badinage, reveals Bussy at his worst, a self-seeker of the most degraded kind.

"MONTPELLIER, *June* 16, 1654

"I have had news of you, Madame. Do you remember the conversation you had last winter with the Prince de Conti at Madame de Montausier's? He tells me that he said some pretty things to you, that he found you much to his taste, and that he intends to tell you so more decidedly this winter. Take care, my charming cousin; the woman who is not guided by interest is sometimes led away by ambition, and she who is able to resist the King's financier may not always be able to withstand his cousin. By the way in which the Prince spoke to me of his designs, I see plainly that he intends to make me his confidant. I suppose you will have no objection to this, knowing as you do, how well I have acquitted myself in that character under other circumstances. For myself, I am delighted with the hope of being his successor; you understand me, my pretty cousin. If, after all that fortune wishes to put in your way, I do not make mine, it will be entirely your fault; but you will surely be careful, for you really must help me in some way. I think you will be somewhat embarrassed between the two rivals; I seem to hear you saying,

"Des deux côtés j'ai beaucoup de chagrin ;
O Dieu, l'étrange peine !
Dois-je chasser l'ami de mon cousin ?
Dois-je chasser le cousin de la Reine ?

"Perhaps you are afraid to attach yourself to the service of princes, and my example may deter you. Perhaps the figure of one displeases you, and perhaps the face of the other. Let me hear something of this latter, and of the progress he has made since my departure. How many free-patents has your liberty cost him?

"Fortune is making you splendid advances, my dear cousin; do not be ungrateful. You are as much infatuated with virtue as if it were a real good, and you despise wealth as if you could never be in need of it. Do you not know that old Senneterre, a sensible man of great experience, said that people of honour go barefooted? We shall see you one day regretting the time you have lost; we shall see you repenting of having so badly employed your youth, and of having with so much difficulty striven to acquire and preserve a reputation which a calumniator may destroy, and which depends more on good fortune than on your good conduct.

"I joined the Prince de Conti at Auxerre. He did not pass by Chaseu [the Comte de Bussy's estate] because he learned that it would take him six leagues out of his way, so my preparations were useless. I have not left him since, and am on the best possible terms with him. We intend to amuse ourselves here for two days, with play, drives, and good cheer, while waiting for the troops to assemble for the purpose of entering Catalonia. I can answer for it, my charming cousin, that you will hear of me in this campaign.

"Adieu, my fair cousin; think sometimes of me, and that you have no relative or friend who loves you so much as I do. I wish—no, I will not finish, for fear of displeasing you, but you know quite well what I wish."

In no other letter of Bussy's does he show quite such black, unrelieved baseness of mind. He was desperately anxious to improve his fortunes, and, untroubled by the least moral hesitation, he urges his young, unprotected cousin to barter her beauty and charm that he may, of her dishonour, make a stepping-stone to advancement! His counsel, his insinuations, his suggestions throughout are villainous, and not even the prevalence of such ambitions among courtiers can excuse him. There were many honourable and noble men even among the class who claimed the proud title, and Bussy's shameless and

THE COMTE DE BUSSY

cynical letter would not deserve quotation if it did not show what a fire of temptation assailed the young Marquise on all sides, even from her nearest relative, who should have held her honour as dear to him as his own. Tried in this fire, however, her purity of life shines the brighter, more especially as the licence of the times was so great that many examples among her daily society would have provided her with ample excuses if she had wished to follow Bussy's advice.

How sadly prophetic he is, too, in saying that a caluminator may easily destroy the reputation which she is so careful to preserve! One may quite certainly say that at this period neither of them dreamed that the base-hearted Bussy would be the caluminator of the cousin he professed "to love better than any relative or friend."

Her answer to this letter has been lost, but we may gather something of its nature from the note Bussy sent her on receiving it—

"FIGUIÈRES, *July* 30, 1654

"Mon Dieu! How witty you are, my dear cousin! How well you write, and how charming you are! It must be owned that, being so modest as you are, you are under a great obligation to me for not loving you more than I do. Faith, I can scarcely keep within the limits you impose. Sometimes I blame your insensibility, sometimes I excuse it; but I always excuse you. I have many reasons for not displeasing you, but I have still stronger reasons for disobeying you. What! You flatter me, my cousin, you say sweet things, and yet you forbid me to have the least tenderness for you. Ah well; I must not then; I must do as you wish, and love you after your own fashion; but some day you will have to answer before God for the constraint I put upon my feelings, and for the evils which will follow in consequence. . . ."

In the next letter to his cousin, written rather more than a fortnight afterwards, Bussy gives us some glimpses of Madame de Sévigné's affectionate character, and of the scorn and indignation with which she regarded coquettes. We also glean a little news of the Surintendant Foucquet, about whom Bussy was continually asking questions, and building, one doubts not, all kinds of airy castles on the subject. It is noticeable, too, that this letter is different in tone from the one he had written at Montpellier. The Marquise, though truly amiable, and hating to wound her cousin, had evidently made him quite aware that such letters were not to her taste.

"The Camp at Vergès, *August* 17, 1654

"You tell me so often that you would regret me greatly if I were dead, and there is something so delightful in the idea of being regretted by you, that I would willingly die, if a few trifling considerations did not make me wish to live. Besides, having never found you out in an untruth, I am quite willing to believe your word in this instance rather than prove it. It is also extremely probable that a person whose eyes fill with tears when speaking of the loss of her friend, would mourn him truly if he were really dead. I believe then, my beautiful cousin, that you love me, and I assure you that I, like you, am entirely satisfied with our friendship.

"But I do not agree with you that your letter, frank, and signed openly as you say, would put to shame all the love-letters in the world; the two things are entirely distinct from each other. You must be satisfied if your friends approve of your style, without depreciating the *billets-doux* that have never injured you. You are ungrateful, Madame, to abuse them after the respect they have shown you. For my part, I am an advocate for the love-letters, but not against yours; I see no necessity to decide between them, for they are entirely different things. Your letters have their graces, and the *billets-doux* theirs; but, frankly speaking, if you would sometimes send us a love-letter, your letters would not be so valued as they are.

"You are strangely indignant against coquettes. I do not know whether this will last till you are fifty, but at all events I shall keep in exercise a few sentiments of love, so that I may have them for use if at any time you should happen to change your mind. Till then, I shall have for you only the purest friendship in the world, since you will have nothing more.

"I am glad that you are satisfied with the Surintendant; it

is a proof that he is returning to reason, and that he does not take things to heart so much as he did. When you will not do as we wish, Madame, we must wish to do what you desire, and consider ourselves too happy in remaining your friends. No one except you in the whole kingdom could persuade a lover to be content with friendship. There are very few who remain friendly when their love has been refused, and I am convinced that a woman who is able to prevent a rejected lover from turning into an enemy, must have extraordinary merit. . . .

"I am delighted to hear that your uncles think well of me. Apart from jealousy, they are excellent men; but there is no one perfect in this world, and if they were not jealous they would perhaps be something worse. With it all, it is not they whom I fear the most; and do you wish to know why, Madame? I fear you so much because you are a hundred times more jealous for your own honour than they can be.

"I shall be obliged to say sweet things sometimes, Madame; I cannot keep from writing them; but there is no danger from the hour that Madame de la Trousse sees my letters. . . . Adieu, my charming cousin, here is enough badinage for this time. Here is the serious part of my letter, I love you with all my heart."

The Marquise, rather alarmed, no doubt, at the licence Bussy was taking in his letters, told him, with the instinct of self-protection, that in future all the letters he sent her would be shown to her aunt, the Marquise de la Trousse. Her uncles, too, one gathers, are prepared to be watch-dogs to their charming young niece, whose greatest safeguard, however, is her own high sense of honour.

Bussy encloses a note to Madame de la Trousse, which shows that he is not abashed in the least at his too-free letters to his cousin.

"I am greatly obliged to you, Madame, for the advice you have given me. Believing that our charming Marquise read my letters by herself, I might perhaps have written some things that I should not wish others to see, and God knows what a life you would have led me on my return, and how ashamed you and I would have been of them. Your prudence has averted that misfortune by telling me that you will read all I write, and has placed things on such a footing that I shall take care to please you always, and never to cause you any annoyance. But, Madame, in reassuring you concerning the too-tender letters, I am ashamed of writing such follies, knowing that you will read them; you who are so wise, and before whom only the *précieuses* are pure. . . ."

CHAPTER X

The escape of Cardinal de Retz—His relative, Madame de Sévigné, acts as intermediary—A letter to her old tutor Ménage—The Comte de Bussy leaves Paris to go to camp—A lively correspondence between the two cousins

SHORTLY after receiving these letters from her cousin Bussy, Madame de Sévigné went, as was her custom, to spend the autumn at Les Rochers, and while there received a letter from Cardinal de Retz which must have caused her much astonishment.

Though personally she had kept aloof from the political and other intrigues of the Fronde, she had a close acquaintance with most of the prominent actors in it, for her kinsman by marriage, Cardinal de Retz (he obtained the hat in 1650), has with much reason been called by historians "the soul of the Fronde." He began his career as "leader of a party"—the phrase is his own—by instigating the Paris mob to rebel against authority on the eve of the famous Jour des Barricades, in August 1648, which was virtually the beginning of the Fronde; and for the next four years he was intriguing, now with this party, now with that, and was, throughout the rebellion, one of its most prominent and truculent figures.

At the conclusion of the Fronde he was confined at Vincennes, and not long after, his uncle, the Archbishop of Paris, died. This was a great opportunity for the Cardinal. All the curés of Paris demanded of the King, in the name of religion, that the Cardinal should be set at liberty to take his rightful place at the head of the clergy and of his flock. The Holy Father at Rome, too, had a voice in the matter, and expressed some indignation that a Prince of the Church should be put in prison, considering that all ecclesiastics claimed immunity from arrest.

But strangely enough, for some inexplicable reason, the Cardinal formally renounced all claim to the Archbishopric of

Paris! He thus gave up all hope of his liberty, and the only result of this quixotic action was his removal from Vincennes to a prison at Nantes, where the Maréchal de la Meilleraye guarded him with so little severity that the Cardinal passed his days in the pleasantest society.

It was probably from motives of policy that the scheming Cardinal was surrounded by diversion, and permitted to receive visits from all the ladies in the neighbourhood, who, after enjoying the comedy which was the usual evening amusement of the Cardinal, would often stay to sup with him. The Chevalier Renaud de Sévigné and his wife, who lived in Anjou, often came to see him, bringing with them Mademoiselle de la Vergne, whom the Cardinal found "very pretty and charming."

But amidst all these diversions the Cardinal was yearning for the only thing they denied him, his liberty. He was a prisoner on parole, but de Retz was always able to juggle with conscience or honour as occasion demanded, and he now made a bold bid for freedom with the aid of Joly, the Duc de Brissac, and his relative the Chevalier Renaud de Sévigné.

It was a romantic flight. He escaped from under the eyes of his gaolers in broad daylight, and while they were trying to open a heavy door which he had shut behind him, he climbed with ropes the walls of a bastion forty feet high, and then descending, mounted a horse which his friends had in readiness on the other side. While hotly pursued he fell from his horse and dislocated his shoulder, but even this did not daunt him. He concealed himself for seven hours in a haystack, and then galloped off again, in spite of the intense pain in his arm. The whole flight was a romance, a series of exciting perils and hairbreadth escapes, till finally, reaching Rome, the escaped prisoner was just in time to bring the drama to a picturesque conclusion by assisting at the election of a new Pope, with all the gorgeous pomp of the Roman Catholic Church.

While he halted on his journey at Machecoul, in his brother's territory of de Retz, he had a short breathing-space in which to reflect on the consequences his flight might have for the Maréchal de la Meilleraye. He dared not write to him personally, for fear of compromising him still more than he had already done by his breach of faith; he may even have found it somewhat difficult to find explanatory phrases for his conduct in addressing the considerate guardian to whom he had given his parole. In his dilemma he bethought himself of his charming young relative, the Marquise de Sévigné. She, he knew, was on friendly terms with la Meilleraye, and he wrote to her an account of his flight, explaining his motives, passing as lightly as he could over his breach of honour, and begging her to use what influence she had with la Meilleraye on his behalf. Fearing this letter might be intercepted, he sent it to Ménage, indicating, at the same time, how it should be used. The letter reached Madame de Sévigné in safety, and on the first of October she wrote to Ménage from les Rochers.

"I have received the letter you sent me from the Coadjutor, and I do not doubt but that it will have a very great effect. I sent it yesterday to Nantes to the Maréchal de la Meilleraye, and I cannot tell you how much obliged to you I am for the promptness with which you have done me this service. In that I recognise your usual habit, and I truly thank you with as much goodwill as of goodwill you have taken such trouble. . . .

"But how delightful it is to find you on good terms with all my family. Six months ago things were not so pleasant. I find that these quick changes have a strong resemblance to those of the court. . . . But, bon Dieu! Where did you make acquaintance with the Grand Prieur, whom M. de Sévigné used always to call 'my uncle the Pirate'? He had the fancy that he resembled him greatly, and I think he was not mistaken. But do tell me what you could have been doing together, as well as with the Comte de Bussy. I have a strange curiosity to learn all about this affair as you have promised me. But there is yet something else. Our Abbé [the Bien-Bon], who hears on all sides that you are loved, gets it into his head that he loves you also, and he has already told me to put a word in here and there on this subject to you. I have promised to do my best, and if it be true that you love those whom I love, and to whom I am under the very greatest obligations, I shall not have much trouble to obtain this favour from you. I will give you time to think of it, and, while awaiting your reply, I assure you that you ought to be as satisfied with me as on that day when I wrote to you a letter worth ten thousand crowns.

"MARIE DE RABUTIN-CHANTAL"

The Marquise could not resist her inclination to coquetry whenever she wrote to her old tutor Ménage, and she refers to the days of her girlhood, when the tutor had declared that one of her letters was "worth ten thousand crowns." A year or two before this she had reproached him humorously for the devotion he was showing to his young pupil Mademoiselle de la Vergne. "But even though she be a thousand times more amiable than I am, you have been ashamed of your injustice, and your conscience has been so remorseful that you have been obliged to divide your affections more equally than you did at first. I praise God for this good feeling, and promise you to agree so well with that amiable rival, that you shall hear no complaint from either of us."

As may clearly be seen from the letter, dated 1654, Ménage, who a few years before had been, in his quality of literary man, an almost daily guest at the Cardinal's table, had become embroiled with his patron during the troubles of the Fronde. Loret refers to it in his chronicle, and it is probable that at the same time he may have quarrelled with the Abbé de Livry also.

"But how delightful it is to find you on such good terms with all my family. Six months ago things were not so pleasant." These cordial phrases show what genuine pleasure it gave the Marquise to find that the friend and tutor of her girlhood was no longer at enmity with her people. With what charming artifice she mentions the Abbé de Livry's desire to be friendly again; how gracefully she insinuates that by meeting him half-way, her old tutor will be giving her a special pleasure! This gentle, peace-loving side of Madame de Sévigné's nature must have been one of her greatest charms; her gracious, kindly spirit was strangely free from the taint of pride or bitterness; she "hated satire," it was said, and she hated, too, all the ignoble passions which mar human intercourse; the discord, strife, and jealousy which, a free-growing crop at all times, flourished especially during the turbulent years of the Fronde.

Madame de Sévigné returned to Paris for the winter season

at All Saints, and in the spring her cousin Bussy came to the capital for a short period. All society was watching with keen and curious eyes for the lady who would be honoured by the preference of the young King. It was more than whispered that Mademoiselle Mancini was the chosen of the King; indeed, it is history now that he would fain have raised her to share his throne. But the Cardinal's ambitions stopped short at this; even Anne of Austria could not countenance this honour for Mazarin at her son's expense, and the project was promptly quashed.

The Marquise de Sévigné was still pursued by the attentions of Foucquet, who was daily increasing in the power that wealth gives, and it is again from Bussy's letters that we gather in what relation the Surintendant stood to Madame de Sévigné. Bussy, who still professed to care for his cousin with a more than cousinly affection, was so occupied with his various " affairs of the heart " that he could not find time to bid her good-bye, till the last hour before his departure for Landrecy. Then, on calling at her house, he found that she had gone to Livry for a few days, as she often did while she was in Paris during the summer. He sent an apologetic letter, but we see from Madame de Sévigné's reply that she has nothing but the most frank and sisterly regard for him, and accepts the excuses for his neglect without the least offence, and is anxious, indeed, only for his honour and distinction.

"LIVRY, *June* 26, 1655

" I did not doubt that you would bid me good-bye sooner or later," she writes, " either at my own house or from the camp at Landrecy. As I am not a woman of ceremony I am quite content with the latter, and had not even thought of being angry because you did not come to see me before you set out. . . .

" I have not stirred from this beautiful desert since your departure, and, to speak frankly, I am not at all sorry to hear that you are with the army. I should be unworthy of so brave a cousin if I were sorry to see you in this campaign, at the head of the finest regiment in France, and in so glorious a post as the one you hold. I believe that you would condemn any sentiments less noble than these; I leave weaker and more tender feelings to other people. Everyone loves in his own way. I profess to be brave as well as you, and am proud to boast of such sentiments. Some ladies might perhaps think this profession a little too much in the old Roman style, 'And would thank God they were not Romans, that they might still preserve some feelings of humanity.'"

"But I can assure them that I am not entirely inhuman, and that with all my heroism I desire your safe return as passionately as they can do. I trust, my dear cousin, that you do not doubt this, or that I pray to God with all my heart that He will preserve you. This is the farewell you would have received, and I beg you to accept it from here as I have accepted yours from Landrecy."

Bussy was a little piqued at these heroic sentiments, however, and would have been much better pleased with timorous doubts as to his safety.

"Your letter from Livry is very pleasant," he writes, "but, as you say, it is not the most loving in the world. . . . When one loves people who go to the army, one has more fear for the dangers to which they will be exposed than joy in the hope of the honours they may obtain."

About a fortnight after this, the Marquise wrote again to Bussy, giving him the most affectionate congratulations on the success of his Guards at Landrecy, an engagement that Maréchal de Turenne had praised before all the Court. She was delighted to hear that her cousin had so distinguished himself, and sent her praises under the form of the badinage he so well understood.

"PARIS, *July* 14, 1655

"Will you always disgrace your relations? Will you never be tired of making yourself the subject of conversation in every campaign? Do you think we are pleased to hear that M. de Turenne has sent word to the Court that you have done nothing worthy of mention at Landrecy? Truly this is most annoying to us, and you will understand how deeply I feel the insults that you bring upon our family.

"But I do not know, my cousin, why I thus amuse myself

with jesting, for I have just now very little leisure, and what time I have I ought to speak seriously. Let me tell you, therefore, how delighted I am to hear of the success you have had in what you have undertaken. . . .

"Adieu, my cousin; the *Gazette* mentions you very slightly; which has given offence to many people, and to me especially, for I am more interested than anyone in what concerns you. . . ."

A few days after this, Madame de Sévigné wrote a long letter to her cousin, of which the most interesting paragraphs are those which relate to the Surintendant Foucquet. In a letter that Bussy had sent her early in July from the camp at Landrecy, he gave her a detailed account of the tender leave-taking between himself and Madame de Montglas, and finished the recital by saying—

"There, Madame, is my *histoire amoureuse*. I believe that that of the Surintendant is neither so gay nor so sad, but whatever it is I beg you to tell me all about it."

The Marquise did not satisfy his curiosity. In her letter answering this she told him very little, and of what she did say she warns him not to gossip, for Bussy had already been helped by the powerful Surintendant to purchase his post of *mestre de camp général*, and, as she took care to remind him, it would not be politic to talk about Foucquet's relations with herself. It is quite probable that Bussy's too-glib tongue occasionally needed a curb!

". . . I never remember to have read anything more amusing than your description of your leave-taking. . . . But though it is very good of you to give me the particulars of this affair, I have not the least inclination to make you a similar confidence concerning what passes between the Surintendant and me; indeed, I should be very sorry to be able to say anything in the least resembling it. I have always in his company the same circumspection and the same fears, and these are a considerable drawback to the progress he wishes to make in my affection. I believe that, in the end, he will be tired of renewing a subject in which he is so little likely to succeed. I have seen him only twice these six weeks because of a journey I have taken. This is all I can, and indeed all I have to say on this subject. Be as careful of my secret as I am of yours; it is as much your interest as mine to keep silence on the matter. . . ."

The journey that Madame de Sévigné mentions was in all probability to Saint-Fargeau, the lonely chateau where La Grande Mademoiselle was still in exile. The Princess mentions this visit in her memoirs. "Mesdames de Montglas, Lavardin, and de Sévigné came expressly from Paris to see me," she writes in July 1655; and she whimsically complains of the curious power she has at this period of making people ill. In many cases when she invited her former friends and flatterers to her chateau, she received, instead of the visits she expected, so many excuses on the score of ill-health that she began to suspect that the real cause of so much illness was her disgrace with the King!

In October, Bussy again wrote to the Marquise, again mentioning the Surintendant, with whom he had evidently had some little misunderstanding, and, reading between the lines, it is not difficult to imagine that Foucquet's leniency, which so surprises Bussy, is due to the powerful influence of the Marquise. It is interesting, too, to note that Maréchal de Turenne, one of the most distinguished heroes in France, was anxious to be on familiar terms with Madame de Sévigné. The little we can learn of this affair is tantalising. We know from her letters that, some years after this, she went to visit him with Madame de la Fayette, we know also that the sympathetic letters she wrote on his death could only have been inspired by a personal acquaintance and a deep admiration, but we do not know whether at this brilliant period of her life he was ever successful in gaining admittance to her *ruelle*.

"THE CAMP AT ANGRES, *October* 7, 1655

"I am very glad, Madame, to receive assurances from you that the Surintendant is inclined to think me in the right in the affair between us. This greatly surprises me, and I think it very extraordinary that he chooses to complain of Madame Martel rather than of me. I assure you also, my charming cousin, that I am very much obliged to him, and that there is hardly anyone in the world against whom I would not declare myself if it were a question of his interests. Judge, if you can, how much I love you for having prevented me from losing such a good friend. . . .

"Two or three days ago, when M. de Turenne and I were chatting together, I chanced to mention your name. He asked me if I saw you sometimes, and I told him that we were first cousins of the same family, and that I saw no other woman so frequently as you. He said that he knew you, and that he had been twenty times to your house without finding you at home. He added that he esteemed you greatly, and that, as a proof of it, he saw no other woman—[the next sentence is missing in the text in every edition]. I told him that you had spoken of him to me, that you were aware of the honour he did you, and that you had told me you were greatly obliged to him.

"While we are upon this subject, Madame, I must tell you that I do not believe there is a person in the world who is more generally esteemed than you. You are the delight of mankind. In pagan times, altars would have been raised to you, and you would assuredly have been created the goddess of something or other. In these days we are not so prodigal of incense, above all for living merit, and we content ourselves with saying that you are the most lovely and virtuous woman of your age. I know Princes of the Blood, foreign princes, great noblemen who keep a princely state, great captains, ministers of state, gentlemen, magistrates, and philosophers, who would be your humble servants if you would allow them. What could you desire more? Unless you envy the liberty of the cloisters you can go no further. . . ."

CHAPTER XI

The Queen of Sweden visits Paris—Her impression of Madame de Sévigné—An infant prodigy—La Fontaine's verses on the Marquise—A ball in her honour—Wax candles carried off by maskers

THESE were indeed the most brilliant and triumphant years of Madame de Sévigné's life. The "princes, ministers of state, and great captains" of Bussy's eulogy are easily recognisable in the Prince de Conti, Foucquet, and Maréchal de Turenne; and it would be interesting, if it were possible, to trace the other dignitaries who he declared were willing, at a sign from her, to become her devoted servants. She had not yet reached her thirtieth year, and was still in the zenith of her extraordinary charm, still enjoying life with the gay abandon that was part of her natural disposition, but which was, however, always kept between well-defined limits of grace and propriety.

During the year 1656 Paris was pleasantly occupied with entertaining that eccentric royal lady, Queen Christina of Sweden. This learned and masculine daughter of Gustavus Adolphus, who voluntarily renounced her throne, was received with enthusiasm and given many fêtes by the French King and his Court; for it has ever been a charming Parisian habit to offer hospitable welcome to kings and queens who were not comfortable in their own kingdoms.

Balls and masquerades, comedies and reviews, followed by sumptuous banquets, were given in honour of the Northern Queen, whose dress, speech, and actions were watched and noted with an amused and eager curiosity. At the balls and festivals she clothed herself something like the Court ladies at least, but there were times, enjoyed by the Parisian crowd, when she donned her usual costume of a man's *justaucorps* of black velvet trimmed with ribbons; a cravat tied with flame-coloured ribbons, which was popularly called a "drôle"; a blue moire skirt edged with deep embroidery; and on her fair hair, cut short like a man's, a black velvet toque decorated with a plume of black feathers.

Among the many diversions provided for the Queen, was that of an exhibition of an infant prodigy, at that time astonishing both Court and town, and who reminds us that there is nothing new under the sun, not even infant prodigies. This strange child was the son of a comedian named Beauchasteau, and at the age of seven or eight, spoke several languages, and improvised verses with extraordinary facility. King, queens, and courtiers, always eager for novelties of any description, crowded to hear the child, who, unabashed by this brilliant assembly, improvised complimentary verses on each in turn. Madame de Sévigné was of the company, and of her he said—

> "Sévigné, suspendez vos charmes
> Et les clartés de votre esprit?
> Pour nous faire rendre les armes,
> Votre extrême beauté suffit."

Poor little prodigy! After receiving a pension of a thousand crowns from Mazarin, and another of three hundred crowns from the Chancellor Séguier, he was taken to Spain, and from thence to England, where he was brought before the Protector Cromwell. He survived all these honours, but his ambitious friends, still not satisfied, wished to introduce him at the Court of Persia, and during his journey into that far country all trace of him was lost.

Queen Christina of Sweden wrote and spoke her impressions of people and things with an almost embarrassing freedom. To Mazarin she wrote that the Court lacked only one thing to make it perfect, "the witty conversation of that rare person Ninon de l'Enclos"! She was evidently quite impartial in her admiration of gaiety and intellect, for she expressed an equally sincere admiration for Madame de Sévigné, and in a letter to the Marquise de Lavardin said so much in praise of her beauty and wit, that Madame de Sévigné was rather annoyed when she found that the Marquise had been showing this letter somewhat freely to her friends. There is, perhaps, a little of this annoyance to be traced in an extract from a curious epistle, half prose, half verse, that she wrote to La Grande Mademoiselle from Les Rochers the same autumn:

"I have lately received twenty-five or thirty letters, which have told me the same thing twenty-five or thirty times; the fine receptions that have been given to the Queen of Sweden, and those which she has given to other people."

Among the many fêtes was a sumptuous entertainment given by Nicolas Foucquet at Saint-Mandé, for the Surintendant had grown in influence and importance as his wealth increased. He kept a superb table, which was supplied with the rarest delicacies from all known quarters; and so exquisite were his banquets, that Mazarin, the Queen-Mother, the young King, and Monsieur accepted the hospitality of this wonderful financier, who seemed to have discovered the coveted secret of turning everything into gold. But, magnificent as Saint-Mandé was, Foucquet's ambition soared yet higher; he would have a palace of art, in which should be gathered all that money could buy or art create, of things that were most rare and precious.

The Surintendant owned the estate of Vaux-le-Vicomte, near Melun, and here he determined should be his Palace of Art. Up to that period, brick faced with stone was considered good enough for any private building, but Foucquet, for his new palace, would have nothing but the finest cut stone. Le Vau, the King's architect, planned the building, and an army of workmen was brought to carry out his advanced ideas. Le Nôtre, the King's gardener, exercised his talent in laying out whole villages in parks, parterres, gardens, and closes; and there was also the tranquil little river Argenteuil to turn into fountains, cascades, and foaming torrents, amid the sylvan silence of the woods and gardens.

Foucquet had inherited from his father, not only a cherished collection of books and rareties, but also the passion for collecting, which he was now able to gratify to its utmost. He bought whole libraries and collections, which he housed at Vaux; he procured the richest tapestries from Mortlake in England and from Flanders; but such an enormous quantity of these precious fabrics was required for the walls and furniture of his new palace, that skilled workmen were brought from Paris, and a manufactory was started at Maincy, a village close to Vaux.

The famous Le Brun decorated his walls and ceilings; sculptors, artists, craftsmen of all kinds, looked to Foucquet as a beneficent patron, and if anything rare or unique were taken to him it was nearly certain to be bought at a good price. Marble basins, vases and groups of figures, were wanted for his fountains; statues were required to people his woods; all the most rare and costly works of art were needed to fitly furnish the rooms of his superb palace. Even his factotum Vatel was unique; there was not such another as he in the kingdom; and the great Mazarin did not disdain to borrow him from Foucquet to superintend the festivities when the Duc de Mantua stayed in Paris.

There was a charm of boyish enthusiasm in all that Foucquet did, a vivid personal charm that seems to have endeared him to all those whom he benefited. He was a generous friend to literary men in the days when, as Pellisson said, "an immortal work would cause a poet to die of hunger." La Fontaine lived at Vaux, and amid the beauties of the woods and gardens watched the habits of the wild creatures of the woods, a knowledge that he afterwards turned to good use in his imperishable Fables. To Scarron, the jovial scoffer, the burlesque poet whose words were winged with venom, he was more than a patron; we have glimpses of him as a kind and thoughtful friend. Foucquet not only allowed him a pension of sixteen thousand crowns, but in 1659 the poet wrote to Foucquet: "Since you sent me the pie, I have received your excellent cheeses. I believe you intend to nourish us on the best fare in the world."

Mademoiselle de Scudéry was another of his pensioners, and also one of his most attached and faithful friends. She is not an altogether lovable person, although she was most wearisomely admirable; for ever talking in her strident voice; for ever laying down rules for the guidance of other women; always posing as an oracle to an admiring circle. But her loyalty to her friends when they were in trouble excuses many of her platitudes. Just as she had been faithful to the Duchesse de Longueville in her disgrace, so, when Foucquet came to his inevitable fall, Mademoiselle de Scudéry was his most ardent helper and advocate, so far as a man in his desperate condition could be helped.

When Vaux-le-Vicomte was finished, Foucquet had an

especial pleasure in gathering round him in his sumptuous retreat, the poets, literary men, playwrights, and artists, to enjoy the exquisite gardens and to wonder at the marvellous fountains, which for their beauty and ingenuity had not their like in France. Molière came with his troupe of players to give his comedies; Le Brun, the painter, would not only paint scenes for their representation, but he would also use his mechanical genius in preparing all kinds of surprises; artists of every degree delighted in giving the generous, kindly Foucquet of their best.

Mademoiselle de Scudéry was a person of much importance at Vaux. She was the pre-eminently successful novelist of the day, whose volumes, as they issued from the press, were veritable events. Here, too, came her declared lover Pellisson—Foucquet's business manager—not as an ordinary lover, of course, but a purely platonic though ardent friend, exactly according to the precepts that Mademoiselle de Scudéry had laid down with so much authority at the Hôtel de Rambouillet.

Madame de Sévigné was an honoured guest at Vaux. Besides the admiration Foucquet had always professed for her, he had great confidence in her intelligence and judgment. "I must consult the Marquise de Sévigné," he said on one occasion, "her conversation throws such a clear light on things that are puzzling."

It is not difficult to picture the Marquise at Vaux, wandering among the beautiful gardens, listening to the murmurous music of the fountains, and walking round with her host to examine and admire all the wonderful works of art he had gathered in his palace.

At these charming reunions, host and guests vied with each other in literary games, *bouts-rimés*, epigrams, madrigals, and *chansons*; and on one occasion La Fontaine, then an unknown, ardent young poet, read a letter for the amusement of the company that he had written in verse to the Abbesse de Mons. The audience was charmed with the wit and easy grace of the letter, and Madame de Sévigné expressed her pleasure to the modest young poet with her usual gracious frankness. Two days afterwards, La Fontaine, delighted with her approval, and knowing that praise of the charming Marquise could not fail to

NICOLAS FOUCQUET

please Foucquet, wrote to him the following prophetic but somewhat obscure lines :—

> "De Sévigné, depuis deux jours en çà,
> Ma lettre tient les trois quarts de sa gloire.
> Elle lui plut, et cela se passa,
> Phébus tenant chez vous son consistoire.
> Entre les dieux (et c'est chose notoire)
> En me louant, Sévigné me plaça . . .
> Ingrat ne suis : son nom sera piéça
> Delà la ciel, si l'on m'en voulait croire."

It was about this time that Mademoiselle de Scudéry published her famous romance *Clélie*, in which she gives a "portrait" of Madame de Sévigné, under the name of the "Princesse Clarinte." It was, indeed, one of the chief points of interest about these novels, that some of the ladies and gentlemen of the fashionable world would be certain to find themselves there, under high-sounding names drawn from Greek and Roman sources.

One can imagine the eager curiosity and interest with which certain people would be recognised, and how the author would be besieged with questions as to who was who. The "portrait" of Madame de Sévigné would be considered a somewhat lengthy description even of a princess in a novel to-day, but the many little details give us an intimate knowledge of this *grande dame* who was so unaffected and charming in her manner.

"The Princesse Clarinte," she writes, "is of that pleasant height and figure which, while being much more than medium, is yet not excessive. Her air also is so free, her actions so natural, her carriage so noble, that immediately one sees her one knows she is of noble birth and has passed her life in the great world.

"She is fair, without being insipid, and her colouring is very suitable to her style of beauty. Her complexion is so admirable that not even the most severe winters can rob her of the beautiful bloom which makes it so lovely, which gives such a fine effect to her marvellous fairness; and one sees there at all seasons that freshness which is only seen at dawn on the most beautiful roses in spring. Her lips are of the loveliest colour; her face is well formed, her eyes are blue and full of fire and expression. . . . Her throat is white, and beautifully formed. As for her mind, I do not know how to make you understand it, but I know well that there never was òne more charming, better turned, more enlightened, or more delicate. She has a lively imagination, and her whole manner is so *galante*, so frank, and so charming, that one could not, without shame, see her without loving her. She, however, confesses that she is sometimes subject to little moods of melancholy without reason, which cause her to make a truce with joyousness for three or four hours only; but these annoyances are so slight and pass so quickly that hardly anyone but herself knows anything of them. Her conversation is easy, amusing, and natural; she speaks well and justly; she has sometimes certain naïve and witty expressions which please infinitely; and though she is not one of those stiff and motionless beauties who have no gestures, all her little actions have no affectation and are only the natural outcome of her vivacious spirit, of the enjoyment of her humour, and of her charming habit of doing everything gracefully. She dances so marvellously well that she delights the eyes and the hearts of all those who see her. Clarinte loves reading, and, what is better, she understands admirably all the best literature without any pretence of being a *bel esprit*. She has even learned the African [Italian] language, with wonderful ease. This princess, besides these rare qualities, has a sweet, true, and charming voice; and what is especially praiseworthy, is that though she sings in a passionate manner, and one might truly say she sings well, yet she sings like a lady of quality; that is to say, without staking all her honour on how she does it, without being begged to do it, and without ceremony: and she does it so gaily that she becomes still more charming, especially when she sings certain little African [Italian] songs, which she likes better than those of her own country because they are more passionate.

"For the rest, Clarinte loves all pretty things, and all innocent pleasures, but she loves glory more than herself; and what is a very great advantage to her, is that she has found the means, without being either severe, shy, or solitary, to preserve the best reputation in the world at a great court where she sees round her the most polished men, and where she awakens love in the hearts of all those who are capable of experiencing it. That same playfulness which becomes her so well, and amuses herself while it amuses others, helps her to retain as friends many who, if they dared, would become her lovers. Her conduct is such that calumny has always respected her virtue, and she has never been suspected of the least gallantry, though no one is more *galante* than she. She sometimes says that she has never been in love except with her own reputation, which she guards jealously.

"What is still more remarkable in this person, is that at her age she directs the affairs of her household as prudently as if she had all the experience that time could give to a most enlightened mind; and what I admire still more is that, when it is necessary, she can leave the world and the court, and amuse herself in the country with as much tranquillity as if she had been born in the woods. . . . I have never seen together so many attractions, so much good-humour, so much politeness, so much enlightenment, so much innocence and virtue; and no one else has ever known better the art of having grace without affectation, cheerfulness without folly, propriety without constraint, glory without pride, and virtue without severity. . . ."

Mademoiselle finishes the portrait by saying—

"She has a friend who has known her since childhood, who is a man of such great merit, who has so much wit, judgment, knowledge, virtue, politeness, and who knows the world so well, that it is not strange that she should have chosen him from the beginning of her life to be the chief among her friends."

This description could only apply to the Comte de Bussy, who, to his world, seemed a polished courtier, a gentleman *sans peur et sans reproche*—the abduction hardly counted—but who was soon to make a startling revelation of his character, in a manner that most seriously wounded the heart and hurt the reputation of the lady who was supposed to be his closest friend.

During the years that immediately succeeded the Fronde, Paris was gradually growing more ardent in the pursuit of amusement exactly in proportion as the young King approached nearer to his full manhood. Never was King more passionately devoted to pleasure in every form than Louis XIV, and at this period, a year or two before his marriage, we find him frequently running about the streets at night during Carnival time, with his young brother the Duc d'Anjou, and a few choice spirits among his courtiers, all masked, or dressed in absurd masquerade costumes, visiting the houses at which they knew balls were being held. It is interesting to find that on one such occasion he visited the hôtel of the Duc de Lesdiguières, who that night was giving a ball, ostensibly to six ladies, though, says the chronicler, "the affair was really given in honour of the widow of the Marquis de Sévigné."

It was a magnificent entertainment. It began with a comedy, which was followed by a ball, and after that the guests sat down to a banquet. The rooms were beautifully decorated, and in the grand gallery there were no less than thirty-six crystal lustres, each holding twelve wax candles. At the hour of the ball, a little group of figures, all closely masked *à la portugaise*, came out of the Louvre and stood on the steps debating as to where they should go that evening. There was the young King, then about nineteen, Monsieur, some chevaliers d'honneur, and a few ladies of the Court, the charming little Rivière Bonœil, Mademoiselle d'Argencourt, and Mesdames de Navailles and de Comminges. It was at first proposed to visit Mademoiselle, but finally they decided to go to the house of M. de Lesdiguières. The maskers reached the house just as the comedy was over, when the ball was in progress; and the host, knowing this band of maskers, gave them welcome, and after dancing for some time they all sat down to a superb collation. But when the King and his distinguished company had left the house, another masked band of a less reputable kind swarmed in, and carried food from the tables and candles from the lustres. These latter had to be replaced several times during the evening, and it was said that the wax candles alone cost the Duc de Lesdiguières more than one hundred pistoles.

These maskers were an extraordinary feature of the second half of the seventeenth century in Paris, and under such convenient disguise, robberies and murders were committed with impunity. Sometimes as many as two hundred maskers would be seen at one ball; and it was a necessity for anyone walking or driving through Paris at night to be accompanied by armed lackeys. So great was the disorder that sometimes the lackeys themselves would turn on the maskers and plunder them; indeed, all kinds of excesses were committed by these dark, mysterious figures, who might be anyone, from the young King, or Monsieur his brother, to the students at the Jesuit or other colleges, escaping for a few brief hours from the rigid rule of their daily life.

CHAPTER XII

The Comte de Bussy in difficulties—He desires to borrow money of the Marquise—A misunderstanding—Madame de Montglas pledges her diamonds—Bussy's mean revenge on his cousin—Molière produces Les Précieuses Ridicules

MADEMOISELLE DE SCUDÉRY was not the only person who considered the Comte de Bussy as one of the staunchest friends of Madame de Sévigné. Had the Marquise been asked who was her dearest, most loyal friend, she probably would have named her cousin Bussy. He never lost an opportunity of telling her—in polished phrase and amusing epigram, it is true, but none the less unmistakably—that he was her very humble servant, always anxious to do her bidding, always hoping that she would return the love he professed to have for her.

Madame de Sévigné, as we have seen, consistently laughed at such professions, and kept him at a safe distance by refusing to take them seriously. Those were the days of exaggerated gallantry, and perhaps it was a legacy from the court of *précieuses* that men should make pretty speeches and women expect them. The Marquise certainly preserved her reputation as a *précieuse* by keeping all her professed admirers beyond a well-defined circle of propriety, and to Bussy she confessed a sisterly love and interest in his honour which he found peculiarly irritating. In 1655 she wrote to him—

"I am told that you have asked permission to stay on the frontiers this winter. As you know, my poor cousin, that I love you with a blunt and honest kind of love, I hope your request may be granted; for this, it is said, is the sure road to promotion, and you know how sincerely I am interested in your welfare and good fortune. But I shall be pleased whatever happens. If you remain on the frontier, true friendship will find there what it expects; and if you return, affectionate friendship will be gratified."

Bussy, as we have seen, was rather piqued by such calm expressions of friendship; he would greatly have preferred to hear that a warmer, more agitated interest filled her with fears for his safety.

The peculiar connection between these cousins, who, said a mutual friend, "were born for each other," was an intimacy of mind, an affinity between their wit and understanding quite apart from their totally diverse characters and principles. The Marquise herself once wrote that "they could hear each other's thoughts before they spoke," and this quick mutual interplay of ideas and expression is so marked in some of their letters, that, without looking at the heading, it is occasionally difficult to say which cousin is writing.

Each, without question, found an especial and piquant pleasure in the other's society. The Comte admired his cousin for many things: her grace, her beauty, her sweet disposition, even for the impregnable virtue which he tried so often to undermine; but above all else he admired her for her instant appreciation of his sparkling wit, to which her own brilliant intellect answered with never-failing responsiveness; his lightest *bon mot*, his most obscure allusion, his most delicate repartee, would always, he knew, be sure of instant comprehension from her, and not infrequently strike an answering fire of wit.

As Bussy told Maréchal Turenne, " he saw no other woman so frequently," and the Marquise was, doubtless, equally glad to see this handsome and polished soldier-cousin who had so many times tried to impress on her the fact that he was her most devoted servant. It would seem incredible that any misunderstanding could arise between these two friends, bound so closely together by ties of kinship as well as by such an unusual affinity of understanding, did we not know that the frail texture of human friendship has often some weak part that gives way under the strain of unusual circumstances.

Bussy, in the month of May 1658, was in Paris, preparing to join Turenne's army in Flanders, and, as the preparation of his equipages and other requirements was an expensive matter, he found himself in desperate need of money. He applied to some of his friends, who probably knew Bussy too well to lend him a sou, and finally he went to the Marquise de Sévigné, who, like himself, had just been left ten thousand crowns by their uncle, Jacques de Neuchèze, the Bishop of Chalon. They had neither of them yet received the money from the executors, and Bussy sent to ask his cousin if she would advance him a thousand pistoles on the money he was to receive.

The Marquise was quite ready to help him in his need, but apparently the Abbé de Coulanges managed all her money affairs, and when she told him of Bussy's application he did not think the matter so simple as did his niece. Money should not be lent even to cousins, said the sage Abbé, without good and solid security; and had Bussy, who played high, who was a spendthrift, who was always squandering money on his pleasures, such security to offer?

Bussy was therefore told that, before the money could be lent him, his affairs would have to be inquired into. It was only a postponement, but Bussy, who was in sore need of money, regarded it as a disguised refusal. Besides, there was no time to wait; his reputation would suffer if he arrived late at the seat of war; and, burning with wrath against his cousin, he went to Madame de Montglas, who, to lend him two thousand crowns, immediately pledged her diamonds.

Having obtained the much-needed assistance, Bussy left for Flanders, more angry with Madame de Sévigné than he would have believed possible. His anger had not cooled when, some time after, he wrote this scathing reflection on his cousin's refusal.

"There are people," he writes to a friend, "who make only sacred things the limit of their friendship, and who will do everything to oblige their friends with the exception of offending God; these people call themselves *friends as far as the altar*. Madame de Sévigné's friendship has other limits. That beauty is only a friend till it is a question of the purse."

Was the Marquise to blame? It is difficult for us to-day to decide how much share she had in the delay, and we know it was the Abbé de Coulanges who counselled prudence. Had she had the control of her own affairs she would probably have advanced the money at once, without further question. But her own and her children's fortunes had already been seriously impaired by her spendthrift husband; it had taken the thrifty Abbé years of careful management "to draw her from the abyss" into which her husband's excesses had plunged her; and there is no doubt that the Bien-Bon thought good money would be thrown away by lending it to a prodigal like Bussy. We know that Madame de Sévigné had a horror of avarice, and that she willingly impoverished herself for her husband and children; indeed, it is quite conceivable that the prudent Abbé used the argument that for her children's sake she must not quite recklessly lend money to a gambler like Bussy without due inquiry. An extract from a letter that she wrote just a year before her death is a touching witness to her generosity of spirit, for it demonstrates plainly that she had stripped herself of almost everything to establish her children, and to pay the debts incurred by their extravagance.

"I die without any ready money," she writes, "but also without debts; it is all I ask of God, and it is enough for a Christian."

But even if some allowance be made for Bussy's anger against the cousin who he thought might have done him this service, the revenge he took a little later was so scandalous, so shameful from every point of view, that the most lenient of his judges could only be shocked at such base, dishonourable conduct.

In the spring of the following year, 1659, the Comte de Bussy, with his friends, had just returned from a campaign, and, eager to join in all the amusements of Paris after the hardships of war, they were greatly annoyed when Holy Week interrupted their plans of pleasure. Vivonne, one of the most reckless of this band, suggested that they should all come with him to one of his country-houses some leagues from Paris, where they might indulge in whatever amusements they desired, unchecked by the religious observances which Paris always devoutly practised in the holy season.

His companions accepted this proposal with enthusiasm, and at his Chateau of Roissy they behaved outrageously; uttering blasphemies against religion, and acting in such a wild, reckless fashion, that Bussy, who had passed his fortieth year, should have been ashamed to chronicle such doings. But Bussy, born without moral sense, had no shame at any time, and he tells us in his memoirs that, in the morning after this wild night, he and his companions agreed to write the worst things they knew of everyone except their friends.

It was then that Bussy, in this disgraceful company, gave rein to his spite and anger against his cousin. He wrote a "portrait," in which he dissected her with a merciless analysis, accentuating her defects, depreciating her charms, and holding her up to ridicule in the manner most calculated to wound her, or any woman, to the depths of the soul.

But retribution was near at hand for Bussy; in fact, this event has been noted by his biographers as the turning-point of his life, when from being a brave, clever captain, with high ambitions for the future, and a brilliant prospect of promotion, he became, first a prisoner, then an exile for long, weary years, seeing one by one his fair hopes and bright ambitions fade to the melancholy actuality of grey, monotonous, empty days at his estate in the provinces, with only the recollection of past successes to feed his vanity.

Rumours, very probably exaggerated, of the orgy at Roissy had reached the ears of the King and the pious Queen Regent, who, as long as she lived, exacted as far as she could an outward respect for religion and virtue, and as a result the offenders were banished, Bussy to his estate in Burgundy. Here, in the long leisure of his solitude, he wrote his scandalous *Histoire amoureuse des Gaules*, which was, in fact, a *chronique scandaleuse* of the Court, with the flimsiest disguise of fictitious names. Bussy knew better than anyone that his cousin had no rightful place among such depraved company, but nevertheless he included her portrait with the others, now polished and sharpened with malicious skill, so that every point was barbed with the worst of venom—the bitter venom of him who has once been friend.

Bussy declared afterwards that he never intended either the *Histoire amoureuse* or Madame de Sévigné's "portrait" to be published; he had only written it, he said, to amuse Madame de Montglas. But of such things, once written, it is impossible to predict the fate. This brochure was found to be so clever, so exquisitely entertaining, by her friends and his own, who had no difficulty in recognising the originals, that it was lent about from one to another, and among others to the Marquise de la

Baume, who privately made a copy of it before returning the manuscript. Copies multiplied, and were passed about, so that the "secret" became very well known in the *beau monde* of Paris.

The Marquise was not long left in ignorance of Bussy's mean revenge. Had it been mere invective or defamation, it would not have been half so damaging. But the clever Bussy had simply analysed his cousin's beauty, and had proved that she, to whom three or four years before he had declared that pagans would have worshipped her as a divinity, had really no beauty at all. The Marquise knew well what laughter the clever sketch would excite among her friends; indeed, no friendship could be proof against it. Even she herself confessed, when time had dulled the acuteness of her annoyance, that "had it been written by anyone else of anyone else I should have enjoyed reading it." Corbinelli, one of her truest friends, who greatly admired and esteemed her, wrote to Bussy his impressions on reading the sketch, and we may be certain that there were many others in that gay social world whose delight would not be tempered by the least sympathy for the victim.

"When I first read it," writes Corbinelli, "I was angry; then, in spite of myself, I laughed heartily. After that, I was ashamed of having laughed. Then I yielded to temptation and read it again. I laughed yet a second time, though I was angry and ashamed all the same."

No wonder Madame de Sévigné said that "the villainous portrait" caused her to pass whole nights without sleep! It was a cruel blow to her friendship as well as to her pride, and for a long time she could neither forget nor forgive it, and would have no intercourse with her despicable cousin, who, in holding up to ridicule his near relative, whose reputation and honour he should have been the first to defend, has heaped such dishonour on himself that it will endure while his name is remembered.

Satire was in the air. Molière, that brilliant satirist of his century, was delighting Paris with his life-like representations of the absurdities around him, and in 1660 he first performed *Les Précieuses Ridicules*. But it must not be supposed that the true *précieuses*, who had shone with such distinction at the Hôtel de Rambouillet, were the people whom Molière held up to the scorn and mocking laughter of the Parisians. Madame de Rambouillet herself and several of her family witnessed the performance. Madame de Sévigné was probably there, and certainly many others of the *précieuses* who were so proud of their title, and it is scarcely probable that they would have gone to see themselves caricatured; besides, all the literature of the day makes it perfectly clear that the *précieuses* of the Hôtel de Rambouillet were ladies worthy of all honour and praise. Since the Fronde that salon had been virtually closed, but Mademoiselle de Scudéry had been holding her "Saturdays" in the rue Vieille du Temple, and one would not dare to say that Molière had not found his absurd *précieuses* there! The conversation was so fervently, so inexorably literary; words, phrases, sentiments, expressions, fancies, and feelings were examined, analysed, and torn to tatters; every form of literary exercise was worked to death, while the hostess talked almost without cessation to her admiring guests.

CHAPTER XIII

The last fête at Vaux—A startling arrest—Letters from Madame de Sévigné found among the private papers of Foucquet—A Parisian scandal—The Comte de Bussy defends his cousin's good name

WHILE Madame de Sévigné was still suffering from the annoyance that her cousin's treachery had caused her, she had to endure yet another attack on the reputation of which she had always been so jealously careful. This time, the scandal did not start up stealthily here and there, like some noxious weed; and instead of learning by the amused and malignant smiles of her acquaintance that they had seen and enjoyed every detail of her latest "portrait," the blow was to fall with the utmost publicity, for the slander was one of the results of an event that astonished not only all France, but all Europe—the sudden and startling downfall from power of Nicolas Foucquet, Surintendant des Finances.

Foucquet was at the very pinnacle of his power in 1661, but he was as yet unaware that he had reached the ultimate point of his splendour. Was not his device, the squirrel leaping upwards from branch to branch, interwoven endlessly in all the decorations of his palace? Was not his motto, *Quo non ascendam?* (To what may I not attain?) ever before his eyes and never absent from his ambitious mind? Mazarin, the ruler of all France, including the Queen-Mother and the young King, was dead, and Foucquet was awaiting an honour which his sanguine spirit looked on as almost a certainty—his appointment to the coveted post of First Minister.

But the astute Mazarin before his death had already planned Foucquet's fall. When the Chateau de Vaux was in course of construction, he had sent an obscure young dependant of his household named Colbert, to give a report of what was going on. Colbert had brought back a detailed account of the stupendous expenditure: an army of workmen, fifteen thousand men at least, employed in building, or on the estate, and many details to correspond; with the conclusion that Foucquet was keeping up his gorgeous state by a system of fraud. He drew up a memorandum and sent it to Mazarin; but if the minister had spies, so also had Foucquet, and the memorandum was stopped in its transit through the post, read by the Surintendant, then re-sealed and sent on to its destination.

In the memorandum, Colbert had suggested that Foucquet should be brought to trial, and forced to refund the money that he had abstracted so freely from the nation's funds. Foucquet at once prepared to resist this intended humiliation, and drew up a wild scheme on paper, which was, not long after, thrown into his desk and forgotten. When it was discovered, however, after his arrest, this absurd document was used by his enemies against him, and proved a terrible witness in the hands of his implacable pursuers, Colbert and le Tellier.

But Foucquet, unaware of the abyss of ruin which his enemies were deliberately preparing for him, had never felt more confident in his good fortune. He was expecting to have the Order of the Holy Spirit conferred on him, as a preliminary to the greater honour of being chosen First Minister in the place of the late Mazarin, and, in buoyant expectation of this great distinction, he prepared a magnificent fête at Vaux for the the King and all the Court, a fête on which he lavished all the resources he had at command.

On that fateful day for Foucquet, August 17, 1661, the royal cortege came from Fontainebleau; King, Queen-Mother, and courtiers, in their carriages, on horseback, in litters; a gay and glittering procession passing under the leafy avenues through the great gates, into the superb grounds of Vaux, then glowing with its mature summer display of brilliant flowers, rare plants and shrubs, and musical with the sound of falling waters.

It was six o'clock when the company arrived, and all, with eager curiosity, wandered from one to another of the superb rooms, where everything that was finest in the arts had been brought together into a magnificent, harmonious whole. Some

THE LAST FÊTE AT VAUX

wandered into the gardens among the orange-trees, or, leaning on the balustrades, listened to the cooling and soothing music of the myriad fountains; or watched with fascinated gaze the wonderful display of water in the big walk that divided the gardens into two. This, perhaps, was the most arresting spot in all these pleasure grounds of enchantment. On each side of it were one hundred columns, out of which water gushed at the height of thirty-five feet, making two straight walls of water; and close by, fifty fountains were playing into separate basins. This cool, murmurous beauty of falling water, irradiated by the declining August sun into millions of sparkling jewels and a rainbow mist of spray, made for King and courtiers a magnificent and novel sight, the like of which had never before been seen in France.

As daylight waned, the company was summoned to a grand collation. The royal guests were served in their own *apparte- ment* with pheasants, quails, ortolans, the choicest wines, the finest fruits and viands that could be procured, all prepared under the skilful direction of the renowned Vatel, and served sumptuously on gold plate, a luxury that the King himself did not possess. The courtiers in other rooms fared no less delicately, while soft music from the twenty-four violins gave a charming and unwonted grace to the feast.

Supper over, the gay, laughing company again hurried into the gardens, now sleeping in the serene splendour of the August evening, anxious to obtain seats for the play—a new, and of course entertaining, comedy by Molière, to be given for the first time. Can we not see that crowd? The young King in close attendance on Mademoiselle de la Vallière; the pious Queen-Mother, drawn in the *calèche* thoughtfully provided by Foucquet; the doll-faced, pretty Monsieur, with his new and charming young wife, the beautiful Henriette of England; and the crowd of attendant courtiers in silks and brocades, the ladies with their hair in bunches of curls on each side of the face, daintily patched, highly rouged, their white throats clasped with pearls, talking, jesting, laughing with their gallants almost as finely dressed as themselves, all sauntering or hurrying towards the theatre; and, chatting with his guests, or in attendance on the King, Foucquet, with his enigmatical smile, the lord of all this Eastern splendour combined with Western ingenuity, pitifully unaware of the tragedy with which this gay and sumptuous fête would end.

What a setting for the play had been chosen! It was given near a grove of fir-trees, with the murmuring freshness of fountains all round; a thousand torches gave a brilliant illumination to the scene, and beyond and round about were the dense, mysterious shadows of the whispering trees. While King and courtiers were waiting expectantly, Molière, as he himself relates, suddenly appeared on the stage in ordinary clothes, and, feigning great surprise, he turned to the King and begged him to excuse the lack of preparation. There was no time, he said, to get ready for the entertainment which his Majesty apparently expected; there were, indeed, no actors; but if the King would only assist by ordering a play!—— It was a comedy within a comedy, a childish artifice which pleased the young King and his young Court, in these early days of his manhood when all pleasures were new, and satiety had not yet dulled the freshness of every delight. The King made a sign; and immediately the famous shell opened, and a Naïde appeared in the car of a goddess, and commanded the boundaries to be removed and the trees to speak, which, naturally, they did at once, at the bidding of so charming a person; Pellisson spoke the inevitable prologue, and at the first entry of the ballet the Naïde, with her train of fauns, nymphs, and satyrs, disappeared into the fairy-land of the surrounding woods. Stale enough to-day, perhaps; nothing but common pantomime; but in those early days of theatrical art in France how exquisitely novel and enchanting!

But as all things, even *Les Fâcheux*, the new comedy by Molière, must come to an end, the King and courtiers turned their steps towards the chateau in the warm dusk of the autumn night. At that instant another surprise awaited them. Suddenly the whole horizon beyond the chateau, near Maincy, was illuminated with soft light, four statues of fire appeared on the hill, and the superb palace of Vaux was brightly outlined by thousands of tiny lamps, an artifice to-day so old, but which to those more than two hundred years ago had the supreme charm of novelty. Dome, statues, carvings, all the wonderful white beauties of this superb castle, stood out in bold relief, and though midnight had struck an hour before, yet King and courtiers stood still to gaze on the fascinating sight. Wonder succeeded wonder, for as they paused in astonishment a countless number of rockets shot up into the vault of heaven; some fell, transformed in their slow descent into fleurs-de-lis, familiar names, monograms; a whale appeared on the canal, from whose body issued rockets, which, shooting up into the air, were transformed into a thousand differing shapes, from which issued fire and water, while trumpets and tambours made a confusing din, giving the illusion that a furious battle was being fought. Just as the King, believing that these wonders were at an end, gave the sign to retire, numberless rockets burst forth from the dome, and, increasing in size as they shot into the air, fell on the other side of the gardens, making an archway of jewelled fire for the King and Court to pass under to the palace. Here another magnificent repast awaited them, after which came a ball that was not ended before the dawn.

Everyone declared that the fête was magnificent, extraordinary, wonderful, fairy-like; but its main object was a failure, it had not given pleasure to the King. Louis had taken note of all the marvels that his host had exhibited for his delight and entertainment, but his comment was somewhat bitter:

"I shall never again venture to invite you to visit me, Monsieur; you would find yourself inconvenienced," he remarked to Foucquet.

It was said, too, that among the allegorical paintings the King had recognised a portrait of la Vallière; but whatever may have been the immediate cause, Foucquet's ruin was a settled thing; Colbert and le Tellier were pursuing him with hatred and jealousy, pointing out to the King how dangerous a man he was; and no one could disguise the fact that the Surintendant was helping himself freely from the public coffers, even as Mazarin, as Richelieu, as all men in power did in those days.

Scarcely more than a fortnight after the fête, Foucquet was arrested at Nantes, where he had been living in a house with a subterraneous passage to the Loire, on which a boat was always in waiting to carry him over to Belleisle. Once there, he hoped to be able to set the King at defiance; a boyish project enough, which was quite in keeping with his character and youthful enthusiasm. Besides this, he had couriers waiting with relays of horses at intervals along the road; but all his avenues of escape failed him, and he was carried off to Angers, a strong prison, which had been prepared, as he blindly supposed, for his rival Colbert.

His superb library was sold, the palace of Vaux was shut up, seals were placed on all his property, and as the Chancellor Séguier affixed them to the furniture of his house, Saint-Mandé, near Paris, he could not resist an epigram. "Foucquet desired the Seals, and he has them now," he said, in reference to the Surintendant's ambition.

Madame de Sévigné was at her Chateau of Les Rochers in Brittany, not far from Nantes, waiting for the news of Foucquet's appointment as Minister, and his election to the coveted honour of the Order of the Holy Spirit, when the sudden and appalling tidings of his arrest was brought to her. We know from her letters afterwards, how keenly she felt her friend's disgrace, and how sincerely she grieved for his fall, but a keener, more personal stroke to herself was presently to shock and harass her yet further. All his private papers at Saint-Mandé had been removed to Versailles for the King to read, and business correspondence, *billets-doux*, and the most intimate communications were eagerly examined. The arrest of Foucquet had been startling enough, but the love-letters of great ladies to the financier was a theme entirely to the Parisian taste. Names leaked out, and *chansons* were sung in the public streets, hawked on the Pont-Neuf, and jested over in the *ruelles*; and while in her Breton solitude, Madame de Sévigné learned with horror and indignation, that letters from herself had been found among the *billets-doux*, that she who had been so careful of her fair fame was held up to public ridicule as being among the crowd of ladies who had not been able to resist the wealth and personal charm of the Surintendant.

Did not all her world know that Foucquet had pursued her with marked attentions? And was it not natural that they should rejoice at hearing that Madame de Sévigné was no better than the rest, in spite of her parade of virtue? Men whom she had repulsed, women who hated her for the honour they lacked, all took up the chorus, and this supposed indiscretion of the virtuous Marquise caused more malicious joy, and tenfold as much scandal, as that of the others, whose notorious gallantries had long ago lost the surprise of novelty.

Madame de Sévigné remembered what letters she had sent to Foucquet, and knew that they were no *billets-doux*, but merely notes concerning her nephew the Marquis de la Trousse. But how prove her innocence to others? It is to be feared that there were men and women of the Court who never were convinced; so difficult it is to demonstrate to others a thing of which they have no conception!

The King himself, struck with the charming and easy style of the letters, said that they did honour to the lady who had written them. Le Tellier repeated this on all sides, but to little purpose; it was so much more piquant and amusing to believe the worst!

The Marquise did not, however, sit down idly under this injustice. She wrote to her old tutors, Chapelain and Ménage, who both exerted themselves in the interests of their esteemed pupil. Chapelain took up the cudgels very warmly on her behalf, but in writing to tell her so, he said hard truths about the Surintendant at which she probably winced; he also referred to Scarron, Pellisson, and Mademoiselle de Scudéry as "interested rabble," which was a harsh judgment on the two latter at least, who proved the most devoted friends of the financier in his adversity. It cannot have been a very agreeable letter to the Marquise, but it at least assured her that he had not waited to be asked to act in her defence, and in a somewhat grandiloquent fashion he finished by assuring her that she had many friends to defend her good name, and "that she might live in repose and sleep in peace."

In a letter that Madame de Sévigné wrote to Ménage, we may trace a little just annoyance that her simple notes should have been placed by Foucquet in a box containing love-letters. She evidently feels that such conduct was a species of treason.

"I thank you, my dear Monsieur, for all your news," she writes; "there are two or three items in your letter that I did not know. As for that of M. Foucquet, I hear nothing else spoken of. I think you understand very well the displeasure I felt at having been included in the number of those who had written to him. It is true that it was neither gallantry nor interest which obliged me to correspond with him, one may perceive quite clearly that it was nothing but the affairs of M. de la Trousse; but that did not prevent my having been very vexed to find that he put them in the same box as his love-letters, and to hear myself classed with those whose sentiments are not so pure as mine. On this occasion it is necessary that my friends should enlighten those who do not know the truth of the matter."

She also wrote on the same subject to the Marquis de Pomponne, the son of Arnauld d'Andilly, who was a personal friend of Foucquet, who, indeed, was included in Foucquet's disgrace and exiled to Verdun in 1662.

". . . But what do you say to all that has been found in those boxes? Would you ever have believed that my poor letters, full of the marriage of M. de la Trousse and of all the affairs of his family, would have been put away so mysteriously? I assure you that whatever credit I may gain from those who will do me the justice to believe that I have never had any other connection with him, I am greatly disturbed to be obliged to justify myself, and perhaps uselessly, with regard to a thousand persons who will never understand the truth. I think you will easily comprehend what grief this causes to a heart like mine. I implore you to say what you know concerning this; I can never have enough friends on this occasion. I am impatiently expecting your brother to console me a little over this strange affair; nevertheless I do not fail to wish with all my heart some solace to the unhappy, and I desire of you always, Monsieur, the continuation of the honour of your friendship.

"M. DE RABUTIN-CHANTAL"

There was yet another defender of her good name to whom Madame de Sévigné had not applied, whom she only remembered, in fact, with indignation and anger. Her cousin Bussy, hearing that letters from the Marquise had been found among Foucquet's papers, bethought himself that they might refer to the office of *mestre de camp général*, in which transaction the Surintendant had advanced him some of the money. He went to le Tellier to explain this affair, and while there took the opportunity to ask the truth about the letters of Madame de Sévigné, which just then were one of the chief subjects of Parisian gossip. Le Tellier assured Bussy that "they were the most honest letters possible, and of a jesting character."

Bussy, already feeling ashamed of his own scandalous behaviour, which he always afterwards had the grace to look on as one of the worst actions of his life, now took up his cousin's cause, and defended her good name on every possible occasion. Society had not forgotten the part he had so lately taken against her, and one day when his brother-in-law de Rouville classed Madame de Sévigné among the mistresses of Foucquet, Bussy quarrelled seriously with him.

De Rouville was astonished at his attitude, and reminded him that after having written such scandal against her, it was hardly in keeping for him to take cudgels in her defence.

"I don't like such reports," retorted Bussy, "unless I make them myself!"

CHAPTER XIV

Foucquet's trial—Madame de Sévigné writes a daily account of it to the Marquis de Pomponne—The Chancellor Séguier—A period of suspense—Foucquet is sent to Pignerol under the escort of d'Artagnan and his famous Musketeers

IN his famous " Instructions to the Dauphin," Louis XIV declared that no act of his reign had given him more pain than the arrest and trial of Foucquet. The Surintendant's ruin was a planned and settled thing, but the bitter animosity of Colbert and le Tellier to the accused, greatly aggravated every circumstance connected with the trial, and contributed, there is little doubt, towards the severity of his punishment.

The letters of Madame de Sévigné to the Marquis de Pomponne, almost the first of importance that she wrote, give a living, moving picture of Foucquet on trial before his judges, some of whom are determined that if possible he shall be made to suffer the extreme penalty of the law. She also, with her wonderful art of fixing the most fleeting impressions, makes us share in the hopes and fears that alternately possessed those of his friends who were watching the trial with such absorbing interest. We see, too, her tender woman's heart resenting the injustice of his judges, and wholly absorbed, as the trial goes on, in the important question, "Will the penalty be death or imprisonment?" Indeed, when Napoleon read these letters in his exile at Saint-Helena, he remarked "that they were very tender letters to be written about a mere friend."

The letters begin—

"To-day, Monday, the 17th of November, M. Foucquet was brought for the second time before the Chancellor. He seated himself without ceremony upon the *sellette* as he did the first time. The Chancellor began by desiring him to hold up his hand, to which he replied that he had already given the reasons which prevented him from taking the oath. . . .

"'But,' said the Chancellor, 'though you will not acknowledge the power of the court, you answer and put questions, and you are now upon the *sellette*.'

"'It is true, I am,' he replied, 'but not voluntarily. I am brought here against my will; there is a power which I must obey, it is a humiliation which God has made me suffer and which I receive from His hands. After the services I have rendered, and the offices I have had the honour to fill, I might have been spared this disgrace.'

"The Chancellor then continued the examination respecting the *gabelles*, to which the replies of M. Foucquet were very satisfactory. As the examination proceeds I shall continue to send you a faithful account of it; I am anxious to know whether my letters reach you safely. . . ."

The Marquise might with reason be anxious about her letters. She was perfectly aware that a rigorous watch was kept on the post, and that all suspected correspondence was seized and read without scruple. It was an unpleasant habit of those in power. Mazarin had found the practice of great service; Foucquet, as we have seen, was glad to exercise it on occasion; and Louis XIV, having a practically inexhaustible capacity for enjoyment, found much diversion as well as profit in reading the private correspondence of his subjects.

But Madame de Sévigné's loyalty to her friends was stronger than her fear, and we must remember that it was no light thing to profess friendship for Foucquet at this period; so many of his friends had been included in his disgrace, while Colbert and le Tellier, his chief enemies, pursued him with the utmost malignity, and were sure to look coldly on those who supported him.

The band of devoted friends who were watching every phase of the trial, in the hope that some miracle would be worked to save him who had been so generous when he was in power, eagerly noticed every circumstance, however trifling, thinking that it might influence the sentence of Foucquet. In the following letter Madame de Sévigné records the little incident of the plaster which Foucquet's mother sent to the Queen, and how much his supporters hoped from it. It is significant, however, that the Marquise, though she desired it, could not hope against her reason.

"*Friday, November* 20, 1664

" M. Foucquet was examined this morning respecting the gold mark. He answered very well. Several of the judges bowed to him, but the Chancellor reproved them, and said it was not the custom|; and to the Breton counsellor he said, ' It is because you are a Breton that you bow so low to M. Foucquet.'

" While passing by the Arsenal, out walking, he asked what the workmen were doing, and he was told that they were making the vase of a fountain. He went to them and gave his opinion, and then returned smiling to M. d'Artagnan, and said to him : 'You are surprised that I should interfere in such things, but formerly I used to understand them very well.'

" The friends of M. Foucquet, and I among the rest, think this tranquillity admirable ; others call it affectation ; such is the way of the world.

" Madame Foucquet, his mother, has given the Queen a plaster that has cured her convulsions, which, to speak correctly, were nothing but the vapours. Many people, believing what they wish, imagine that the Queen will seize this occasion to intercede the King for pardon for the unfortunate prisoner ; but I, who hear a good deal of talk of the tenderness in that quarter, do not believe a word of it. The noise that plaster has made is wonderful ; everyone says that Madame Foucquet is a saint, with the power of working miracles. . . ."

Day by day, as the trial proceeded, Madame de Sévigné gave a clear and lucid account of it to Foucquet's exiled friend Pomponne, always with the most tender sympathy for the accused man, and often with much indignation against his judges. In the following letter she gives a glimpse of the Chancellor Séguier at his devotions, for everything was of importance to the friends who were watching the trial ; even the Chancellor's visit to a convent might have a bearing on the case, and it will be seen that the lady Abbess did not miss the opportunity of speaking a word for Foucquet. The interest for us of to-day lies in the record of an instance of the intense religious fervour that was one of the distinguishing features of this great century, and so conspicuously lacking in the centuries that followed. Saint Francis de Sales and Saint Vincent de Paul had a holy influence on their countrymen that is absolutely incalculable; both were filled with a spiritual fervour that acted like leaven throughout the kingdom. The one, well-born and rich, had his own particular sphere of influence; the other, the humble and pious Père Vincent, was laughed at by the courtiers whenever he appeared at Court, for his shabby appearance and plebeian aspect; but the record of his life's work reads like the chronicle of an early Christian saint, before the love of worldly things had come to mar the simple faith as it came from their Master. His practical Christianity in caring for the sick and poor, when those unfortunates were regarded as absolutely of no account; his work among the devastated villages after the Fronde; his eloquent and successful appeal on behalf of *les enfants trouvés*, are among the most moving and glorious chronicles of his brilliant century.

The convent of the Visitation in the rue Saint-Antoine was one of those founded by the Blessed Chantal, Madame de Sévigné's grandmother, under the direction of Saint Francis de Sales, whom the Marquise once jestingly referred to as "our spiritual grandfather." "Puis" is the Chancellor Séguier; for it was not safe to mention the judges by name in such a recital.

Monday, November 24, 1664

". . . Two days ago I dined at Sainte-Marie de Saint-Antoine. The mother superior related to me the details of four visits that Puis has paid her during the last three months, at which I am greatly astonished. He came to tell her that the now blessed Bishop of Geneva [Saint Francis de Sales had been beatified in 1661] had obtained for him such especial mercies during his illness that summer, that he felt under the greatest obligations to him; and he requested her to ask the prayers of the community for the deceased. He gave her a thousand crowns for the accomplishment of his desires, and entreated her to show him the Bishop's heart. When he was at the grating he fell upon his knees, and remained more than a quarter of an hour bathed in tears, apostrophising the heart, and praying for a spark of the Divine fire of the love of God that had consumed it. The mother superior at his side wept also, and when he left she gave him a reliquary full of relics of the blessed one. He wears it always, and during his four visits appeared so earnest about his salvation, so disgusted with the Court, so transported with the desire of being converted, that a person more clear-sighted than the Abbess would have been deceived. She contrived to introduce carefully the affair of M. Foucquet, but he answered like a man who was interested in nothing but religion: that he did not know; that he would see; and, finally, that justice would be done according to God's will, without considering anything else. I was never more surprised than at this conversation. If you ask me what I think of it, I must tell you that I do not know; that it is quite unintelligible to me; and, on the other hand, I cannot see the good of this comedy; and if it is not a comedy, how can he reconcile his fine speeches with all the steps he has taken since then? These are things that only time will explain, for by themselves they are entirely enigmatical. Do not mention it, however, for the mother superior has begged me not to talk of the circumstance."

In the next letter we find that M. d'Ormesson, whom the Marquise refers to as the "Reporter," is speaking boldly on the prisoner's behalf. Madame de Sévigné was connected by marriage with this famous lawyer (whose *Journal* is one of the most trustworthy records of the period), and during the trial she begged him to use his influence in Foucquet's interest. D'Ormesson would give no definite reply to the Marquise, probably because he saw more clearly than she did the inroads that the Surintendant had made on the national funds. The lawyer was, however, on the side of justice and mercy, and, in fact, he defended Foucquet so well that his own disgrace, which occurred not long after, was supposed to be the result of his zeal at this trial.

In all her letters on the trial there is nothing more delightful than the picture she gives of herself and the little band of ladies—Mademoiselle de Scudéry, Madame du Plessis Guénégaud, Madame Scarron, perhaps, for we can only conjecture—standing masked, opposite the Arsenal, to see their unfortunate friend, as he was escorted back to prison by d'Artagnan and the fifty Musketeers that Dumas has made so famous.

Thursday, November 27, 1664

"The examination was continued to-day on the subject of the grants. The Chancellor had the kind intention of driving M. Foucquet to extremities and of embarrassing him, but he did not succeed, for M. Foucquet acquitted himself admirably. He did not come into the Chamber of Justice till eleven o'clock, because the Chancellor made the Reporter read as before, and in spite of all that fine devotion of which I told you, he said the worst he could of our poor friend. The Reporter always took his part, because the Chancellor evidently leaned to the other side. Finally he said, 'Here is a charge which the accused will not be able to answer.' 'Ah, sir,' said the Reporter, 'here is a plaster which will cure that weakness'; and he gave an excellent justification, adding, 'Sir, in the place I hold I shall always speak the truth, no matter in what form it presents itself to me.' The allusion to a plaster made the audience smile, as it reminded them of the one that has lately made so much noise. The accused, who remained only an hour in court, was then brought in, and when he left, M. d'Ormesson was complimented by several people on his firmness.

"I must now tell you what I myself did. Guess which ladies of my acquaintance proposed to me to go to a house exactly opposite the Arsenal, where we could see the return of our poor friend. I was masked, but I saw him almost as soon as he came in sight. M. d'Artagnan was walking beside him, and fifty Musketeers were thirty or forty paces behind. When I saw him my legs trembled, and my heart beat so violently that I could scarcely bear it. In approaching us to re-enter his dungeon, M. d'Artagnan touched him, and pointed out that we were there. He then saluted us with that bright, smiling countenance you know so well. I do not believe he recognised me, but I confess I was strongly affected when I saw him enter that little door. If you knew the misfortune of having a heart like mine I am sure you would pity me, but I do not think you have much advantage of me in that matter. . . ."

Day by day hope and fear succeeded each other, as the trial went well or ill. Madame de Sévigné's well-balanced mind was stronger than her affectionate heart, which desired Foucquet's acquittal so intensely; we gather from her letters that she was never carried away by the illusions which so misled his relatives and some of his friends. When Mademoiselle de Scudéry, a woman of quite unusual intellect, and looked up to by all her circle as a very oracle, hopes and believes that things are going well, the Marquise is not deluded by a similar optimism; her faculty of fearlessly facing the truth will not allow her even this consolation. On December the 9th she writes—

"I assure you the days are very tedious, and that this uncertainty is a frightful thing, but it is an evil to which the whole family of the poor prisoner has become accustomed. I have seen them, and admire them. One would think they had never known, never read the events that have happened in past times; and what surprises me still more is that Sappho is the same; she whose wit and penetration are unequalled. When I think over this circumstance, I deceive and persuade myself, or at least I try to persuade myself, that they know more of the affair than I do. On the other hand, when I reason with others less interested, whose judgment is reliable, I find the measures against him so just that it will be a real miracle if the affair terminates in the way we desire . . . we sometimes lose by a single vote, but that vote is everything. . . . Yet at the bottom of my heart I still have a little hope; I do not know whence it comes or where it leads, nor is it sufficient to make me sleep in peace. Yesterday I was talking over the affair with Madame du Plessis; I cannot endure anyone just now but those with whom I can speak, and who have the same feelings as myself. She hopes as I do, without knowing the reason why. 'But why do you hope?' 'Because I do.' These are our answers. Are they not reasonable? I told her with the greatest sincerity in the world that if the sentence should be as we desire, the height of my joy would be to despatch a man on horseback to you instantly with the delightful news, and that the pleasure of picturing your happiness on hearing it would make mine complete."

But Madame de Sévigné was to have no such pleasant news to communicate to her exiled friend. Foucquet had defrauded the State of immense sums—even the Marquise admits that "the measures against him are so just"—and the young King intended to make a signal example of him. Richelieu and Mazarin had both grown rich on the public money, and it was a well understood rule that those in power helped themselves liberally as occasion offered. But Louis XIV meant to have neither Richelieus nor Mazarins; he intended above all things to govern by himself, and to understand the affairs of his kingdom. Colbert, whom Madame de Sévigné called the "North," was not so amiable as Foucquet, but he was a man of unquestioned integrity. It is a noticeable fact that during the reign of Louis XIV there were no more ministers who out-shone the King in splendour; no Richelieu keeping up kingly state while the true King sat at his devotions in a badly furnished palace, disregarded even by his courtiers; no grasping Mazarin to hoard the nation's wealth, to lavish it on works of art, or to squander it among the men who were his tools; no Foucquet to live in royal splendour, and to give with more than royal generosity. From the day of Foucquet's arrest, all the glory, splendour, wealth, honour, and power of every kind centred in the Roi Soleil; and if the nobles gave grand fêtes it was for his pleasure and approval, and it probably was his pleasure that they nearly ruined themselves in doing so.

Foucquet was a doomed man from the beginning. Colbert and le Tellier, who had caused his arrest, were determined on his ruin. Maréchal Turenne was talking to a man who blamed the violence of Colbert, and praised the moderation of le Tellier. "True, sir," answered Turenne; "M. Colbert has most desire that he should be hung, and M. le Tellier most fear that he should not be."

By the middle of December, the case had been so far tried that his sentence became the subject of consideration. D'Ormesson suggested that Foucquet should be banished for life, and all his property confiscated. Sainte-Hélène judged that the prisoner ought to suffer the death-penalty, but that the King might be merciful. Madame de Sévigné, with her usual graphic impressionism, gives Pomponne a glimpse of the suspense which all the friends of Foucquet suffered at this crucial time.

"Everybody is interested in this important affair. People talk of nothing else. One reasons, draws inferences, counts his chances on the fingers; one hopes, pities, fears, wishes, hates, admires, is overwhelmed; in short, my dear sir, our present situation is most extraordinary, but the resignation and firmness of our dear friend is admirable. He knows everything that goes on, and every day volumes might be written in his praise."

On Saturday, December 20, the verdict was at length given, and the Marquise writes this short postscript to her letter—

"Praise God, Monsieur, and thank Him; our poor friend is saved. Thirteen were of M. d'Ormesson's opinion, and nine of Sainte-Hélenè's. My mind is so relieved that I am nearly beside myself."

Two days after, the Marquise sent further interesting details to the Marquis de Pomponne, in which we find that Foucquet kept his attitude of defiant resistance to the last. His physician Pecquet and his servant Lavalée were greatly attached to their master, and it is significant of the rigour and personal enmity with which Foucquet was pursued, that these two perfectly innocent men were thrown into the Bastille, and kept there for a year and more, merely because they were the devoted servants of their unfortunate master.

" Monday

"This morning at ten o'clock M. Foucquet was conducted to the chapel of the Bastille. Foucaut held the sentence in his hand. 'You must tell me your name, sir,' said he, 'that I may know whom I address.' 'You know very well who I am,' replied M. Foucquet; 'and as for my name, I will not give it here, just as I refused to give it in the Chamber of Justice; by the same rule, also, I protest against the sentence you are going to read to me.'

"Foucaut put on his hat and read out the sentence, while M. Foucquet listened bareheaded. Pecquet and Lavalée were afterwards separated from him, and the cries and tears of these poor men melted every heart that was not made of iron. They made such a terrible noise that M. d'Artagnan was obliged to go and console them, for it seemed to them as if a sentence of death had just been read to their master. They were both taken to a room in the Bastille, and it is not known what will be done with them.

"M. Foucquet went to M. d'Artagnan's apartment. . . . At eleven o'clock a coach was ready, into which M. Foucquet entered with four guards. M. d'Artagnan was on horseback with fifty Musketeers; he will conduct him to Pignerol, where he will leave him in the care of Saint-Mars, who is a very worthy man; he will have fifty soldiers as a guard. I do not know whether our friend will be allowed another servant; you can have no idea how cruel it seems to everyone that Pecquet and Lavalée should be taken from him; some draw dreadful conclusions from it. May God preserve him as He has done hitherto. We must trust in Him, and leave our friend under the protection of that Divine Providence which has been so gracious to him. They still refuse to allow his wife to join him, but have permitted his mother to remain at Parc with her daughter the Abbess."

There was not much real mercy shown to Foucquet. He was spared the death-penalty, and that was all; and probably to linger for sixteen years in a dungeon at Pignerol, dead to his friends, with not even his wife to share his solitude, was worse, save for the disgrace, than death itself. We hear a few more last words of him from Madame de Sévigné, whose affection followed him step by step on his melancholy journey, and whose brilliant pen shows him to have been a man of singular fascination, with a bright, buoyant, and unconquerable spirit, that not even his long imprisonment in the Bastille, nor the dread prospect of Pignerol, was able to subdue.

"Pecquet and Lavalée are still in the Bastille," she writes to Pomponne a few days later. "Can anything in the world be more dreadful than this injustice? They have given another servant to our unfortunate friend. M. d'Artagnan was his only comfort on the journey. . . .

"La Forêt, his old esquire, came to speak to him as he was going away.

"'I am delighted to see you,' said Foucquet. 'I know your fidelity and affection. Tell the ladies of my family that my courage remains, and that I am in good health.'

"Truly this is admirable. Adieu, my dear sir; let us, like him, have courage. . . .

"Madame de Grignan is dead."

When the Marquise wrote this last piece of news to Pomponne, she had no idea of what an influence it would have on her own life. Madame de Grignan was Angélique d'Angennes, whom she had seen so often at the Hôtel de Rambouillet, and was the first wife of the Comte de Grignan. This latter, after marrying another wife, and losing her also, was destined to become the son-in-law of the Marquise de Sévigné.

The prison doors of Pignerol shut on Foucquet, and though he lived for a time in the hearts of the many whom he had befriended, little was ever heard of him again.

He who had loved all the material pleasures of this world, who had surrounded himself with every luxury that art could produce to delight the eye or to gratify the senses, spent the last sad years of his life in a bare and miserable dungeon, which looked out on to a desolate courtyard where no one ever passed. Whether his bright, eager, kindly spirit chafed behind his prison bars, and hoped vainly for release, or whether, in answer to his pious mother's prayers, his thoughts turned to spiritual things, will never be known—we only know that after fourteen long years of bitter expiation for his offences, Foucquet died.

CHAPTER XV

Madame de Sévigné introduces her daughter at Court—"A beauty who will set the world on fire"—Mademoiselle de Sévigné dances with the King—Verses in her honour

DURING the three years that Foucquet was in the Bastille, awaiting his celebrated trial, the Marquise experienced one of the greatest pleasures of her life, that of introducing her lovely young daughter Françoise to the Court and to the polite world of Paris.

It is a little strange that though Madame de Sévigné was devoted to her children, and to her daughter especially, we hear very little of either of them during their childhood. Fortunately, the Abbé Arnauld, the son of the Port Royalist Arnauld d'Andilly, and brother to the Marquis de Pomponne, has written a charming miniature pen-portrait of the mother and her two lovely children, who were then nine and eleven years respectively. The Abbé was on a visit to Paris, and was staying at the house of the Chevalier Renaud de Sévigné.

"It was during this visit," he writes, "that M. de Sévigné introduced me to the illustrious Marquise de Sévigné, his niece, whose very name is dear to those who value wit, charm, and virtue. . . . I fancy I can see her still as she appeared to me on the day when I first had the honour of seeing her. She arrived in an open carriage with her son and daughter beside her, all three like the poets paint Latona accompanied by the young Apollo and the little Diana, so striking was the beauty of the mother and her children. She did me the honour to promise me her friendship from that time, and I consider myself particularly fortunate to have preserved till now a gift so dear and precious."

Madame de Sévigné herself records the impression that her children made on Pomponne, the Abbé's brother, at about the same period. Nearly twenty years after, he recalled it while talking over bygone times with the Marquise, who, writing to her daughter that same evening, repeated his pleasant little reminiscence.

"Monsieur de Pomponne remembers the day when he saw you as a little girl at my uncle Sévigné's house. You were at a window with your brother, more beautiful, he says, than an angel. You were pretending to be a prisoner, a princess banished from her father's house. Your brother was as handsome as you. You were then nine years old. [She was eleven.] He reminded me of that day, and has never forgotten any of the times when he has seen you."

Françoise de Sévigné had been brought up chiefly under her mother's loving and wise superintendence, though we gather, from a few words of regret written by Madame de Sévigné, that for a short time at least her little daughter, then about ten years old, was sent to the convent of the Visitation at Nantes, naturally one of the establishments founded by her great-grandmother, the Blessed Chantal.

She was taught Latin and Italian by the Marquise, and, under her almost constant supervision, received a solid and thorough education; but she did not wear her learning with so light and winsome a grace as did her charming mother, who, it has been well said, "knew a great deal without professing to know anything." As she grew older the Abbé de la Mousse, a doctor of theology, was her tutor, or perhaps not so much a tutor as a friend in the household, whose learned and wise conversations were of great benefit to the expanding intelligence of the young girl. Under his influence she became a fervent disciple of Descartes, whose philosophy was frequently discussed in certain fashionable salons where Madame de Sévigné and her daughter often visited before the latter's marriage. Drawn by a natural affinity, she turned to the Cartesian theories of cold reason with all the ardour of a strong intellect, unillumined and unwarmed by the generous heart which gave such grace and glow and tenderness to all the dainty blossoms of her mother's witty and cultivated mind.

We get one slight reference to her as a child, which is not particularly pleasant; but it is only justice to her to recall the fact that the other child concerned, Mademoiselle du Plessis

Argentré, her neighbour at Les Rochers, must have had a quite peculiar gift of irritation, for even the Marquise, with her equable temper, continually mentions in her letters what an unmitigated nuisance she is. "Ah!" she exclaims many years later, in a letter to her daughter, "how few people there are who are absolutely *true*! Consider the word a little and you will like it. The divine Plessis is most completely *false*. I do her too much honour even in speaking ill of her; she plays all kinds of characters; the devotee, the skilful, the timorous, the indisposed, the amiable, but above all she mimics me in such a manner that it amuses me as much as would a glass that distorted my face, or an echo, like that of Hudibras, which answered nothing but nonsense."

As a child this person cannot have been very charming, but the incident, as related by Madame de Sévigné, reveals the weakness of her maternal affection, and how almost impossible it was to her to believe her daughter in fault.

"Finally we talked of Mademoiselle du Plessis, of the foolish things she used to say, and we recalled that one day, when she had made some absurd remark to you, with her face close to yours, you did not stand on ceremony, but gave her such a box on the ear that it made her stagger; and how I, to smooth matters a little, remarked, 'How roughly these little girls play!' And how afterwards I said to her mother, 'Madame, these two young creatures were so rough, that they actually fought this morning; Mademoiselle du Plessis irritated my daughter, and my daughter slapped her; it was most amusing.' And by the way in which I represented it, I delighted Madame du Plessis with the idea that the two little girls were so merry together."

It is a much pleasanter reminiscence when she recalls to her daughter the occasion when the two drove together to visit the famous Mont Saint-Michel with its beautiful monastery and castle. Nearly thirty years later, while staying at Dol, she writes to Madame de Grignan: "From my room I can see the sea and Mont Saint-Michel, that noble hill which you have seen so proud, and which has seen you so beautiful; I dwell on the remembrance of that journey with much tenderness." Françoise de Sévigné was only thirteen years old at the time, but she already gave promise of great beauty, for a Counsellor of Parlement, who visited Mont Saint-Michel a week later, wrote to a friend at this date: "For the last month I have had the advantage of being the near neighbour of Madame de Sévigné, whose house is only two leagues from ours. This favourable situation has given me the opportunity of becoming better acquainted with her than merely by the well-deserved report of her worth. . . . Mademoiselle her daughter is another marvel, of whom I will say nothing further than—

> "Vous la verrez, si vous ne l'avez vue,
> Vous la verrez, de mille attraits pourvue,
> Briller d'un éclat sans pareil;
> Et vous direz, en la voyant paraître :
> C'est un soleil qui ne fait que de naître
> Dans le sein d'un autre soleil."

Mademoiselle de Sévigné must have been an exquisitely lovely girl when her mother first took her to Court. She was then sixteen, for life began much earlier for girls in France of the seventeenth century than it does to-day. Her beauty was of a blonde type, with the colouring of the hair and eyes slightly darker than that of her mother, which emphasised the delicate perfection of her features and dazzling complexion. Tréville, who at Court was regarded as an oracle on such matters, declared that "her beauty would set the world on fire"; and her cousin Bussy, with the pardonable pride of a relative, called her "the prettiest girl in France." As we look at her portrait, painted by Mignard more than ten years later, it is easy to understand what an exquisite flower-like loveliness the living, animated original must have possessed in all the dainty freshness of youth, when she first appeared among the powdered, patched, and highly rouged dames of the Louvre.

In these years at Court before her marriage, her beauty won for her a brilliant and undisputed success, and whenever she appeared in the great world, a chorus of praise and flattery greeted her on all sides, which probably gratified the heart of her loving and indulgent mother more than any tribute to her own charms had ever done. But even this triumphant, unquestioned loveliness had its drawback, plainly in this instance the defect of its fair quality. It is the Marquise who tells us this intimate little secret, and at the same time we discover that she too had suffered the same overwhelming annoyance in her own youth. Long years after this, when writing of her granddaughter, she says—

"It is a very fortunate thing that Pauline has not the defect of blushing. It has been, as you say, a real drawback to your beauty, as it was to mine when I was young. When I found that I was not troubled with this ridiculous inconvenience, I would not change myself for anyone else. This is a persecution inflicted by the devil upon vanity. In short, my child, it forced you to leave balls and assemblies, though everyone constantly spoke of you as a beauty. .... I really think people do not blush so much as they used."

But blushing in a beauty of sixteen is rarely regarded by other people as a grave defect, in spite of the real annoyance caused to its victim; and Mademoiselle de Sévigné, who had inherited from her mother the grace of perfect dancing, had been only a short time at Court when she was chosen by the King to dance in the ballets given at the Palais Royal. At no time in the history of France, or indeed of any other nation, have ballets been given under quite the same circumstances as during these and the few following years. The Grand Monarque who ruled so autocratically, who gradually broke the pride of his courtiers and nobles till there was only one will at Court—his own; who was looked on as the source of all good and evil, and who, even by the bold, rebuking Bossuet, was once referred to as a deity—this Grand Monarque appeared before his courtiers, foreign ambassadors, and those of the wealthy bourgeoisie who were fortunate enough to gain admittance to the fêtes, as a dancer, in the same plays as Molière and other actors! Well might the cynical la Rochefoucauld remark that "Everything happens in France!" Of course ballads were made on the subject and sung by the Parisians, "Pont-Neufs" as they were called, because all scandals or events of importance found their way into ballads and songs, which were hawked by thousands on the Pont-Neuf; and Madame de Motteville records that all libels against the Court, and presumably other libels too, were placed on a conspicuous post on the same famous bridge.

As everyone knows, there had been ballets before this. They had been given during the reign of Louis XIII, and in the

Regency; but never had such care, such resources, such expenditure been lavished upon them, since never before had the King appeared as a public dancer. The ballet was not merely a play; it was a superb *mélange* in which the art of the decorator, of the poet, of the musician, and of the actor was called forth to its uttermost. Benserade, the Court poet, composed the verses, but the brilliant Molière frequently aided him with flashes of suggestion, and was often among the players. The scenery, the decorations, the costumes, were the most superb that could be procured, and the great hall of the Palais Royal on evenings when the ballets were given appeared a veritable fairy-land.

The audience itself was part of the glittering spectacle. It is not difficult to imagine that great crowd of brilliant courtiers; the ladies in velvets, rich brocades, and silks, their hair "dressed in a thousand curls"; patched, rouged, and powdered, with priceless jewels gleaming from their necks and arms and hair, or sewn with cunning embroidery among the laces of their corsage. Can we not hear those dainty, perfumed, smiling dames as, with bright eyes gleaming above their fans with mischief, or love, or malice, they whisper comments, criticisms, and satires to the admiring gallants near them? Those gallants who, in their silken and velvet garments, their lace ruffles, their shoes with red heels and diamond buckles, their plumed hats and short embroidered mantles, were not one whit behind the ladies in the matter of gaudy plumage! What a privilege it was to those who were not of this brilliant world to be allowed to witness these wonderful representations! Sometimes, by good fortune, foreigners were admitted to the ambassadors' seats, and it is from the journal of two young Dutchmen that we have a record of one such memorable evening.

They were so anxious to obtain good seats, that they went as early as three in the afternoon, though the ballet did not begin till nine. Through their eyes we see the *grande salle* lighted with so many candles in the chandeliers that the hall is as brilliant as if it were broad day; we see young nobles showing guests to their seats, and giving them a copy of the *vers du ballet*, which ran to fifteen pages, printed by Robert Ballard, the famous printer of music to the King, whose descendants inherited the valuable privilege, till the Revolution came and abolished privilege of all kinds. But the Revolution was as yet undreamed of! Was not the Roi Soleil about to dance before the eyes of his adoring courtiers?

It was on January 8, 1663, when Mademoiselle de Sévigné was sixteen, that she first danced in a ballet with the King, the famous *Ballet des Arts* about which so much has been said and written and sung. An infant daughter of the King and Queen, aged six weeks, had died just ten days before, but all the preparations had been made for the ballet, and such an unimportant event as the death of one of his legitimate children was not allowed to interfere with the amusement of the King!

The representation was given in the great hall of the Palais Cardinal, that superb mansion built by Richelieu, which is known to-day as the Palais Royal. In the first *entrée* the King came on as a shepherd, dancing with the most lovely shepherdesses of the Court. There was Madame, the wife of Monsieur the King's brother, the gay and gracious Princesse Henriette, young, laughter-loving, frivolous, who, with the King, was constantly seeking and inventing new pleasures and diversions; the brilliant and haughty Mademoiselle de Mortemart, on the eve of becoming Madame de Montespan, as yet unaware of her future rôle in France; the beautiful Mademoiselle de Saint-Simon, *parfaitement belle et sage*, said her brother, the prince of chroniclers; and the young, exquisitely fair Mademoiselle de Sévigné, who surpassed them all in absolute perfection of feature.

Benserade, the Court poet, wrote flattering verses for all these fair ladies, and of Mademoiselle de Sévigné he said—

> " Déjà cette beauté fait craindre sa puissance,
> Et pour nous mettre en butte à d'extrêmes dangers,
> Elle entre justement dans l'âge où l'on commence
> A distinguer les loups d'avecque les bergers."

In the seventh *entrée* of the ballet the King and these same ladies came on again; and this time Madame was Minerva, while the demoiselles de Mortemart, de Saint-Simon, and de Sévigné were her attendant Amazons, with Mademoiselle de la

Vallière, who to her shame and life-long sorrow loved the King too well.

We may imagine something, though scarcely all, of Madame de Sévigné's maternal pride and delight in the brilliant success of her lovely young daughter, who, as she confessed, was "the only passion of her heart, the pleasure and sweetness of her life." Years after, she recalled these triumphs to her daughter, and reminded her of the almost unique representation at which she had assisted. "There were," she wrote, "four persons, including the late Madame, whom it would be difficult to replace in whole centuries for their beauty, their exquisite youth, and for their dancing. Oh, what shepherdesses! what Amazons!"

The *Ballet des Arts* was superb, said everyone, and the King, well pleased at its undoubted success, gave it again early in the following year, with the same shepherdesses and the same Amazons. A month after, in 1664, Mademoiselle de Sévigné had the honour of being chosen to take part in another representation. This time she was a sea-nymph in the ballet entitled *Amours déguisés*, and her companions were Madame de Montespan, Madame de Vibraye, and Mademoiselle d'Elbœuf. Monsieur the King's brother was a sea-god, and the Marquis de Villeroy and the Marquis de Rossan were sea-gods also. In the verses for Mademoiselle de Sévigné on this occasion, Benserade included her mother also—

> "Vous travestir ainsi, c'est bien être ingénu,
> Amour ! c'est comme si, pour n'être pas connu,
>   Avec une innocence extrême,
>   Vous vous déguisiez en vous-même.
> Elle a vos traits, vos feux et votre air engageant,
> Et, de même que vous, sourit en égorgeant.
>   Enfin qui fit l'une a fait l'autre ;
> Et jusques à sa mère, elle est comme la vôtre."

As may be seen from these lines, Madame de Sévigné was not eclipsed even by the brilliant beauty and attractions of her young daughter. Poets still sang the charms of the Marquise, who, although she was thirty-six when she first introduced her daughter at Court, yet appeared to her admirers "always fresh and always fair"; and with her gay wit and cheery wisdom, her warm and generous heart, which gave such a genial grace to her

charming manner, she was welcomed wherever she appeared, and was unquestionably much more popular in society than her beautiful and clever daughter.

In 1665, Mademoiselle de Sévigné danced yet once again with the King. In the *ballet royal* of the *Naissance de Vénus* the King came on in the second part as Alexander, the Marquis de Rossan was Hercules, Madame was Roxana, and Mademoiselle de Sévigné was Omphale. From Benserade's verse on the latter we gather something of the success of the young beauty in that brilliant Court—

> " Blondins accoutumés à faire des conquêtes,
> Devant ce jeune objet si charmant et si doux,
>   Tous grands héros que vous êtes,
> Il ne faut pas laisser pourtant de filer doux.
> L'ingrate foule aux pieds Hercule et sa massue ;
> Quelle que soit l'offrande, elle n'est point reçue :
> Elle verroit mourir le plus fidèle amant,
> Faute de l'assister d'un regard seulement.
> Injust procédé, sotte façon de faire,
> Que la pucelle tient de madame sa mère,
> Et que la bonne dame, au courage inhumain,
> Se lassant aussi peu d'être belle que sage,
> Encore tous les jours applique à son usage,
>   Au détriment du genre humain."

It would have been scarcely possible, scarcely human, indeed, for the brilliant young beauty to have passed through such public triumphs without attracting marked and dangerous attention. It was a great distinction to have been chosen to dance with the King, but when to this was added her "exquisite youth," her delicate beauty, her graceful figure and perfect dancing, it is not surprising to learn that she roused a good deal of interest among the Court gallants. The King's favourite, the handsome young Marquis de Villeroy, who, from his personal attractions and notorious gallantries, had been nicknamed "the charming," paid assiduous attention to this fresh young beauty, and the circumstance was quickly noted by watchful eyes at Court. From the Court, as was the invariable custom, the news spread to the town, and *chansons* on the subject were sung in the streets and sold on the Pont-Neuf. But what else could have been expected?

"Who plays, pays," and particularly when one plays on a public stage! But Madame de Sévigné kept a jealous watch over her daughter, and however undesirable and annoying it might be to find her the subject of street songs, she took every precaution to guard her from all actual harm or evil. These were the humiliating penalties exacted by such a pronounced public success; for Court life in those days was so public, so exposed to the curious among the multitude, that few events escaped the popular eye or tongue. Indeed, it has been said that no history of that time could be complete without consulting the street ballads.

In spite of these drawbacks, however, Mademoiselle de Sévigné everywhere reaped the triumphs of her striking and undisputed beauty; and these were brilliant years both for the Marquise and her daughter. But unalloyed success and unbroken happiness is no one's portion for long, and Madame de Sévigné, in the height of her triumph at her daughter's success and distinction at Court, was deeply wounded again by a disgraceful affair which she had been led to believe was finished.

CHAPTER XVI

A reconciliation between the Marquise and her cousin Bussy—Letters of explanation—The Marquise writes a clear summing-up of his offences—The Comte finally sues for mercy, and is pardoned by his cousin

WHEN, at the time of Foucquet's arrest, the innocent letters of Madame de Sévigné to the Surintendant were causing so much undeserved gossip and scandal in Paris, the Marquise had been especially grateful to her cousin, the Comte de Bussy, for the valiant defence he had made of her good name. She was particularly touched that, in spite of their serious quarrel concerning her "villainous portrait," he had apparently forgotten all the rancour her indignant reproaches might have caused him, to come forward as her champion against their too-censorious world. Then, having been assured that the offending manuscript had been burned at the house of Madame de Montglas, the Marquise, whose spirit was too generous to harbour resentment long, allowed herself to be reconciled to her cousin. She, whom he had called so avaricious, so miserly towards her friends, had even lent him four thousand francs, when Bussy, in perennial need of money, went in August 1663 to join the army in Lorraine. Their friendship was apparently on as firm a foundation as ever. In the autumn of 1664, Bussy met his cousin at her manor of Bourbilly in Burgundy, and, as the Marquise herself declares, she was "more than ever enchanted with his society."

But this happy renewal of friendship was not to last long. As we have seen, though the original manuscript of the *Histoire amoureuse* had been burned, a copy of it had been taken by a spiteful woman, Madame de la Baume, whom Bussy had once loved and then neglected. To revenge herself, she treacherously allowed copies to be taken of her copy; nor was this the worst. Bussy had disguised the heroes and heroines of his *Histoire amoureuse* under fictitious names, and though the originals were easily guessed at, the artifice gave at least a little clothing of decency, thin mask though it was, to the disgraceful facts; but even this was now thrown aside. Scandalous truths were added; libels on the King, Queen, and ladies of the Court were inserted; a key, giving the real names of all the fictitious persons, was appended, and in this aggravated form, infinitely worse than the original, the book was printed at Liège early in the year 1665.

The consternation and wrath of those who were thus publicly, without the least disguise, held up to ridicule, and worse than ridicule, may be imagined without difficulty. They demanded punishment for Bussy; they declared that these libels on the King and Court came from his hand; and Bussy was conducted to the Bastille. Madame de Sévigné, deeply wounded at what she considered the fresh treachery of her cousin, was annoyed beyond measure at this new development. It had been humiliating enough to know that her portrait in manuscript had circulated among the society she daily frequented, but now, as she said, to find herself in the libraries, to meet her portrait everywhere, was almost beyond endurance. Perhaps, however, someone represented to her that Bussy had not been quite so blamable as appeared at first; for we find that a year after, when Bussy, seriously ill, was allowed to leave the Bastille to undergo an operation, Madame de Sévigné was the first among his friends who visited him. Then when Bussy, leaving the house of Dalance, his surgeon, in September, was allowed to retire to Chaseu, his estate in Burgundy, in place of being confined in the Bastille, the Marquise, grieving that his career should be broken by exile just at the time when his bravery and long service should have been rewarded by promotion, wrote him sympathetic letters, which reveal a true interest in his welfare, though the old tone of confidence is lacking. In 1667, she says, "The whole Court is at camp, and the whole camp is at Court. . . . My heart has felt most favourably towards you since I have seen so many people eager to begin, or rather, to recommence the profession in which you gained so much honour during the time you were occupied in it. It is a sad thing for a man of courage to be confined at home when there are such great doings in Flanders. As you feel, no doubt, all that a man of spirit and bravery can feel, it is not very wise of me to revive so painful a subject. I hope you will pardon me in consideration of the great interest I take in your affairs.

"It is said that you have written to the King. Send me a copy of your letter, and give me a little information concerning your mode of life; what you do to amuse yourself, and whether the improvements you are making in your house do not greatly contribute to it. As for me, I have spent the winter in Brittany, where I have planted a great number of small trees, and a labyrinth where one will require Ariadne's clue to find the way out of it. I have also purchased some land, to which I have said, as usual, 'I shall make you into a park.' I have extended my walks, too, but this has cost me very little. My daughter sends you a thousand remembrances. I send mine to all your family."

The correspondence between the two cousins was continued for some time, but there was no longer the old buoyant delight and mutual sympathy. Once, when Bussy had waited six months for an answer to one of his letters, he reproached her with the delay, and Madame de Sévigné took the opportunity of reminding him of the Italian proverb, "The offender never pardons." Taking this for a text, Bussy writes her a long, grieved letter, in which he says, "Why tell me that I do not forgive the wrong I have done you, since I have asked your pardon a thousand times, and you have promised as many times to think no more about it? It seems to me, however, that from time to time you repent of having pardoned me."

This intuition of Bussy's was probably very near the truth. Madame de Sévigné must have occasionally felt that he had transgressed against her almost beyond complete forgiveness; and when, in the same letter, he accuses her of withholding her friendship and interest because he is in exile, and "out of fashion," she could no longer contain the just indignation, the bitter sadness of heart, that his base conduct had caused her. About seven weeks after, she writes him a letter in which she places all the circumstances of their difference before him, and then asks him to judge impartially, as if he were a third, uninterested person, *who* is the real offender.

"PARIS, *July* 26, 1668

"I wish to begin by answering in two words your letter of the 9th of June, and then our case will be finished. . . .

"Learn from me, my cousin, that it is not customary to accuse me of indifference towards my friends. I have many other faults, but not that. Such a fancy exists only in your imagination, and I have before this shown proofs of generosity towards people who were in disgrace which have done me honour among many I could name if I wished. I do not believe, then, that I deserve this reproach, and you may strike this item from the list of my shortcomings. But let us talk of you.

"We are relations, and of the same blood. We please each other, we love each other, we are each interested in the other's welfare. You asked me to advance money to you on the ten thousand crowns which you were soon to receive as a legacy from M. de Chalon. You say I refused you, while I say I lent it to you; for you know well, and our friend Corbinelli is witness to it, that my heart was at once willing, and that while we were settling some formalities to obtain the consent of Neuchèze that I might receive the legacy instead of you, you became impatient. Then, having unfortunately found me sufficiently imperfect in body and mind to be a subject for you to make a very pretty portrait of, you made it; and you preferred the pleasure of being praised for your work to our old friendship, to our name, and even to justice itself. You know that a lady, a friend of yours, generously obliged you to burn it. She believed you had done so, and I believed it also; and some time after, hearing that you had done wonders in the affair of M. Foucquet and me, this conduct completely brought me round. I was reconciled to you on my return from Brittany, and you know with what sincerity! You remember also our journey to Burgundy, and with what frankness I gave you again all the share you had ever had in my friendship. I came away delighted with your society. There were people who said to me at that time, 'I have seen your portrait in the hands of Madame de la Baume; I have seen it.' I answered them only by a disdainful smile, pitying those who were so absurd as to believe

A SUMMING-UP OF BUSSY'S OFFENCES 165

their own eyes. 'I have seen it,' I was told again a week after, and again I smiled. I repeat it laughingly to Corbinelli. I again put on the incredulous smile which has already served me on two occasions, and I remain for five or six months in this ignorance, pitying those who laughed at me. At last the unhappy day came when I myself saw, and with my own 'parti-coloured' eyes, what I had refused to believe. If horns had grown out of my head I should have been less astonished. I read and re-read that cruel portrait. I should have thought it very clever if it had been written of anyone else than me, or by any other person than you. I even found it so well introduced, and so appropriately placed in the book, that I had not the consolation of believing it could have been done by any other than you. I recognised it by several things I had heard rather than by the painting of my character, which I entirely disown. Finally, I saw you at the Palais Royal, where I told you that the book was in circulation. You tried to persuade me that someone had made that portrait from memory and had it printed. But I no longer believed you. . . .

"To be in the hands of everyone; to find oneself in print; to serve as a book of amusement for all the provinces, where such things cause irreparable harm; to meet oneself in the libraries, and to receive this injury from whom? I will not extend my reasons further; you have a good understanding, and I am sure that if you reflect for only a quarter of an hour, you will see them, and you will feel them as I do. Nevertheless, what did I do when you were arrested? With utter sadness in my soul I force myself to make you compliments; I complain of your misfortune; I even talk of it in society, and speak my opinion of the behaviour of Madame de la Baume so freely, that I become embroiled with her. When you come out of prison I visit you several times; I bid you good-bye when I set out for Brittany; I have written to you, since you have been at home, quite freely and without bitterness. . . .

"This is what I wish to say for once in my life, and to beg you to erase from your mind the idea that I am in the wrong. Keep my letter and read it again if ever the fancy occurs to you to believe such a thing, and be as just as if you were judging a case between two other persons. Do not let your interest see what does not exist; confess that you have cruelly offended against the friendship that was between us, and I am disarmed. But do not believe that if you merely answer I can always remain silent, for that would be impossible; I shall never cease to write, and in place of the two words I promised you I shall write two thousand; and at last I shall do so much by letters of a cruel length and mortal dulness, that I shall compel you, in spite of yourself, to beg for pardon, that is to say, to sue for your life. Do so, then, with a good grace.

"For the rest, when you were bled I felt the effect of it. Was it not the 17th of this month? Exactly: it did me all the good in the world; pray accept my thanks for it. I am so difficult to bleed that it is a charity on your part to allow your arm to be bled instead of mine...."

This last is a little bit of nonsense of Madame de Sévigné's, who always declared that there was such an affinity between herself and her cousin, that when anything happened to the one it affected the other. She probably wrote it at the end of her long arraignment in order that the whole letter might not have a bitter flavour throughout.

The Comte de Bussy, with more leisure than he wished in his exile, the same day he received this letter wrote an answer to Madame de Sévigné fully as long, justifying himself where he could, explaining that what had made him so angry over the desired loan was the attitude of her lawyer, who talked of sending to make inquiries in Burgundy, while he was in pressing, immediate need of the money to take him to the seat of war at once, that he might not be regarded as a laggard. He also gave a new version of how the portrait got into print.

"I pass by your condemnation of the portrait, Madame, for no one could possibly blame me for that more than I blame myself; but you ought to learn something else about it that you do not know. That friend so generous, who, you say, obliged me to burn the portrait, obliged you very cheaply. First, after having enjoyed the pleasure of having heard it read, she begged me to tear it up; and this I did into a thousand pieces in front of her. To tell the truth, I had not left the room when her husband, who was present, gathered together the pieces, to the tiniest morsel, and put them together again so well that he copied it, and showed it to me three days after. I confess to you that I was seized with the desire of having it again, and that some time after, being on friendly terms with Madame de la Baume, she had the ridiculous brochure from me, which she published as you know. . . ."

It was a sordid story in whatever form the Marquise heard it; a story of bad faith, treachery, and meanness that must have made her own frank and noble heart sick with disgust. Bussy goes on trying to justify himself with his plausible and subtle skill, but such repetitions and justifications, however interesting they may have been to the two cousins, are of little interest to us of to-day. One circumstance, however, that Bussy mentions, gives us a piquant glimpse of the fashion in which prisoners at the Bastille received visits. " All my friends except you," he tells her with reproach, "came to see me at the moat near the windows of the Bastille. . . ."

Madame de Sévigné, when she answers this letter at her leisure, scorns his excuses, and refuses to receive them. She does not approve of his efforts at sheltering himself behind the ladies of his acquaintance. " Do not tell me again," she writes, "that it is the fault of anyone else; it is not true . . . the fault is entirely your own." Indeed, the whole letter is very bracing, though there is not a trace of malice or ill-feeling. She merely shows him, by the plainest demonstration, what a disloyal friend and faithless relative he has been.

Bussy feels himself vanquished, and at last sues for his life, as she had demanded. " I have begged for life, and you would kill me at your feet; that is a little inhuman. I did not think that pretty women could be so cruel except in love affairs. Cease then, *petite brutale*, to desire to whip a man who throws himself at your feet, who confesses his fault and beseeches you to pardon him. If you are not yet content with the terms I use in this encounter, send me the model of the satisfaction which you desire, and I will return it to you written and signed with my own hand, countersigned by a secretary, and sealed with the seal of my arms. What more would you have? . . ."

The Marquise did not desire more. She had written to him fully of all the grief and chagrin and unhappiness his conduct had caused her; she had had that satisfaction, so dear, it is said, to women, of proving her opponent in the wrong, and, what was more, of making him confess it; and now she was her own gracious, kindly self again, willing to send him a full, free pardon.

"PARIS, *September* 4, 1668

" Rise, Comte; I would not kill you at my feet, or take your sword to renew the combat. But it is better that I should give you life, and that we should live in peace. I exact only one condition; that is, that you should own the thing just as it happened. This is a very generous proceeding on my part, and you can no longer call me a *petite brutale*. . . . Adieu, Comte. Now that I have conquered you, I shall say everywhere that you are the bravest man in France; and whenever remarkable duels are talked of I shall relate ours. . . ."

CHAPTER XVII

Suitors for the hand of Mademoiselle de Sévigné—A vain young beauty—The Duc de Caderousse — Monsieur de Mérinville — "The prettiest girl in France" unmarried at twenty-three—She is betrothed to a widower with two young daughters

BY an odd, malign chance, it was during the time when the Comte de Bussy's malice and treachery was bearing its most bitter fruit, that Madame de Sévigné was, by her daughter's social success, most prominently before the society of the Court; and to the Marquise, so keenly sensitive to impressions, the trial must have been exceptionally severe. But probably her own annoyance was partly atoned for by her daughter's success. Each year some fresh distinction awaited the young beauty. In 1666 La Fontaine dedicated to her his *Lion amoureux*, which was not, however, published till 1668. It begins—

> "Sévigné, de qui les attraits
> Servent aux Grâces de modèle,
> Et qui naquîtes toute belle,
> A votre indifférence près . . ."

The rather spoiled young lady had already shown herself to be cold and proudly indifferent to those who sought her smiles, and La Fontaine made a gentle and guarded allusion to this, which was, however, well enough understood. The gallant Ménage, always delighted to pose as the slave and adorer of pretty young girls, addressed to her a madrigal in Italian, the language which he had taught her mother; and the hunchbacked poet, Saint-Pavin, whom she often met at Livry, now wrote epistles in verse to the daughter, as years before he had written them to Marie de Rabutin-Chantal.

But Mademoiselle did not receive all this homage with the gracious and winning charm that had so endeared her mother even to some of those whose advances she had been obliged to check. She was cold and slightly haughty in her manner, with much more intellect than heart. She would probably have been something of a bluestocking if social affairs had not fully occupied her time. Among her brother's friends was the Comte de Saint-Paul, that youngest son of the Duchesse de Longueville who had been born at the Hôtel de Ville, and the story goes that he paid a good deal of attention to the clever young beauty, who one day, in reply to his *fleurettes*, flippantly quoted in Latin, " Saul, Saul, quid me persequeris ? "

Her mother records, too, that another time when a foreigner, M. Dietriechen, was mentioned, Mademoiselle de Sévigné gave her opinion :

" He is very much like the Duc de Beaufort," said she, " except that he speaks better French ! "

A witticism that was received with delighted laughter, for the Duc de Beaufort was noted for his coarse language, which was more suited to the streets than to the polished society of his compeers.

She was fond of argument, too, and quite willing to uphold a bad cause for this reason ; in which she was singularly unlike her mother and her brother, who always greatly preferred to agree with their friends. And in many other qualities she was a complete contrast to the charming Marquise. We never find a trace of personal vanity in Madame de Sévigné's letters ; on the contrary, she frequently laughed at her little defects, and pretended to see her own flat-tipped nose in that of her granddaughter Blanche. But Mademoiselle, her daughter, was no such unconscious beauty. She, whose face was so perfect in form and colouring that she might well have left the care of it to Nature, was over-anxious to preserve it in all its freshness ; and, quite unintentionally, the Marquise has told for all time the little artifices that her daughter practised. They are by no means grave faults in a girl, however. They merely amusingly serve to show that vain beauty is singularly alike in all ages and conditions of life, whether the means used be the latest concoctions of the " beauty doctors," or the simpler methods of the seventeenth century, before vanity was so systematically exploited by business cunning.

"What is become of the time when you would eat nothing but a woodcock's head for fear of becoming too fat?" she asks years afterwards. And another time she whimsically recalls how, as a young girl, her daughter, in anointing her face to get rid of her pimples, "had contemplated herself in essence, like a chicken in a pie."

The Abbé de la Mousse, her tutor, noting one day some exhibition of girlish vanity, reminded her of the fleeting nature of beauty. "Mademoiselle," he remarked gravely, "those charms will all decay some day."

"That may be, Monsieur," pertly replied his pretty pupil, "but they are not decayed yet!"

When Mademoiselle de Sévigné had been some years at Court, and was about twenty-one or twenty-two, it was whispered by jealous and malicious tongues that the King, visibly colder to la Vallière, was thinking of choosing Mademoiselle de Sévigné as her successor! His Majesty was at this period undoubtedly giving great distinctions to the young lady and her mother. On the 18th of July 1668, they were both guests at the famous fête given at Versailles in the chateau and gardens, as yet in an unfinished condition. Only three hundred ladies were invited to this *fête galante*, which was one of the most exclusive given at Versailles by Louis XIV. The guests, already dressed in festive costume for the day, drove, early in the morning, from Paris to Versailles, where they found that the apartments had been specially decorated and perfumed for the occasion, and, so that the visitors might not be embarrassed by the laws of etiquette, the King and royal family had retired to a pavilion in the gardens. On their arrival, the guests sat down to a repast; after which they descended to the gardens, where small carriages were in waiting to drive them, accompanied by the young Queen, round the park and gardens. These carriages, in fact, were placed all day at the service of the visitors, to convey them from one entertainment to another without fatigue or loss of time. There were many English at this fête, the most notable of whom was the ill-fated Duke of Monmouth, who paid conspicuous attention all that day to the equally ill-fated Madame, the beautiful Henriette of England. No entertainment at that time was complete without a comedy, and the famous *Georges Dandin* by Molière was given for the first time in the park of Versailles.

But the chief event of the day, or rather the evening, was the supper; and at this banquet both Madame de Sévigné and her daughter were at the King's table, a distinction that we may be sure was commented on freely. Curiously enough, Mesdames de la Vallière, de Montespan, and de Maintenon, were all at this fête; de Montespan already scheming to supplant de la Vallière, and the humble "widow Scarron" was suing for a small pension, entirely unaware of the barren and disappointing splendour the future held for her.

These and similar distinctions from the King set the Court gossips on the *qui vive*. Already reports of the King's attentions to Mademoiselle de Sévigné were finding their way into letters. Madame de Montmorency, who sent to Bussy in his exile all the gossip and scandal of the Court, wrote on the 15th of July, three days before the fête, that the King was paying attention to Mademoiselle de Sévigné with the intention of making her the successor to Mademoiselle de la Vallière. "But this is still very feeble," she added. Bussy answered this at once, and he, always seeking his own advancement, frankly declared the pleasure the news gave him: "I should be very glad if the King did become attached to Mademoiselle de Sévigné," he wrote, "for that young lady is among my very good friends, and he could not do better than take her for a mistress."

Bussy's troubles had not changed him. This nobleman of long and honourable descent, who openly confessed that he sought his own advancement when advising his cousin to smile graciously on the attentions of Foucquet and the Prince de Conti, now rejoices that his lovely young relative is attracting the notice of the King; for through her, one guesses without difficulty, he hopes to repair his damaged fortunes, and to get release from his wearisome exile.

But Madame de Sévigné kept faithful guard over her young daughter, and she who had been so jealous of her own reputation would not lightly have allowed her daughter to be robbed of womanhood's most precious jewel. "Her devotion to her young sovereign had its limits," sagely remarks a biographer.

Nor had she waited till then to instil into her daughter the precepts of honour and virtue. Mademoiselle de Sévigné had been too well brought up to buy any grandeur at the expense of her good name. She has been reproached by many writers with too much indifference; of being so cold by temperament that she found it no temptation to resist the King's advances. But the firmness that repels has nothing picturesque or dramatic in its quality; and those who can lightly bewail the lost virtue of the frail and gentle Louise de la Vallière, or write with pleasant deprecation of the magnificence of the haughty and venal Montespan, would probably find such firmness a trifle too austere for interest. But one doubts not that M. de Grignan had full satisfaction in the unassailable honour of his wife, and that he probably did not object to her coldness to others—it was not a common fault at the Court of Louis XIV!—since she was a loving and faithful wife to him. The line of simple duty and virtue has never made much stir in the world.

Many people, including the Comte de Bussy, have accused the Marquise de Sévigné with being cold, and "too much in love with her own reputation"; but her solicitous care that that jewel of price should never be dimmed, has preserved, not only for those of her own day, but for millions of posterity, a striking and praiseworthy example. She was a woman of brilliant attractions, with a frank enjoyment of the pleasures of the world, and was not indifferent to its honours; she was sought by a crowd of seductive triflers, and surrounded by potent temptations, but she has come through the fire unstained and untainted, a shining example of purity in a Court and society where absolutely impregnable virtue was not reckoned among the most estimable or popular attractions. How different would have been the effect of the life of Madame de Sévigné, had either she or her daughter succumbed to the evil influences that beset them in the Court of Louis Quatorze!

Besides belonging to the exclusive circle near the person of the King, Mademoiselle de Sévigné was taken by her mother to many of the salons of Parisian society where the Marquise had long been a welcome guest. Madame de la Fayette was always ailing, but she was nevertheless always at home to some of the "best talkers" in Parisian society; and though the

Marquise and her daughter were among her most frequent visitors, we hear more of the evenings they spent at the Hôtel de Nevers, which had taken the place, in some degree, of the Hôtel de Rambouillet. At this period there was no more celebrated hostess in Paris than Madame du Plessis Guénégaud. Foucquet had been an intimate friend of the family, and M. du Plessis Guénégaud, who was Secretary of State, and enormously rich, was for a time involved in Foucquet's disgrace and sent into exile. But in 1665, when the late Surintendant was under safe keeping in a dungeon at Pignerol, M. de Guénégaud was permitted to return to Paris, and the Hôtel de Nevers once again opened its hospitable doors to a polished and brilliant society.

Madame de Sévigné always called her intimacy with Madame du Plessis Guénégaud a *reflected* friendship, because they had become acquainted though the Marquis de Pomponne, over their mutual distress and interest at Foucquet's trial. But the Marquise was soon welcomed on her own account, and was frequently at the Hôtel de Nevers. When Pomponne was recalled from exile, in 1665, he wrote a letter describing an evening he had spent there after his return. Among the numerous company were Madame de Sévigné and her daughter, Madame de la Fayette, and the Duc de la Rochefoucauld; Boileau the critic, who pricked so many bubbles of reputation with his caustic pen, was there also, reading one of his satires before publication; and Racine read a part of his *Alexandre*, which was not played till the end of the year. The Great Century was now in its golden prime; the King, though furiously devoted to pleasure, was governing well and wisely; encouraging the development of arts and manufactures, and by his gracious approval and patronage stimulating the literary men to give of their best. In place of Voiture, the Scudérys, and all the lesser lights of the Hôtel de Rambouillet, there was now at the Hôtel de Nevers, Corneille, the one star of magnitude that had given a glory to the former salon, and, in addition, Molière, Racine, La Fontaine, de la Rochefoucauld, and Boileau—a very constellation of brilliant literary stars, the like of which was never before seen at any other period of French history.

Graceful little literary games were played at the Hôtel de Nevers, in which Mademoiselle de Sévigné and the two young daughters of the house eagerly took part. Here, too, came the Duc de Caderousse, who became one of the suitors for the hand of Mademoiselle de Sévigné. But the Marquise, whose good sense and penetration were rarely at fault, did not overlook the fact that he was a dissipated young man who was a gambler, and not likely to make a good husband; therefore, in spite of his great position, this suitor was refused. The Duc de Caderousse, however, determined to have one of this charming group of girls, married the elder of the daughters of Madame du Plessis Guénégaud, and in a few short years the unhappiness of this marriage proved how wise the Marquise had been to refuse the alliance.

Sometimes in summer the Marquise and her daughter would pay a visit to Madame du Plessis Guénégaud at her country-house at Fresnes, for two or three months at a time. Many of their friends from Paris came there also, and little romances and fairy-tales were played, in which the Marquise frequently acted, and gained considerable success and applause. In a letter to the Marquis de Pomponne, who had recently been appointed Ambassador to the Swedish Court, Madame de Sévigné gives a delightful little glimpse of the pleasant society at Fresnes. " I have M. d'Andilly at my left hand, which is the side of the heart," she writes; " I have Madame de la Fayette at my right; Madame du Plessis is in front of me, and is amusing herself with daubing little pictures; Madame de Motteville, a little farther away, is deep in thought; while Madame de Caderousse, her sister, and Mademoiselle de Sévigné keep flitting in and out like bees."

But, singularly enough, the lovely young Mademoiselle de Sévigné, with all her beauty and unusual distinction, backed up by the appreciable advantages of good birth and a rich dowry, had considerable difficulty in finding a suitable husband. After the Duc de Caderousse had been refused in 1665, another Provençal presented himself. He was the son of the Comte de Mérinville, Lieutenant-General of Provence; and this marriage was brought very near to a conclusion, but Madame de Sévigné, finding that her daughter did not greatly care about the match, and that she herself did not wish her child to be settled in such a distant province, broke off the marriage as diplomatically as she could.

Another suitor was the Comte d'Etauges, who was rich, it was said, "but something of a fool." Nothing came of this, however; and the Marquise began to be somewhat weary, as well as surprised, at still having her beautiful young daughter to chaperon; and when the Comte de Bussy asked in one of his letters about "the prettiest girl in France," his cousin wrote in reply, "The prettiest girl in France sends you her compliments. It is a charming name, but I am tired of doing the honours of it!"

Perhaps, like many another beauty, Mademoiselle de Sévigné began by being too exigeant. Saint-Pavin, in a letter to the Marquise, glances lightly at the truth in graceful, facile verse—

> "Votre fille est le seul ouvrage
> Que la nature ait achevé.
> . . . . .
> Aussi la terre est trop petite
> Pour y trouver qui la mérite;
> Et la belle, qui le sait bien,
> Méprise tout et ne veut rien."

Françoise de Sévigné was not the first beautiful girl who has illustrated the truth of the homely proverb anent the crooked stick. After seven years in which to make a choice, after refusing a rich and handsome young duke, a rich young count, and probably others, she became affianced to a man who had been married twice before, who, it was remarked, "abused a man's privilege of being ugly," and who was burdened with debt. Yet, let it be said at once, it was an entirely happy marriage, which in all probability brought more solid satisfaction than either of the others would have done. And it is also only justice to add that the proud, cold young beauty, who as a girl had been so vain and selfish, ripened into a thoughtful and capable woman, entirely devoted to her husband and children, and to the interests of the family into which she married.

Not long before the marriage took place, Madame de Sévigné wrote the news to Bussy; she had probably not thought it prudent to tell him sooner, although negotiations had been going on for some time previously.

"PARIS, *December* 4, 1668

"I must tell you a piece of news that I am sure you will be rejoiced to hear; it is that at last the prettiest girl in France is

MARRIAGE NEGOTIATIONS

to be married, not to the handsomest youth, but to one of the worthiest men in the kingdom—to M. de Grignan, whom you have known for a long time. All his wives died to give place to your cousin, and, by extraordinary good fortune, even his father and his son died too, so that he is richer than he has ever been. Being besides, by birth, establishment, and by his good qualities, everything that we could wish, we have not bargained with him as is usual on such occasions, but have relied on the two families which have preceded us. He seems very well pleased with the alliance, and as soon as we have heard from his uncle, the Archbishop of Arles, the affair will be concluded before the end of the year, as his other uncle, the Bishop of Uzès, is here. As I am a lady who loves decorum, I could not fail to ask your advice and approbation. The public seems satisfied, which is a great deal, for we are so foolish that we are nearly always governed by its opinion."

The "advice and approbation," which the Marquise so decorously asked from Bussy, were asked for at a somewhat late date, seeing that the arrangements for the marriage were nearly concluded, but the etiquette that demanded such empty compliments was apparently satisfied by the merest show of attention.

CHAPTER XVIII

Mademoiselle de Sévigné is married to the Comte de Grignan—An ancient and honourable family—An imprudent mother—Charles de Sévigné—His campaign in Candia against the Turks

FRANÇOIS ADHÉMAR, Comte de Grignan, who to Madame de Sévigné seemed such a desirable husband for her daughter, was the eldest son of an ancient and illustrious family of Provence. He was descended from the House of Castellane, and this family, being connected with the Adhémars of Monteil, took the name and arms of Grignan in 1563, when they inherited the Comté de Grignan. The Adhémar family dated further back than the Crusades, and the exploits of one of their ancestors in these wars were immortalised by the poet Tasso. The Marquise was well pleased at having arranged such a distinguished alliance for her daughter, and she delighted in reading up the records of the family greatness.

"I see an Adhémar," she wrote to M. de Grignan, "who was one of the greatest seigneurs six hundred years ago. His death threw an army of three hundred thousand men into mourning, and made all Christian princes weep. I see also a Castellane, but he is not so ancient; he is modern; it is only five hundred years ago since he made such a grand figure in the world."

The family of Grignan was still influential, with numerous connections in good positions. Two uncles of M. de Grignan were distinguished prelates, the Archbishop of Arles and the Bishop of Uzès. Two of his brothers were also in the Church; the elder, the Coadjutor of the Archbishop of Arles, and the other an abbé, who became Bishop of Evreux. He also had two brothers in the army, one a captain of a company of Light Horse, and the other a Chevalier of Malta.

M. de Grignan was between thirty-seven and forty years old at the time of his marriage to Mademoiselle de Sévigné, but his exact age is not known. He was not handsome; indeed, his pronounced plainness is frequently referred to by the Marquise, who set a high value on her daughter's loveliness, and passionately admired beauty and grace wherever she saw it. But notwithstanding this intense and innate love of beauty, she knew that good qualities were of infinitely greater importance in the matter of her daughter's happiness; and, for the rest, M. de Grignan had a tall and fine figure, his manners had the polish of good breeding and the refinement that had been acquired in the school of the Hôtel de Rambouillet. He was an accomplished musician, and, of more importance than all else, he was an honourable and good man, who made her daughter an excellent husband. "He was," said the Marquise, "the most desirable husband, and very agreeable in society"; later, too, he gave her daughter a great position, which, in the Marquise de Sévigné's estimation, had only one drawback, it was far away from Paris and from Court. M. de Grignan had two little girls at the time of his marriage with Françoise de Sévigné, the daughters of his first wife, Angélique Claire d'Angennes. His second wife had died in giving birth to a son who did not live.

But the Marquise had not been quite her usual prudent self in arranging this marriage. Perhaps the alliance appeared to her so desirable from all other points, that she wilfully shut her eyes to one important fact. She had written to the Comte de Bussy, "we have not bargained with him as is usual on such occasions, we have relied on the two families which have preceded us"; and she had evidently written in the same strain to Cardinal de Retz, who, as head of her husband's family, was one of the chief persons to be consulted about the marriage. The Cardinal saw no reason for such blind confidence, and in his reply he gave her a warning which was only too well justified by the events of after years.

"Great as are your daughter's fears concerning the wedding day," he writes, "I doubt whether they can be equal to mine in regard to what is to follow, since I see by one of your letters that you have neither had, nor expect, any explanations, and that you have, in a manner, trusted yourself to Destiny, who is often most ungrateful, and ill requites the confidence placed in her."

Notwithstanding this warning, it was a time of optimism and pleasurable anticipation for Madame de Sévigné, even though in the marriage contract, signed two days before the wedding, it was agreed that of the two hundred thousand livres which the Marquise gave in ready money as part of her daughter's *dot*, one hundred and eighty thousand livres should be handed over to be used in payment of the Comte de Grignan's debts!

The Marquise was wealthy at this period of her life; her estates were in a prosperous, flourishing condition, and all her pecuniary affairs had been kept in most excellent order by the Abbé de Coulanges. Happily for her she could not foresee the future married life of her daughter, which, ominously begun by payment of the bridegroom's debts, was, through luxury, ostentation, gambling, and much needless vanity, to bring debt and discomfort to the chief persons concerned, and to reduce the Marquise to comparative poverty.

But all this was far enough away when the wedding took place on January 29, 1669, the day of Saint Francis de Sales, as Madame de Sévigné reminded her daughter. It was doubtless attended by a numerous company of friends and relatives, as more than sixty persons signed the wedding contract. The Comte de Bussy's name is absent from the list, not because he was in exile and unable to attend, but because he was greatly annoyed that the Comte de Grignan had not written to him as a near relative of the bride. Bussy had put himself beyond the pale of all honest men's regard by his scandalous conduct in general, and to Madame de Sévigné in particular; and it is quite conceivable that the Comte de Grignan, who was not conspicuously humble, considered that he did not deserve the usual civilities. Bussy, swift to take offence, and always willing to credit any coldness or neglect to the fact of his exile rather than to his own shameful behaviour, wrote to the Marquise to air his grievance. "Madame de Grignan has reason also to complain of me; I ought to have written to her after her marriage, and I beg her pardon and frankly confess the debt. I must also be frank with you concerning M. de Grignan. From whatever point you look at it, particularly when he marries the daughter of my first cousin, he ought to write to me first (for I suppose that being persecuted does not exclude me from this favour; there are a thousand people who would write to me all the more willingly on that account), his omission is not like the politeness of the Hôtel de Rambouillet. I know well that friendships are free, but I was not aware that the things which concern good breeding were equally free. This is what comes of being so long away from Court, one unlearns everything in the provinces. . . ."

The Marquise replied to this in gay mood, and cheerfully tried to make peace between her relatives; telling Bussy of the bridegroom's happiness, and that if the latter did write, he would probably only bore him, the Comte de Bussy, with a list of her daughter's perfections, as was the custom of the newly-wed. Madame de Grignan would, she assured him, write instead of her husband.

The young Comtesse did write, but not so graciously or so tactfully as her mother had done. "M. de Grignan has not written," she says, "and so far from understanding that he ought to send you a letter, he thinks it rather lacking in courtesy on your part that you have not condescended to send your compliments, because he is so happy he thinks that everybody should congratulate him. These are his reasons, and I am vain enough to repeat them to you myself."

The Comte de Bussy made a quite considerable grievance of this petty affair, for in the long days of exile he probably exaggerated his own wrongs and the shortcomings of his friends. He thought the Comtesse de Grignan's letter "very sharp," and he consequently wrote a long, bitter complaint to the Marquise, who, though only so recently reconciled to him, found to her dismay that, owing to his vanity, they were now on the verge of another quarrel.

"Ah! Comte, was it you who wrote the letter I have just received?" she replied soon after. "I was so astonished while reading it that I felt distracted, and could not believe what I saw. Is it possible that the most foolish letter in the world could be taken in that manner by a man who understands raillery as well as you, and who also knows how to give such excellent explanations when a letter needs them?"

Then she explains, almost sentence by sentence, the meaning and intentions of the offending letter, and finishes with the little reproach, "Not only have I not recognised my blood in your style, but I have not recognised yours."

Bussy, only half appeased, finally did write first to M. de Grignan; but coolness had again sprung up between the cousins, and the correspondence ceased for some months, till in the next year, 1670, the President Frémyot died, leaving part of his fortune to Madame de Sévigné. Then Bussy, probably missing her friendly and charming letters during his interminable, empty days of exile, wrote to congratulate her. The Marquise, whose bright, healthy spirit was incapable of bearing malice, replied to his letter almost immediately, saying, "I thank you for having reopened the door of our intercourse, which had entirely lost its handle. Incidents are always happening between us, but we mean well, and perhaps we shall laugh at them some day."

It is a little curious that during all this time there is scarcely a mention, either in memoirs or correspondence, of Charles de Sévigné, the only son of the Marquise. There is no indication in all Madame de Sévigné's letters as to where or by whom he was educated; we only know that, like his sister, he received a good and thorough education, and that, from his mother, he inherited an enthusiasm for literature, though in his youth he loved nothing but plays and romances; and sometimes, when he was with the Marquise, we find her gaily complaining in her letters that he lured her from more serious reading to listen to the romantic novels of Calprenède, or to the many comedies that he read so well.

In character, Charles de Sévigné was in all surface qualities very like his mother, having an abundance of those charming graces that make for success in society. "He accommodates himself to the humour of everyone," wrote the Marquise, "and always agrees with the last speaker."

In his delightful letters we catch more than a hint of Madame de Sévigné's own felicities of style; he has the happy faculty of saying the right thing in the most pleasant fashion; he is always amiable, perhaps a thought too amiable, and he takes the second place in his mother's affection with the most graceful humility in the world. He was undoubtedly in all superficial charm more like the Marquise than her haughty and reserved daughter, and some biographers have said that Madame de Sévigné would have done well to bestow her greatest love on him. But even had she been able to love at will, she knew his amiable, unreliable character too well, and must often have unwillingly noticed his resemblance to his father in the mad follies to which he gave up his youth. She was very patient ; she paid his debts, and bore with all his youthful faults and excesses; but though with the true mother-spirit she accepted the present with resignation and hoped all things for the future, she could not give her dissipated, erring son the honour and respect which she gave in such full measure to her daughter, and which must necessarily be the foundation of any great love.

Perhaps, since so many people say so, Madame de Sévigné may have loved her daughter a little unwisely, but that is a matter upon which it is impossible to dogmatise. Is any great love wise, measured by ordinary, practical standards? Hers was truly a great love, poured out without stint, one of the world's most celebrated, most unselfish loves, giving all and asking little in return—a love which has enriched literature and humanity with some of the finest letters in the world. And as we read those letters, we cannot fail to grasp the difference in character between her two children.

Between the lines we may discern some indication of the clever, thoughtful mind of Madame de Grignan. Her mother could write to her, sure of entire comprehension, of complete understanding; sure, from her absolutely upright character, that she would never be betrayed. Could she have written with the same freedom of maternal love to her son Charles, even if she had had the same tenderness of feeling for him? Impossible. She would never have known whether some mistress, who had empire over him for the moment, might not obtain possession of her most cherished secrets! Madame de Sévigné's experience of men had not been calculated to inspire her with much trust in them. Her husband, on whom she lavished all the best of her young, unspoiled faith and affection, was base, faithless, and utterly untrustworthy through his weakness. Her cousin Bussy, between whom and herself the tie of kindred was unusually strong, had, in a fit of pique, coldly and with wicked deliberation held her up to the ridicule of the world among whom she lived. Her son, as he grew to manhood, handsome, witty, brave and charming though he was, had yet the weak and fatal amiability of character that made him always ready "to agree with the last speaker," with apparently no solid or settled convictions of his own.

He was a little over twenty when he joined the heroic and adventurous expedition to Candia, which the Duc de Roannes led to the assistance of Venice against the Turks. More than four hundred young gentlemen volunteers, belonging to the greatest families of France, took part in the campaign, and Charles de Sévigné was in the brigade commanded by the young Comte de Saint-Paul, that son of the Duchesse de Longueville who had been born in the Hôtel de Ville.

Though Françoise de Sévigné's betrothal had not been mentioned at the time of her brother's departure in August 1668, we know that before he set out he left a power of attorney with the Abbé de la Mousse, so that he might sign in his place in his sister's marriage contract. After he left, Madame de Sévigné wrote to tell the news of his departure to the Comte de Bussy, and we see the anguish of her true mother-love at the first long separation from her son:

"You do not know, I believe, that my son is gone to Candia with M. de Roannes and the Comte de Saint-Paul. He took this fancy very strongly into his head, and consulted M. de Turenne, Cardinal de Retz, and M. de la Rochefoucauld—you see what important personages! All these gentlemen approved of it so highly that it was settled and rumoured about before I knew anything of the matter. In short, he is gone. I have wept bitterly; I am terribly afflicted by it, and I shall not have a moment's peace during the whole expedition. I see all its dangers, and am frightened to death by them, but I have not been mistress; on such occasions as these, mothers have not much voice in the matter.

It turned out to be a disastrous expedition. The brave young volunteers knew little of the art of war, and a terrible loss of men was the natural result. Then the pestilence broke out, and carried off many of the men that battle had spared; but, fortunately for Charles de Sévigné and his mother, he returned unhurt by wounds or pestilence, and with a reputation for bravery in this his first campaign.

CHAPTER XIX

The Comte de Grignan is appointed Deputy-Governor of Provence—Madame de Sévigné's grief and disappointment—Model letters from a mother-in-law—The Comtesse de Grignan remains a year in Paris with her mother—The Bishop of Marseilles

ONE of the greatest advantages of her daughter's marriage to the Comte de Grignan was, in Madame de Sévigné's eyes, that their home was in Paris, and that, in all probability, they would remain there. M. de Grignan had influential friends and relatives, he was a man of solid worth and good abilities, and they hoped that in time he would secure some position at Court. There is no doubt that in her visions of the future the Marquise had dreamed of being always near her beloved daughter, rejoicing in her happiness and success, helping to lighten her troubles, and soothing her inevitable sorrows with tender love and experience. The Comte was Lieutenant-General of Languedoc, it is true, but as there were two other lieutenants-general and a governor-general of the province, it was hardly probable that he would be often called upon for military service.

But Madame de Sévigné did not enjoy one whole year of this tranquil, undisturbed happiness, which she hoped would have lasted for her lifetime. On the 29th of November 1669, the Comte de Grignan was appointed Lieutenant-General of Provence.

It was the same title that he had held in Languedoc, but with a wide difference in the office. The Duc de Vendôme, who had succeeded his father as Governor of Provence, was only thirteen years old, and consequently unable to govern in person. In his absence the chief President of Parlement, the Baron d'Oppède, was a kind of provisional governor, but the Bishop of Marseilles had so arrogantly taken advantage of this circumstance to usurp legal authority, that it was imperatively necessary for some recognised government to be immediately established in the name and authority of the King.

This was a great position for the Comte de Grignan and for Madame la Comtesse his wife; it was practically the government of a little kingdom, with all the pomp and authority belonging to the office. But to Madame de Sévigné all the joy and honour of the prospect were swallowed up by the grief of the imminent parting. In these days of swift and easy travelling it is so difficult for us to imagine what a wide gulf of separation lay between Paris and Provence! It took more than a fortnight to get from one place to the other, and there were real dangers in crossing the impetuous Rhone, in the bad roads, and the many possible mischances of travel.

It was a sudden and distressing disappointment to all Madame de Sévigné's hopes, and an overwhelming grief to be compelled to part with her daughter. But that painful duty was deferred for some months after the Comte de Grignan's departure, which was a respite to the Marquise, embittered, however, every day by the thought of the approaching separation. M. de Grignan left Paris for Provence at the end of April 1670, but as his wife was not then in a fit state of health to travel, he left her in Paris with her mother till the end of the year. We gather from Madame de Sévigné's letters afterwards that the young wife, parted from her husband, was so determined to be entirely faithful to him, that instead of dressing herself in beautiful costumes, as she had formerly done when she appeared at Court, she now wore most unbecoming clothes. "Do you not remember," her mother writes some time after, "how you used to weary us with the sight of that wretched black mantle? That negligence was the action of a virtuous woman. M. de Grignan might well be obliged to you for it, but it was most annoying for those who saw it."

Though the Marquise was delighted to have her daughter in Paris for a time longer, she was too wise to wish to cause any resentment from a sense of being neglected on the part of the Comte de Grignan. She wrote frequently to him, and her letters are a model of what the letters of a mother-in-law should be. They are most delicately diplomatic, saying with instinctive tact all the things he would most desire to know. She dwells on her daughter's love for him, she takes the second place in her daughter's affection, she tells him that everyone speaks of her correct and regular conduct, and dwells insistently on her daughter's desire to be with him.

"PARIS, *August* 6, 1670

"Is it not true that I have given you the prettiest wife in the world? Can anyone be more virtuous, more regular in her conduct? Can anyone love you more tenderly? Can anyone have more Christian sentiments? Can anyone desire more ardently to be with you? Can anyone be more devoted to her duties? It is rather ridiculous of me to speak so well of my own daughter, but it is because I admire her conduct as much as other people do; and perhaps more, because I have more opportunities of seeing it. To tell you the truth, whatever good opinion I had of her on all important points, I did not think she would be so scrupulous as she is on all minor matters. I assure you everyone does her justice, and she loses none of the praises that are her due.

"It is an old theme of mine, for which I shall be stoned one day, that the public is neither foolish nor unjust, and Madame de Grignan has too much reason to be satisfied with it just now to dispute it. She has been in inconceivable anxiety about your health, and I am delighted to hear that you have recovered, for love of you as well as for love of her. I beg you, if you expect any more attacks of your disorder, to prevail on them to wait till after my daughter is confined. She complains every day that we keep her here, and declares very seriously that it was extremely cruel to have separated her from you. One would suppose that we had put two hundred leagues between her and you for pleasure. I beg you to calm her mind on that point, and to tell her what joy it gives you to hope that she will be happily delivered here. It was absolutely impossible for her to have accompanied you in her condition, and nothing will be so good for her health as to be confined with the care she has here, nor for her reputation as to remain in a place where her conduct is so admired. If, after this, she desired to become giddy and coquettish, it would be more than a year before anyone would believe it, as she has given everyone such a good opinion of her wisdom. I call on all the Grignans who are here to bear witness to the truth of what I tell you. My joy in all this accords well with yours, for I love you with all my heart, and I am delighted that the result has so well justified your choice. I shall tell you no news, as that would be trespassing on my daughter's rights. I only beg you to believe that no one can be more tenderly interested than I am in everything that concerns you."

It is almost impossible not to admire the Marquise from almost every aspect, and in relation to almost every duty of life! In the world she is brilliant, witty, amiable, and graceful; to those who have the happiness of being near her heart she is most tenderly affectionate; as wife, mother, niece, friend, she is as nearly perfect as faulty human nature may be; even to this difficult character of mother-in-law, which has been the butt of vulgar wit since the beginning of the world, she adds a new dignity, and invests it with a wise and thoughtful tenderness; showing an acute avoidance of giving offence that might well be copied by those unhappy, untactful mothers-in-law, who by an overweening, selfish affection for their daughters have wrecked their happiness for life.

In another letter, written a few days after this, she tells him that she writes so frequently to him only on condition that he will not answer her letters. She rejoices in the honours that are paid to him in his new office of lieutenant-general, and again she writes most about his wife, knowing that of this subject he will not soon tire. "I see that such a lively correspondence is kept up between a certain lady and you that it would be absurd of me to pretend to give you any news. There is not the least hope of being able to inform you that she loves you; all her actions, all her conduct, all her cares and anxieties tell you so plainly enough. I am rather difficult to please in matters concerning love, and profess to know something about it; and I own to you that I am perfectly satisfied with what I see, and that I should not wish it to be different. Enjoy this pleasure to the uttermost, and do not be ungrateful. If any little vacant place remains in your heart, allow me the pleasure of occupying it, for you hold a very considerable place in mine. . . . I have given my daughter a book for you, you will find it very beautiful; it is by an intimate friend of Pascal's; he writes nothing that is not perfect; pray read it with attention. I have also sent you some beautiful airs till I can get the other music. Do not neglect either your voice or your fine figure; in a word, continue to be amiable since you are loved so well."

The intimate friend of Pascal, of whom she writes, is Nicole, the author of *Essais de morale*. Madame de Sévigné greatly admired his writings, and she read and re-read his books many times in the long leisure of her days at Les Rochers. He was one of the celebrated band of writers at Port Royal, the headquarters of Jansenism in Paris. The Marquise was a good Jansenist, as were so many of her friends. She always speaks with love and reverence of the good Arnauld d'Andilly, who, in spite of his almost aggressive Jansenism, was looked on with favour by the King, though the latter, by his mother's training and his early education, leaned towards the Jesuits in doctrine.

Again, in September, Madame de Sévigné writes to the Comte de Grignan to assure him of his wife's health and wellbeing, and above all of the love she shows for her absent husband. These are by no means the most witty, or humorous, or clever of her letters, but they record her tender anxiety to foster the best possible feeling between the Comte and Comtesse, so that this favour of having her daughter near her for these few months shall not in any way cause unhappiness between them. In nothing else that she has written does she show herself more tenderly tactful, more affectionately desirous of her daughter's truest well-being and happiness.

"PARIS, *Friday, September* 12, 1670

"I do not write with the idea of beginning a correspondence with you; I should be cautious of doing so, knowing how you are overwhelmed with that from Madame de Grignan. I pity you for having such long letters to read; I never saw anything so lively, and I believe that you would gladly have her with you to be delivered from them, to such a state has she reduced you by her importunity. She has just now separated herself from us and retired to a corner of the room with a little table and desk before her, not thinking M. de Coulanges or I worthy of approaching her. She is in despair because you have written to me; I have never seen such a jealous and envious woman. However, I defy her, let her do what she will, to interrupt our friendship. You have a great part in the care I take of her health. . . ."

About two months later, on November 15, 1670, Madame de Grignan gave birth to a daughter. They had all greatly desired a son, but Madame de Sévigné, one may easily guess, and M. de Grignan too, there is little doubt, were so happy to find the young Comtesse out of danger that there was not much room for regret. The baby was baptized Marie Blanche, and for some time stayed with Madame de Sévigné, who called her granddaughter her "little heart." The child had for godfather the Archbishop of Arles, and for godmother the Marquise de Sévigné, who showed more tenderness to the child than its own mother, who had so ardently hoped for a son, that, with a coldness that was part of her nature, she was not very satisfied with her baby daughter. Perhaps, too, she, who was so beautiful herself, was rather piqued at the baby's plainness; it is a point on which young, foolish mothers are sometimes ridiculously sensitive. Madame de Sévigné, with a soupçon of mischief, tells her son-in-law that his third daughter resembles him rather than its mother. "Malicious people," she writes, "say that Blanche d'Adhémar will not be an extraordinary beauty, and the same people add that she is very much like you. If this be the case, you will not doubt that I love her dearly."

Every week regularly, while her daughter was convalescent, the Marquise wrote to M. de Grignan, giving him details of her health and the news his wife was unable to write. In one of these letters she gives him such excellent counsel that we read in and between the lines a little of that art of *savoir vivre* of which Madame de Sévigné was so completely mistress, and at the same time we get a passing hint of that amiability, and peace-loving feminine charm, which was one of the many graces of her beautiful character.

The Bishop of Marseilles, who, through his arrogance and

usurpation of power, had been the immediate cause of the Comte de Grignan's appointment to the vice-government of Provence, had evidently been mentioned to the Comte as likely to cause him a considerable amount of trouble in his new office. He had probably told this to Madame de Sévigné, and her advice as to how to treat the Bishop is so admirable, so packed with epigrammatic wisdom and knowledge of human nature, that it might with advantage be taken as a rule of conduct in similar difficult circumstances.

"PARIS, *Friday, November* 28, 1670

"Let us speak no more of this wife of yours, we love her beyond all bounds of reason. She is very well, and I want to write to you entirely on my own account. I wish to talk to you about Monsieur de Marseilles, and to beg you, by all the confidence you have in me, to follow my advice in your conduct respecting him. I know the manners of provincials, and I know the pleasure they take in fomenting quarrels, so much that unless we are always on guard against the discourse of these gentlemen, we insensibly adopt their sentiments, which are very often unjust. I can assure you that time, or other reasons, have greatly altered M. de Marseilles's disposition. For some days he has been very mild, and if you do not treat him as an enemy, you will not find him one. Let us take him at his word till we find he does something to the contrary. Nothing is so likely to destroy a good intention as to show a distrust of it; to be suspected as an enemy often suffices to make a man one; everything is then at an end, and there is no further hope of management. Confidence, on the contrary, prompts us to do good actions; we are pleasantly affected by the good opinion of others, and will not willingly lose it. In God's name be openhearted, and you will be surprised by a behaviour you did not expect. I can never believe that this man conceals any venom in his heart, when we consider all the professions of friendship he has made us, and of which it would be better to be the dupes rather than to be capable of suspecting him unjustly. Follow my advice; it is not mine only, several capable persons recommend this conduct to you, and assure you that you will not be deceived. Your family is convinced of it; we see better into these things than you; and so many people who love you, and who have not a little good sense, can hardly be mistaken."

It was excellent advice, but it is uncertain whether the Comte de Grignan adopted it. If he did, the result did not justify Madame de Sévigné's expectations; as for many years the Bishop of Marseilles proved a veritable thorn in the flesh to M. de Grignan and Madame his wife.

CHAPTER XX

A celebrated letter—La Grande Mademoiselle and M. de Lauzun—A royal love-story—Madame de Sévigné visits the Tuilleries, and is the confidante of La Grande Mademoiselle—A Princess in tears

JUST one month after the birth of Blanche d'Adhémar, and while the Comtesse de Grignan was still staying with her mother, an event occurred which threw Parisians into an almost inconceivable state of excitement. Never had such a thing been dreamed of before! The Court was indescribably agitated by the news; it was the only possible topic in the salons and *ruelles*, in the Louvre and in the Luxembourg; in short, all Paris was as excited as if the town had been on the point of being besieged. Madame de Sévigné, who was greatly attached to the principal personage in the drama, wrote what is perhaps her most famous letter, on the occasion, to her cousin Emmanuel de Coulanges, who was then staying at Lyons.

"PARIS, *December* 15, 1670

"I am going to tell you of an event which is the most astonishing, the most surprising, the most marvellous, the most miraculous, the most magnificent, the most bewildering, the most unheard-of, the most singular, the most extraordinary, the most incredible, the most unexpected, the greatest, the least, the most rare, the most common, the most public, the most private till to-day, the most brilliant, the most enviable; in short, an event to which there is only one parallel to be found in past ages, and even that not an exact one; an event which we cannot believe in Paris (how then can it be believed in Lyons?); an event which makes everybody exclaim, 'Lord, have mercy upon us!' an event which causes the greatest joy to Madame de Rohan and Madame d'Hauterive; an event, in fact, which will take place on Sunday next, when those who are present will doubt the evidence of their senses; an event which, though it is to happen on Sunday, may perhaps not be accomplished on Monday. I cannot persuade myself to tell you. Guess what it is! I give you three guesses. Do you give it up? Well, then, I must tell you. Monsieur de Lauzun is to be married next Sunday at the Louvre—guess to whom! I give you four guesses, I give you ten, I give you a hundred. Madame de Coulanges says, 'It is not very difficult to guess, it is Madame de la Vallière.' You are quite wrong, Madame. 'It is Mademoiselle de Retz then.' No, it is not; you are very provincial. 'Dear me, how stupid we are,' you exclaim, 'it is Mademoiselle de Colbert, of course.' You are farther off than ever. 'Then it must be Mademoiselle de Créqui.' You are no nearer. Well, I find I must tell you. He is to marry on Sunday at the Louvre, with the King's permission, Mademoiselle, Mademoiselle de—Mademoiselle—guess the name! he is to marry Mademoiselle, my faith! by my faith! my sworn faith! Mademoiselle, la Grande Mademoiselle; Mademoiselle, daughter of the late Monsieur; Mademoiselle, granddaughter of Henri IV; Mademoiselle d'Eu, Mademoiselle de Dombes, Mademoiselle de Montpensier, Mademoiselle d'Orléans; Mademoiselle, first cousin to the King; Mademoiselle, once destined for the throne; Mademoiselle, the only person in France worthy of Monsieur. Here is a fine subject for conversation. If you cry out, if you are beside yourselves, if you say we are deceiving you, that it is false, that we are laughing at you, that it is a pretty joke, that it is a very poor invention; if, in fact, you abuse us, we shall say you are right, for we have done the same ourselves. Adieu. You will see by the letters you receive by this post whether I am telling you the truth or not."

This amazing romance of royalty is almost too well known to mention, were it not that Madame de Sévigné has given the most inimitable account of it, and was, besides, as nearly a personal friend of the Princess as anyone could be who was not of royal blood.

There is no more prominent, and, in some respects, no more

HENRIETTE
DUCHESSE D'ORLÉANS

THE DUCHESSE DE MONTPENSIER
"LA GRANDE MADEMOISELLE"

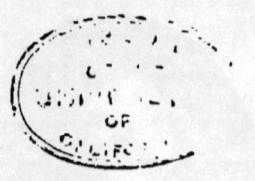

LA GRANDE MADEMOISELLE 195

romantic, figure than that of La Grande Mademoiselle in all the pageant of great personages who defile before us as we read the history of France's great century. The daughter of Gaston, Duc d'Orléans, she was the cousin of the King, and when he was born called him "her little husband," till Richelieu scolded her, then a girl of twelve, and told her she was too old for pleasantries in such bad taste. Nevertheless, Mademoiselle for many years cherished the hope of sharing the throne of France, till that great day of the battle of Saint-Antoine, when she earned her name of "Heroine of the Fronde" by opening the gates of Paris to the King's enemies, and by turning the cannon of the Bastille on the King's army. As Mazarin heard the thunder of the cannon, he remarked with grim humour, "Mademoiselle has killed her husband!" And, truly enough, in place of sharing her young cousin's throne, she was very shortly after exiled to Saint-Fargeau, one of her numerous estates, where Madame de Sévigné was among the few friends who were loyal enough to visit her during her disgrace.

Whom was not Mademoiselle to have married? Charles II of England, living in exile at Saint-Germain, would have been glad of the vast wealth of this Princess, but he was then a prince in poverty and exile, with not sufficient French to plead his cause, though his mother was eloquent and anxious enough on his behalf. Unluckily for him, at this time Mademoiselle's head was somewhat turned with the chimerical hope of marrying the Emperor, and a bashful, out-at-elbows Prince, metaphorically speaking, without even a kingdom, was quite eclipsed by those dazzling imperial splendours which were brought so tantalisingly near only to be snatched away. After the failure of this brilliant scheme she had hoped to marry the Great Condé. His wife was alive at the time, it is true, but so near to death that Mademoiselle almost exultingly wrote in her diary how slender were the chances of her recovery. She did recover, however, and Mademoiselle had to look elsewhere for a husband. There was some talk of a Prince of Bavaria; but who was a petty prince, when Mademoiselle had hoped to marry an Emperor? Then came the Prince de Savoie, Alphonse VI of Portugal, then Monsieur the King's brother, who had just lost his wife, Henriette of England, the gay and graceful Princess who had danced in the *ballet royal*, where Mademoiselle de Sévigné had figured also, only a few years before.

Monsieur was some thirteen years younger than Mademoiselle, who was then over forty years of age. But disparity of age had never been any bar to Mademoiselle's matrimonial schemes; indeed, there was some talk of an alliance with the Comte de Saint-Paul, who had just returned with Sévigné and others from the expedition in Candia, and he was a full twenty years her junior! These plans, however, came to naught, for at the mature age of forty-three she had fallen deeply, violently, irresistibly in love for the first and only time in her life. She who had scoffed at love for so long as a bourgeoise passion, " unworthy of a noble soul," was now to succumb to its autocratic power with an abandonment of heart as reckless as could be shown by the meanest of her tiring-women or kitchen-maids. Her love would have been more dignified, more worthy of respect, had she given her heart to a man who was morally or physically attractive; but it was a part of the adverse fate of Mademoiselle, who, in marriage at least, was always near to great things and always missing them, that her grand passion, when it swept her away from all the artificial moorings of royalty and left her a mere human woman, ready to sacrifice everything for her love, should be roused by a man who would have been utterly ridiculous, had it not been for a certain sinister power which was largely the result of giving way to his mad impulses without an ordinary sane fear of consequences. This M. de Lauzun, who by his projected marriage with Mademoiselle gained more distinction than his own qualities could ever have brought him, made his appearance at Court as a cadet of Gascony, under the protection of his uncle the Maréchal de Gramont. He was inconceivably impertinent and audacious, but as audacity is said to be one of the ingredients of success, he soon made his way, and short and plain though he was, he was soon quite a favourite among the ladies. He was more than ordinarily insignificant in stature; "the smallest man that God has ever made," wrote the Comte de Bussy to Madame de Sévigné; and Mademoiselle's own portrait of him when he was thirty-seven is not attractive, though she saw him with the eyes of love.

"He is a small man," she writes, "but no one can say that his figure is not the straightest, prettiest, and most agreeable. His limbs are fine, and he has a good air in everything he does. 'His hair, which is blonde, mixed with grey, is rather scanty; it is badly dressed and somewhat greasy; he has fine blue eyes which are generally red; he has a shrewd mien and a pleasing countenance. His smile is agreeable. The end of his nose is pointed and red; there is something elevated in his physiognomy; he is very negligent in his attire, but when he thinks it worth while to be careful he looks well. Behold the man!"

Saint-Simon gives us his moral attributes, which are even less attractive. "A courtier who was equally insolent, spiteful, and obsequious; full of mean intrigues to gain his ends, and for that reason dangerous to ministers; feared by all at Court, and ever ready with sarcasms as witty as they were cruel, sparing no one." The same authority tells us that he was full of ambition, whims, and fancies; that he was jealous of every distinction, and, sullen and morose, he was never satisfied with anything; that he had no knowledge of letters or mental culture, and even when he was a good friend, which was seldom, he was a dangerous man.

Mademoiselle, who gives all the details of her love-affair quite ingenuously and frankly, paints for us only too clearly the fact that it was herself who made all the advances, and that when this strange little person saw what advantages would really be his by marriage with this tall spinster of royal blood, who was so enormously wealthy, and of such personal distinction as to be next the Queen in consideration, he fell in with her plans more from a spirit of ambition than from any genuine affection. It was long before Mademoiselle could bring herself to believe that she, the granddaughter of Henri IV, whose strongest article of faith was her blind belief in the divine superiority of royalty, could stoop so low as to become the wife of a noble whom she regarded as definitely, tangibly, immeasurably inferior to herself in the scheme of the universe. It is one of the celebrated romances of the world; a touching story of a woman's great renunciation, though in the Memoirs of Mademoiselle the pathos often gets perilously near to bathos, as she innocently exhibits her amusing conception of the divinity of royalty; but as she was close to the throne in the reign when royalty in France reached its apotheosis, her times are probably more responsible for this than she is.

When Mademoiselle had come to this great decision, and had told Lauzun of the great honour she intended to confer on him, there was yet the King's permission to obtain. Louis XIV neither forbade her nor gave his consent, but begged her to reflect well on what she was about to do. She implored and entreated him still more urgently, and at length the King sent word to her by the Duc de Montausier that she might do as she pleased. The messenger, a wise man, knowing much of Court intrigue and of royal indecision, urged Mademoiselle to get married at once, that very night, before the King should have time to change his mind. Mademoiselle might perhaps have done so, but the vain little Lauzun refused to forego the triumph of a grand wedding, at which all the Court would be present to witness his semi-royal grandeur; and they delayed fatally. Madame de Sévigné tells the story so graphically, with such a warm, breathing human interest in the Princess and her romantic marriage, that while reading her letters the centuries fall away, and for the time we are at the Tuilleries, sharing in La Grande Mademoiselle's triumph, her bitter disappointment, and her despairing grief. Before M. de Coulanges had received his cousin's letter, giving him the news of the "most astonishing" marriage, the Marquise wrote him another containing a surprise which was almost as dramatic.

"PARIS, *Thursday, December* 19, 1670

"What is called falling from the clouds happened last night at the Tuilleries; but I must relate things farther back. You have already heard of the joy, the transport, the ecstasies of the Princess and her happy lover. The affair was made public on Monday, as I told you. Tuesday was passed in talking, astonishment, and compliments. On Wednesday Mademoiselle made a deed of gift to M. de Lauzun, with the design of giving him certain titles, names, and dignities necessary to be inserted in the marriage contract, which was drawn up that day. She gave him, then, four duchies till she could bestow something better on him; the first was that of the comté d'Eu, which entitles him to rank as the first peer of France; the dukedom of Montpensier, of which he bore the title all that day; the dukedom of Saint-Fargeau, and the dukedom of Châtellerault, the whole of which is valued at twenty-two million livres. The contract was then drawn up, and he took the name of Montpensier. On Thursday morning, which was yesterday, Mademoiselle was hoping and expecting the King to sign as he had said, but about seven o'clock in the evening the Queen, Monsieur, and several old dotards had so persuaded the King that his reputation would suffer in the affair that he resolved to break it; and sending for Mademoiselle and M. de Lauzun, he announced to them in the presence of Monsieur that he forbade them to think any further of the marriage. M. de Lauzun received the prohibition with all the respect, submission, firmness, and, at the same time, with all the despair one might expect at such a great reverse of fortune. As for Mademoiselle, she gave vent to her feelings. She burst into tears, cries, lamentations, and the most violent expressions of grief; she has not left her bed all day, and takes nothing but a little broth. What a fine dream is here! What a splendid subject for a romance or a tragedy, but, above all, what a subject for reasoning and talking eternally! That is what we do, day and night, evening and morning, without end and without intermission. We hope you will do the same, and with this I kiss your hand."

Madame de Sévigné greatly appreciated the dramatic value of the whole incident, and on Christmas Eve, writing again to her cousin de Coulanges, who was so witty that he often called forth her most sparkling letters, she tells him that they think it a story well adapted for a tragedy, following all theatrical rules. "The other day we laid out the acts and scenes, and taking four days instead of twenty-four hours, the play was complete." A week later she gives him a few more interesting details, and we see how familiar she was with the proud Princess, who doubtless was glad to pour some of her sorrow and disappointment into the sympathetic and discreet ear of Madame de Sévigné.

"PARIS, *Wednesday, December* 31, 1670

"I have received your answers to my letters. I can easily understand your astonishment at what happened between the

15th and the 20th of this month; the subject well deserved it. I admire also your penetration and judgment in thinking that so great an affair could not possibly hold out from Monday till Sunday. Modesty prevents me from praising you on this point, because I said and thought the same things as you. I remarked to my daughter on Monday, 'This will not go on happily till Sunday; I will wager that though everyone talks of nothing but this wedding it will never happen.' In fact, the sky was overcast on Thursday, and at about ten in the evening, as I told you, the cloud burst. That same Thursday I went at about nine in the morning to Mademoiselle's house, having been informed that she was going out of town to be married, and that the Coadjutor of Rheims was to perform the ceremony. These were the plans on Wednesday evening, but affairs had been determined otherwise at the Louvre since Tuesday. Mademoiselle was writing; she told me to enter, and when she had finished her letter she made me kneel at her bedside. She told me to whom she was writing, and why; she told me of the beautiful presents she had given the evening before, and the titles which she had conferred; that there was no match for her in the Courts of Europe, and that she was determined to provide for herself. She related to me, word for word, a conversation that she had had with the King; and appeared transported with joy at the thought of making a man so happy. She spoke to me with tenderness of the worth and gratitude of M. de Lauzun, and to all this I said, 'Mon Dieu, Mademoiselle, you seem very happy, but why was not this affair promptly finished on Monday? Do you not perceive that such a great delay will give time to the whole kingdom to talk, and that it is tempting God and the King, to put off such an extraordinary affair for so long?' She told me that I was right, but she was so full of confidence, that what I said made hardly any impression on her at the time. She spoke again of the family and of the good qualities of M. de Lauzun.... She embraced me tenderly. This conversation lasted an hour, and it is impossible to repeat all that passed between us, but I may say without vanity that my company was very agreeable to her, for her heart was so full that she was glad to talk to anyone. At ten o'clock she devoted her time to the rest of France, who came to pay their compliments upon the marriage. She waited all the morning for news from the King, but none came.

"After dinner she amused herself with putting M. de Montpensier's rooms in order with her own hands. You know what happened in the evening. The next day, which was Friday, I went to see her, and found her in bed; she redoubled her cries on seeing me, she called me to her, she embraced me, and made me all wet with her tears. 'Alas!' she said, 'do you remember what you said to me yesterday? Ah, what foresight! what cruel, cruel foresight!' She made me weep to see her weep so violently. I have been to see her twice since; she is in great affliction, and she always treats me as a person who sympathises with her grief, and in this she is not mistaken, for I feel for her on this occasion such sentiments as one rarely feels for people of such exalted rank. All this, however, is between ourselves and Madame de Coulanges; for you can understand how entirely ridiculous these things would sound to other people. Adieu."

It is generally supposed that Mademoiselle married Lauzun privately, but in any case the strange little man, after ten years at Pignerol, in the cell above that of Foucquet, treated the Princess so badly when he was released, that with all her love and desire for self-sacrifice, she made the resolve, and kept it, of never seeing him again.

CHAPTER XXI

A bitter parting—The perilous journey to Provence—A tender mother—" A pretty pagan "—Spring at Livry

UNDERLYING all the excitement and interest that Madame de Sévigné felt in the dramatic affair between La Grande Mademoiselle and Monsieur de Lauzun, was the sad prospect, daily growing nearer and more formidable, of parting with her idolised daughter. In early December she already laments the need for separation, and whimsically says to M. de Grignan, with a light reference to her grief when she first heard of his appointment, "I shall soon be in the same state that you saw me in last year. I must love you greatly to send my daughter to you at this inclement season. How foolish it is to leave a good mother, with whom you assure me she is so satisfied, to go to find a man at the farthest end of France! Nothing could be more indecorous than such conduct!"

As Madame de Grignan daily regained her health, there was, however, no longer any reason for detaining her in Paris, and her departure was fixed for the 10th of January 1671. The journey was nevertheless postponed a little longer because of the heavy rains, and Madame de Sévigné writes a most apologetic letter to her son-in-law, assuring him with such full and detailed reasons that she had no joy in keeping his young wife now that she ought to be in Provence with him, that the most unreasonable husband should have been convinced.

"Alas!" she writes on the 16th of January, "the poor child is still with me, for it was utterly impossible for her to have set out on the 10th of this month as she had intended. The rains have been, and are still, so violent, that it would have been the greatest folly to have attempted it. All the rivers have overflowed; all the highroads are under water; all the carriage-tracks are so hidden, that she would have run the risk of being overturned at every ford."

Another reason for delaying the departure was that the Coadjutor of the Archbishop of Arles, the Comte de Grignan's brother, with whom the Comtesse was to travel, had been commanded by the King to perform the marriage ceremony between Mademoiselle d'Harcourt, a cousin of the Grignans, and the Duc de Cadaval, a Portuguese nobleman. Madame de Sévigné was most anxious that her daughter should be accompanied by her brother-in-law, partly as a protection for the young Comtesse, partly for the sake of *les convenances*, and was greatly disturbed at the postponement of the marriage.

"The affair has been put off day after day," she goes on, "and may not be concluded this week. However, I see that my daughter is so impatient to be gone that the time she now passes with us cannot be called living, and if the Coadjutor does not excuse himself from this marriage, I can see that she is quite ready to commit the folly of going without him. It would be so extraordinary to travel by herself, and, on the contrary, such a fortunate thing to have the company of her brother-in-law, that I shall do my utmost to arrange for them to travel together, and in the meantime the waters may have somewhat subsided. But I assure you that I have no pleasure in her company; I know that she must leave us, and all that she does now are her duties and the preparations for departure. We see no society; we go to no amusements; our hearts are always heavy, and we talk of nothing but rains, bad roads, and melancholy stories of people who have lost their lives in travelling on them. In a word, though I love her as you know, our present condition is dull and disagreeable. We have had no pleasure in these last few days. I am greatly obliged to you, my dear Comte, for all the friendship and sympathy you feel for me. You understand better than anyone else what I suffer, and what I shall suffer. I should be sorry, however, that the joy you will have in seeing her should be troubled by thoughts of that. These are the changes and sorrows with which life is chequered. Adieu, my dearest Comte. I weary you to death with my long letters, but I hope you will understand the reason why I write them."

It was almost three weeks after this charming letter of apology was written that Madame de Sévigné endured the first terrible parting from her daughter, a separation that to her loving and sensitive heart seemed to contain nearly the bitterness of death. On the 5th of February Madame de Sévigné held her daughter in her arms for the cruel farewell, weeping, "without knowing what she did." One of the Marquise's most faithful and affectionate friends was there to assist them in those little welcome offices at parting, when the principals are too absorbed in grief to remember necessary details; the good d'Hacqueville, the kind, officious friend who divided his days among so many friends, who so multiplied himself in their service that he was sometimes, in affectionate mockery, spoken of in the plural as "les d'Hacqueville." He had been a college friend of the Cardinal de Retz, and through him had become acquainted with Madame de Sévigné. He was devoted to her and her daughter; he was sometimes even too attentive, but always with such praiseworthy intentions, that when most annoyed they could only laugh at him and his bad writing and his stale news, and love him for his kind, unselfish devotion. When everything necessary for the long journey had been packed into the travelling carriage—a bed, which the Chevalier de Grignan, another of her husband's brothers, had lent her, food, kitchen utensils (the coffee-pot was unluckily forgotten!), besides books for the long monotonous days of travelling— Madame de Sévigné saw the man who was to drive her daughter bringing his horses round, and, her eyes streaming with tears, she went to implore him to take care of her daughter. She asked him his name, and when he had told her—

"'Monsieur Busche,' said I, sobbing all the time" (it is the Marquise who tells this afterwards to her daughter), "'I recommend my daughter to your care; do not overturn her, I pray; and when you have taken her safely to Lyons, come and tell me the news and I will give you something to drink.'"

Even when the good-byes had all been said, and Monsieur Busche was just driving off, Madame de Sévigné could not let her daughter go without one last anguished embrace, then, watching her from an upper window as she finally drove away, she felt, as she afterwards declared, "fit to throw herself out of the window after her."

Distracted at her loss, she went from her own desolate house to the Convent of Sainte-Marie, in the Faubourg de Saint-Jacques, and in this retreat she remained for hours, unable to do anything but weep. The next day she wrote to her daughter, and in her own vivid words we recognise the sincerity and depth of her grief.

"PARIS, *Friday, February* 6, 1671

"My grief would be very light if I could give you a description of it; I shall not therefore attempt it. I search everywhere in vain for my dear child, and I find her not; every step she takes carries her farther away from me. I went to Sainte-Marie, half dead, and weeping all the way; it seemed to me that my very heart and soul had been torn from me. Mon Dieu! what a cruel separation! I begged to be alone; and they took me into Madame du Housset's room, where they made me a fire. Agnes stayed with me, but without speaking, for that was our bargain; and I remained there till five o'clock without ceasing to weep; every thought brought death with it. I wrote to M. de Grignan, you may easily guess in what style. Then I went to Madame de la Fayette, who redoubled my sorrows by sharing in them. She was alone, and ill and sad, because of the death of a sister, a nun, which was exactly as I would have wished to find her. Monsieur de la Rochefoucauld came in, and we talked of nothing but you, and of the good reason I had to be in distress. . . . At about eight o'clock I came home, but, bon Dieu! can you understand what I felt on going upstairs? The doors were open of that room which I always entered with such happiness, but everything was in disorder and desolate, and only your poor little girl was there in place of mine. Can you understand all that I suffered? The night passed in mournful vigils, and the returning light brought me no peace of mind. . . ."

The abandonment of grief that Madame de Sévigné felt for the absence of her daughter has probably been endured by thousands of mothers at bitter separations, but which of them has ever painted her grief in such living, convincing words?

"I thought my very heart and soul had been torn from me," "every thought brought death with it." Can anyone who has endured like partings fail to recognise the wonderful word-painting of a passion which is generally too overwhelming, too numbing to be articulate? There is perhaps nothing more astonishing in Madame de Sévigné's charming letters than this extraordinary faculty of giving definite and clear expression to the most fleeting thoughts, the most ephemeral and vague impressions, common enough to most people, but which rarely take form either in speech or in writing.

A few days after this the Marquise received the first letter from her daughter, and she is touched and delighted at her expressions of love. "I am in tears while I read them," she says, "my heart feels as if it would be torn in two. You love me, my dear child, you love me; and you tell me so in a way that makes my tears flow in torrents. . . . You think of me then, you speak of me, you like better to write your sentiments to me than to talk of them. In whatever way they come they are received with a tenderness and emotion known only to those who love as I do. You make me feel the greatest tenderness for you that it is possible to experience; but if you think of me, my poor darling, be assured that I am continually thinking of you; it is what devotees call an habitual thought; it is what we ought to have for God if we did our duty. Nothing is capable of diverting me from it; I see your carriage continually driving on, never coming nearer to me; I am always on the highroads, and sometimes I fear that the carriage will be overturned. The violent rains we have had these last three days have reduced me to despair; the very thought of the Rhone gives me horrible fears. . . . I have a mass said for you every day, and this is no superstitious devotion. . . ."

The Comtesse de Grignan has so often been called cold, and unworthy of her mother's great love, that it is a distinct pleasure to trace in Madame de Sévigné's letters the growth of the daughter's love in response to the mother's passionate outpourings of tenderness. We get a glimpse in the above extract of the more reserved, colder nature of the young Comtesse, who found it impossible to express her affection for her mother in phrases when she was with her, but who, as soon as she had been

THE COMTESSE DE GRIGNAN

separated from her a single day, could send warm, loving words that were so sweet and affecting to the elder woman. As a young girl Mademoiselle de Sévigné had, without doubt, been wrapped in a youthful armour of pride and egotism—but are not most girls Undines more or less till love and sorrow have awakened their better selves?—she had, in vain girlish fashion, given much attention to her beauty; for beauty is not usually unconscious, though poets would sometimes have us think so; and, surrounded by adulation and constant flattery, even from her mother, it is scarcely surprising that she appreciated her charms at their due value. But when the Marquise, many years later, reminded her how careful she had been of it, she added at the same time, "who would have thought then that you would have grown into such a sensible and superior woman!" An addition that should not be overlooked in the estimate of Madame de Grignan's character.

The Comtesse was probably not far from the truth when she accused her mother of being a curtain that concealed her. "I will not have you say that I was a curtain that concealed you," writes Madame de Sévigné in reply, "so much the worse if I did hide you; you appear still more amiable now the curtain is drawn aside; you require to be discovered to appear in your true perfection; this is what we have said of you a thousand times."

It is quite conceivable that the brilliant social gifts of the Marquise de Sévigné did eclipse those of her daughter, and had the double effect of making her appear proud and almost disagreeable in comparison. The Marquise delighted in being amiable and gracious to everyone, from her friends at Court to the gardeners and workmen on her estate; she had the charming instinct of wishing to please, which is one of the most valuable birth-gifts that the fairies can bring to a baby's cradle; "she loved to be loved," said her malicious but astute cousin Bussy; she had, moreover, an exquisite talent for expression, not only in writing, but in speech and action. "The simplest compliments of politeness from you seem like protestations of friendship, and all who leave your presence remain persuaded of your esteem and goodwill, without being able to explain to themselves what evidence you have given to them of either." That delicate little piece of analysis by Madame de la Fayette tells us so much of Madame de Sévigné's radiant personal charm, and, in a manner, explains much of her social success, but not all; for we who see her life whole, as it were, and know of her loving, generous heart, her fine and penetrating intellect, her sane common-sense and practical wisdom, her spotless integrity, her constant aspirations towards the truly spiritual life, her Christian goodwill to all the world—save those one or two people who had wronged her beloved daughter!—we know that Nature is not prodigal of such women, and that not for centuries, perhaps never again, will she reproduce that subtle fusion of heart and mind, of body, soul and spirit, of wondrous gifts and graces, known as Madame de Sévigné. What wonder that her daughter, who was her precise opposite, her complement, in whose qualities of heart and mind she found the most complete satisfaction, did not shine beside this radiant mother! In place of Madame de Sévigné's magnificent health, and consequent energy, the Comtesse had been an ailing and delicate child, difficult to rear, and often languid and indolent. Her loving mother, following with the eyes of affection all her duties and pleasures in her new character of Madame la Gouvernante de Provence, wonders how she manages to indulge this indolence, and gives us a passing glimpse into her habits.

"But what becomes of your indolence amid all this stir and bustle? It suffers, it retires into some little room, it is almost dead with apprehension of losing its place, it waits for some leisure moment in which you may remember it, to give you a word in passing. 'Alas!' it says, 'but you have forgotten me. Remember that I am your oldest friend, the one who has never abandoned you; the faithful companion of your most happy days, that which consoled you for all pleasures, and who sometimes have made you hate them. It was I who prevented you from dying of *ennui* when you were in Brittany. . . . Sometimes, indeed, your mother would interrupt our joys, but I knew I should have you again; besides, too, she respected me. But now I do not know where I am, the dignity and importance of your husband will be the death of me if you do not take care of me.' I think I hear you say a little friendly word to it in passing, you give it some hope of possessing you at Grignan, but you go very quickly and have not the leisure to say more.

Duty and reason are round you, and do not give you a moment's repose."

Where Madame de Sévigné was brilliantly expressive, her daughter was thoughtful and reflective as a natural result of this indolence. She was somewhat seriously intellectual too, and would certainly have been called a *bas bleu* had the term been invented. As we have seen, she was a devoted disciple of Descartes; and when she was yet in her early twenties she began a translation of Tacitus, and, though there is no record of its completion, it was an indication of the solidity of her intellectual tastes. She was, too, it must be remembered, a woman of strict virtue in the days when, more than at any other period of her century, vice was the royal road to preferment for a favoured few. She fulfilled with credit all the duties of her great position, she was an excellent wife, and though she certainly did not spoil her children with excessive fondness—indeed, her maternal coldness is one of her greatest faults—she brought them up well. But beside the glowing and positive charms, mental and moral, of her mother, her virtues seem dull and negative, and as a consequence she has scarcely received justice from some of Madame de Sévigné's biographers. The Marquise herself, who had a discriminating, intuitive judgment of character, had the highest opinion of her daughter, and she was not so entirely blinded by her love as some would have us believe; indeed, a careful study of her letters brings one to the conclusion that her love, like all great and worthy and lasting love, was founded on a firm basis of honour and respect, and that the Comtesse de Grignan was one of those people whom the many find unattractive, but who for a few chosen spirits have a compelling charm at which others can only wonder. In the first few days of their separation, the Marquise scolds her daughter gently for having so rarely expressed her affection. In her grief of parting she hungers for expressions of love and tenderness. "You must be aware," she says, "that in the way you write I cannot read your letters without weeping. To understand how I love you, join to my natural inclination and affection for you the little circumstance of realising that you love me with equal warmth, then judge what I must feel. Wicked girl! Why do you sometimes hide from me the precious treasures of your heart? You fear that I shall die of joy, but ought you not rather to fear that I should die of grief when I imagine the contrary? D'Hacqueville will bear witness to the state in which he has formerly seen me. . . ."

In the empty days of grief that followed the parting, the Marquise spent much of her time in writing to her daughter, and in trying to satisfy her heart-hunger by the letters she received from Madame de Grignan, which seemed, to her impatient love, so long in coming. "How I should like to have a letter from you!" she exclaims. "It is nearly half an hour since I received the last!"

It is scarcely surprising that Madame de Sévigné's friends should sometimes blame her gently for the excessive devotion she gave to her daughter. On one occasion she repeated to Madame de Grignan the reproof that the good Arnauld d'Andilly had given her when she dined with him at the house of his son, the Marquis de Pomponne, on her way to Livry.

"I set out early yesterday morning from Paris," she writes, "and went to dine at Pomponne, where I found our good old man, who awaited me; I would not on any account have gone without bidding him good-bye. He is more pious than ever; I am astonished at him; the nearer he approaches death the more holy he becomes. He scolded me very seriously, and, in the warmth of his zeal and friendship, he told me how wrong it was not to think of changing my course of life; that I was a pretty pagan, and that you were the idol I had set up in my heart; that this kind of idolatry was quite as dangerous as any other, though it might appear less criminal to me; and he concluded by admonishing me seriously to consider my state. He said all this so impressively that I had not a word to say. After six hours of very agreeable, though very serious, conversation, I left him, and came here, where I found May in all the triumph of its beauty; the nightingale, the cuckoo, and the linnet have already brought spring to our woods. I have devoted part of this afternoon to writing to you in the garden, where I am almost deafened by three or four nightingales which have perched just over my head. This evening I shall return to Paris, and make up my packet to send to you."

CHAPTER XXII

Baron de Sévigné—His dissipated life in Paris—"He wears the chains of Ninon"—An actress' love-letters—"A fool in head but not in heart"—Description of a fête at Chantilly—The death of Vatel

WHEN the Baron de Sévigné, as Madame de Sévigné's son was called during her lifetime, returned from the fruitless expedition into Candia, he was stationed for some time at Nancy. His mother had bought for him the post of cornet in a company of Gendarmes-Dauphin, which was commanded by his cousin, the Marquis de la Trousse. In February 1671 he returned to Paris, where he stayed during the spring and early summer.

It is at this time that we get the first real introduction to the young Baron; we see his disposition, his tastes, his habits, all faithfully and unconsciously painted for us by his mother's pen as she writes those intimate letters to her daughter. They are almost too intimate for other eyes to see; one sometimes feels a sensation of eavesdropping as one reads what Madame de Sévigné would assuredly never have written to anyone else about the follies and indiscretions of her son, whom she loved with true maternal tenderness, though the first place in her heart, as they all recognised, was held by his sister. Indeed, these letters, read in full, give a hint of an explanation at least of the preference the Marquise always showed for her daughter. "We think," once said the Marquise de la Fayette, meaning the Duc de la Rochefoucauld and herself, "that your son is not made of the wood by which strong passions are kindled; nothing would give him greater pleasure than to die for a love he did not feel." And he was no more able to rouse a strong passion than to feel it.

His first letter of which there is any record is to his sister, and reveals at once something of his light, pleasure-loving nature, besides introducing us to some of the company among whom he spent his days.

"I take the opportunity," he writes to his sister, "in the interval of two repetitions, to let you know that I have just come from a most delightful concert given by the two Camuses and Ytier. You know that music generally has the effect of softening the soul, but though I have no need for that in your case, yet it has recalled a thousand little circumstances that one would have thought our long separation might have sent into oblivion. But do you know what company I have been in? There were Mademoiselle de l'Enclos, Madame de la Sablière, Madame de Salins, Mademoiselle de Fiennes, Madame de Montsoreau, and they were all at Mademoiselle de Raymond's house. After this if you do not think me a fine fellow you will be to blame; for you have not the same reason as they have for thinking otherwise, since from where you are you cannot see my black wig, which makes me look frightful; but I shall have another to-morrow which will make amends for it, and give me the air of a gallant cavalier. Adieu. I congratulate you on having escaped the perils of the Rhone, and on the grand reception you received in your kingdom of Arles. I made Monsieur de Condom [Bossuet] shudder by giving him an account of your adventure; he loves you always with all his heart."

Most of these ladies mentioned by the young Baron had a reputation more or less damaged; and Ninon had for thirty years been a celebrity in her own particular, disreputable way, for her wit and beauty, her free-thought and free life. We gather from the letter to his sister that Sévigné, then about twenty-three, was rather proud of frequenting such company; we also find that Ninon is now "Mademoiselle" de l'Enclos, and that ladies of birth seek her society.

Madame de Sévigné was at this time sorely troubled by her son's dissipated habits. She sadly recalls that it was Ninon who led his father astray; but his mode of life was so common, so general among young gentlemen of fashion, that she occasionally makes light of his follies and laughs at them in her letters to her daughter. A few days after this, she tells Madame de Grignan of her brother's infatuation with Ninon, and in the same letter she reproduces a little scene in the Luxembourg, where, it will be seen, La Grande Mademoiselle held her miniature court with all the minute distinctions of honour that were observed at the Louvre; and which were accompanied, it will be noticed, by the same petty jealousies, the same absurd eagerness to do the most trifling service for royalty.

"PARIS, *March* 13, 1671

". . . I enclose you a letter from M. de Condom, who sent it to me with a very pretty note. Your brother wears the chains of Ninon, and I fear they are no good to him. There are minds who consider her worthless; she corrupted the morals of his father. We must commend him to God. A Christian, or at least one who wishes to be a Christian, cannot view these irregularities without concern. Ah Bourdaloue! what divine truths did you not tell us to-day on the subject of death! Madame de la Fayette was there for the first time in her life, and was carried away by her admiration of him. She is delighted with your remembrance of her, and embraces you with much affection. I have given her a beautiful copy of your portrait, it decorates her room, where you are never forgotten. Adieu, my amiable daughter. Should I tell you that I love you? It would be folly to tell you that again; however, as I am enchanted when you tell me of your affection, I will assure you of mine in order to give you happiness if you feel about those things as I do. . . .

"A circumstance occurred yesterday at Mademoiselle's which gave me considerable pleasure. Who should come in but La Gêvres, pretty, charming, and elegant. I fancy that she expected me to offer her my place, but, my faith! I owed her a little grudge for her conduct to me the other day, and I paid her with interest, for I did not move. Mademoiselle was in bed, and Madame de Gêvres was obliged to place herself at the lower end of the room, which was most annoying to her. Something was brought to Mademoiselle to drink, and it was necessary to present the serviette. I saw Madame de Gêvres drawing the glove from her thin hand, upon which I touched Madame d'Arpajon, who was above me. She understood at once, and taking off her glove she advanced a step, and, with a charming grace, got in front of the Duchess, took the serviette, and presented it. The Duchess was quite embarrassed and ashamed of her part in the affair. She had mounted on the *estrade* and pulled off her glove, only to be able to see a little closer Madame d'Arpajon present the serviette. My dear child, I am very wicked, but this has delighted me, it was so very well done. Would anyone have thought of depriving Madame d'Arpajon of a little honour that was naturally her due as she was in the *ruelle*? . . . As for Mademoiselle, she did not dare to look up, and my own countenance was not very straight. After this a thousand kind things were said to me about you, and Mademoiselle commanded me to tell you that she is very glad to hear you escaped being drowned, and that you are in good health.

"I shall send you the two volumes of La Fontaine, even though I make you angry by so doing. There are some charming, very charming passages; and some that are dull. We are never satisfied with having done well, and in trying to do better we do worse."

Shortly after this the Marquise wrote again to her daughter, still distressed about her son and the influence Ninon has over him—

"I have been greatly amused with our hurly-burly head-dresses," she writes; "some of them look as if they could easily be blown away. Ninon said that La Choiseul looked as much like the sign-painting of spring outside an inn as one drop of water is to another, and the simile is excellent. But how dangerous she is, that Ninon! If you only knew how she argues about religion you would be horrified! Her zeal to pervert the minds of young men is like that of a certain M. de Saint-Germain whom we once met at Livry. She says that your brother has the simplicity of a dove, and that he resembles his mother. It is Madame de Grignan, she says, who has all the *sel* of the family, and who is not so foolish as to be so docile. A certain person would have taken your part, and robbed her of the esteem she has for you, but she told him to hold his tongue, and that she knew more of the matter than he did. What depravity! Fancy! Because she knows you are handsome and witty, she must needs endow you with that other good quality without which, according to her maxims, one could not be perfect! I am greatly concerned because of the harm she does my son in this matter, but do not say anything to him about it. Madame de la Fayette and I do our best to draw him from this dangerous entanglement."

Besides spending much of his time with Ninon, whose daring opinions on free-thought made her so dangerous to young men, Sévigné was often in the company of the actress Champmeslé, who in the preceding autumn had enchanted all play-going Paris with her acting in the play of *Bérénice*. Racine, it was said, wrote his plays for Champmeslé; and the Marquise on another occasion bore witness to her fine acting. "She is, in my opinion, the best performer I ever saw; as for me, though I am supposed to have some talent for acting, I am not fit to light the candles when she appears. When you come near her she is ugly, but when she recites verse she is adorable." Sévigné frequently gave suppers to the poet and the actress, while the witty Boileau, the cynic and satirist, often made a fourth. The young Baron made no attempt to keep his excesses from his mother's knowledge; in fact, he not seldom made her his confidante; laughing meanwhile at his own follies, making her laugh, resolving sometimes to give them up, and inevitably committing the same follies as soon as the temptation presented itself. Almost every letter the Marquise writes to her daughter at this period contains some reference to her son, and to the wild oats he was sowing so freely.

"He made no Easter, no Jubilee," she writes sadly; "and the only good thing I know about him is that he avoids sacrilege; indeed, I do my best to persuade him from it. God directs all for the best, and I hope this journey into Lorraine will break up all these shameful connections. . . . He relates all his follies to me; I scold him and insist on hearing no more, and yet I still listen. He amuses me, he does all in his power to please me, and I know he has a kind of regard for me. He professes to be delighted with the affection you show for me, and often laughingly accuses me of the preference I have for you; and I confess to you, my dear child, that it is great, even when I hide it. And I will confess yet another thing: it is that I believe you love me also; you appear to me to be steadfast, and I believe that your word may be relied on; in a word, I esteem you highly."

While the Marquise makes her daughter the confidante of her fears and vexations regarding her son, she paints for us his character in all its pitiable weakness; and it is easy to understand that Madame de Sévigné can place no reliance on his word or his promises; that she cannot help drawing comparisons between his failings, and the more solid, though not so agreeable, qualities of her daughter. Sometimes he tells the Marquise that he is intensely sick at heart of his own conduct, and his mother declares frankly that he makes her sick at heart too. " He agrees to all I say while I am talking to him, and then goes on exactly as before." Through all his confessions, which must indeed have made her mother-heart ache, she throws in "a little word of God," which the young man receives quite amiably, and even, by his compliance and reception of her good counsel, deludes her into the belief that he means to lead a more manly and Christian life.

But occasionally the Marquise had to use sharp measures to induce her son to act honourably. He was not even sincere in his attentions to the actress; though, because it was the fashion, he would profess to be dying of love for her, and the moment he left her he would turn her into ridicule. He once gave the letters she had written to him to Ninon, and when the Marquise heard of this, she talked to him with the horror that her just mind felt at such dishonourable conduct, even towards an actress and a light woman.

"When your brother told me what he had done," she writes, " I represented to him how base it was to treat the poor girl so badly for merely having loved him . . . that it was shameful treason, base and unworthy of a man of quality, and that there was a degree of honour to be observed even in things that were dishonourable in themselves. He admitted the justice of this, and ran to Ninon's lodging, and partly by cunning, partly by force, got the poor girl's letters out of her hands, and I made him burn them directly he came home. You see by this what a regard I have for the name of an actress. It is a little like the Visionary in the play. She would have acted just like this.

My son has told all his follies to M. de la Rochefoucauld, who loves originals. He approved of what I said to him the other day, that my son was not a fool in head but a fool in heart; his sentiments are all true and all false; all cold and all warm; all deceitful and all sincere; in short, it is his heart that is so foolish. We laughed a good deal at all this; my son with the rest, for he is very good company and always agrees with what the others say. We are on very good terms. I am his confidante, and I keep this disagreeable office which brings me very disagreeable confessions, merely to have the opportunity of telling him freely what I think of his conduct. He listens to me as well as he can, and begs me to give him advice, which I do as a friend. He wishes to go with me to Brittany for five or six weeks, and if there is no camp in Lorraine I shall take him."

Madame de Sévigné hoped that by taking her son to Brittany she "would restore him body and soul," and in the meantime she and the Abbé de la Mousse prevailed on him to go to confession as had been his habit. What a picture we get in these letters of the anxious, tender mother-heart of the Marquise! She listens to her son's sorry confidences with a deep sadness underlying all the lightness, thinking, perchance, that he may have inherited his taste for vicious companions from his father; and to the daughter, whom she loves with an overwhelming, unquiet affection, she gives advice with a gentle unobtrusiveness on those points where it is most necessary. She begs her to be careful how she treats the ladies of Provence, to be sure to give each her due in the matter of precedence and the little attentions that befit their rank; she reminds her frequently of the people she ought to mention in her letters to Paris; while, on her own part, she remembers her duty as a grandmother, and sends to Provence frequent details of the little Blanche d'Adhémar, whom the young mother naturally wishes to hear about. She tells her daughter that she has procured such a nurse for the child as has not been known since the days of Francis the First, that she pays her 250 francs a year, with food and clothing—the last "quite modest." She describes how the baby is brought in all her finery to do the honours of her room, and she begs the baby's mother to send a pleasant message to "little Pecquet," the physician who was so faithfully attached to M. Foucquet, and who was now attending the child with much care.

Madame de Sévigné was heedful of her servants' interests as well as of those of her children. In her household was a man named Hébert, a good, reliable man, who evidently deserved a better situation than she was able to give him. She mentioned him to Gourville, that Gourville who had been a servant of the Duc de la Rochefoucauld, till the turmoils and intrigues of the Fronde revealed him as a man of infinite resource, judgment, cunning, and calm prudence; who was so clear-sighted that he could see straight to an end, which would probably have to be gained by the most tortuous turnings. He was one of the very few who had risen in the upheaval of the Fronde, and he was now a man of considerable property and much quiet influence, who gave suppers and country-house parties at his estate Saint-Maur, and was on terms of equality with the great world.

A few weeks after, when Madame de Sévigné had forgotten her request, Gourville told her that he had obtained a place for Hébert at Chantilly, to look after the linen in the house of the Prince de Condé. But he kept this place only a very short time, because of the death of the *maître d'hôtel* who had engaged him, which happened at Chantilly, and of which the Marquise gives a most realistic account.

It was the fashion at this time to give magnificent entertainments to the King; and the Prince de Condé, who in the Fronde had resisted his Majesty with so much determination, was now most anxious to prove his loyalty by giving a grand fête to the King at Chantilly. The Marquise, who knew that her daughter, in the depths of Provence, liked to hear all that was going on at Court, sends her a detailed description of the brilliant affair.

"*Friday evening, April* 24, 1671
"AT M. DE LA ROCHEFOUCAULD'S HOUSE

"Here then I make up my packet. I had intended to tell you that the King arrived yesterday evening at Chantilly; and that he hunted a stag by moonlight. The illuminations were wonderful; the fireworks were a little eclipsed by our friend the moon, it is true, but the evening, the supper, and the entertainment, all went off admirably. . . . But what do you think I learned when I came here? I am not yet recovered, and hardly know what I write. Vatel, the great Vatel, late *maître d'hôtel* to M. Foucquet, and now acting in that capacity to M. le Prince, that man of such distinguished capability above all others, whose abilities were equal to governing a State; this man whom I knew so well, finding that the fish did not come, ran himself through with a sword. . . ."

On Sunday the Marquise, having learned more details, continues the story—

"I wrote to you last Friday that he had stabbed himself, and here are the particulars of the affair. The King arrived there on Thursday evening, and the hunt, the illuminations, the moonlight, the promenade, the banquet in a place strewn with jonquils, were all that could be desired. Supper was served, but there were some tables at which there was no roast meat, because Vatel had had to provide several dinners that had not been expected. This greatly troubled Vatel, who was heard to say several times, 'I have lost my honour; I cannot endure this disgrace!'

"'My head is quite bewildered,' he said to Gourville; 'I have not slept for twelve nights; I wish you would help me to give orders.'

"Gourville did all he could to assist and console him, but the failure of the roast meat—which, however, did not happen at the King's table, but at some of the other twenty-five—was always in his mind. Gourville mentioned it to the Prince, who went to Vatel's room, and said to him—

"'Everything is admirably managed, Vatel; nothing could be better than the King's supper.'

"'Your goodness overwhelms me, Monseigneur,' replied Vatel, 'but I know there was no roast meat at two tables.'

"'Not at all,' said the Prince; 'do not distress yourself, and all will be well. . . .'

"At four o'clock the next morning, Vatel went round and found everyone asleep. He met one of the under-purveyors, who had just brought in a load of fish.

"'Is this all?' asked Vatel. 'Yes, sir,' said the man, who did not know that Vatel had ordered fish from all the seaports round.

"He waited for some time, but the other purveyors did not come; his head grew distracted, he believed there was no more fish to be had. He then went to Gourville and exclaimed—

"'Sir, I cannot outlive this disgrace; I shall lose my honour and reputation'; but Gourville only laughed at him.

"Vatel, however, went to his room, and, placing the hilt of his sword against the door, after two ineffectual attempts, succeeded the third time in forcing the sword through his heart, and he fell dead.

" At that instant the purveyors arrived with the fish, and search was made for Vatel to distribute it. They went to his room; they knocked, and, receiving no answer, they broke open the door, and discovered him lying in a pool of blood. . . ."

Poor |Vatel! Some praised, some blamed his courage ; the Prince de Condé said to the King that he had acted from a high sense of honourable pride; while the King declared that he had delayed coming to Chantilly for five years entirely because of the expense and embarrassment it would cause; and that two tables would have been sufficient; but, as the Marquise remarks, "it was too late for poor Vatel!"

CHAPTER XXIII

The Marquise and her household go to Brittany for the *belle saison*—Her cavalcade of carriages, pack-horses, and postilions—The tenantry assemble on the wrong day to welcome the young heir—Dancing Bohemians—Sévigné leaves for the camp in Lorraine

"I FANCY you will like to know of what my travelling equipage consists, so that you may see me pass by as I have seen M. Busche. I shall have two coaches, seven carriage-horses, a pack-horse for my bed, and three or four men on horseback. I shall be in my own carriage, drawn by my two beautiful horses; and the Abbé will sometimes be with me. In the other, which will have four horses and a postilion, will be my son, the Abbé de la Mousse, and Hélène. Sometimes the Abbé will take a second place, and make room for a certain breviary of Corneille's which both Sévigné and I are longing to repeat."

Just five days later, after having had a friendly farewell supper given in her honour by her cousin Emmanuel de Coulanges, she writes to Madame de Grignan on May 18, 1671: "Just going to set out. At last, my dear child, I am ready to step into my carriage. There! I am in. Adieu."

Thanks to the Marquise's desire that her daughter should know exactly how she travelled to Brittany, we also, more than two hundred years after, are able to picture the stately procession of carriages, and fine horses, and postilions in livery, that accompanied this charming *châtelaine* with her friends and dependants, as they rattled along the rough roads to spend the *belle saison* at her beautiful estate Les Rochers in Brittany. It is a long journey from Paris for one day now, even by a fast train, and in those leisurely, spacious, far-away days—before the wildest imagination had dreamed of the trains and motor-cars that were to be evolved from the keen brains of posterity—it meant constant, wearisome travel for more than a week; and on this particular journey we find that they did not reach Les Rochers till May 27, but they had stayed for a day at Malicorne, where M. de Lavardin, the son of one of her intimate friends in Paris, had a beautiful estate. On the way she lost one of her fine horses from the heat, and she herself declares that she needed all the water Malicorne could supply to refresh her after the dreadful heat they had endured while travelling. They tried to forget the monotony of travelling by reading Corneille and Nicole's *Essais*; but it was a long, fatiguing journey, and the Marquise says that if people always kept in the same mind that they found themselves at the end of a journey, they would never travel again. A vexatious little mistake, too, occurred at Les Rochers. The tenantry had all been assembled by Vaillant, the land-steward, to give a welcome to the young heir, who had not been there for some years—but, as usual, the Marquise tells the story so well that paraphrase would spoil it.

"The people here intended to give a triumphal reception to my son. Vaillant had called out more than fifteen hundred men under arms, all well dressed, with new ribbons at their necks, and they awaited us in good order about a league from Les Rochers. But what do you think happened? Monsieur the Abbé had written to say that we should arrive on Tuesday, and then forgot to mention it to us. Accordingly the poor people were waiting all Tuesday till ten o'clock at night, when they returned to their homes very disappointed; and the next day, which was Wednesday, we came in quite peaceably, without dreaming that a little army had been brought out to meet us. We were greatly vexed at this mistake, but there was no help for it."

Perhaps Madame de Sévigné is never more charming than when we see her, through the medium of her letters, in the gracious and soothing solitude of her country home. She had not stayed there for five or six years, and we see how, step by step, she renews her acquaintance with all the old, delightful, familiar haunts and people. At first she is saddened by the sight of her daughter's rooms, by her books, her little ornaments, the trifles which she had prized as a young girl. "Can I see these walks, can I look at these ornaments, this little study, these books, these rooms, and not die with grief?" But she does not

LES ROCHERS

MADAME DE SÉVIGNÉ'S HOME IN BRITTANY

dwell too long on these sad recollections. We see her talking to Pilois, her good, sensible gardener, whom she loves to help when he is planting trees, and laying out fresh walks in her park and garden. She is as eager about her grounds as the most enthusiastic "garden-wife" of to-day, but there is something of her own grand and stately times in the way she plants magnificent allées and labyrinths, and waits patiently for the growth of her young trees. She tells her daughter, too, of the mottoes that are hung about; one is *Vago di fama*, All for fame ; another *Bella cosa far niente*, How sweet to do nothing ! for just then mottoes were the "high mode"; like epigrams and maxims, they were in the air, and most of her young and intelligent visitors were looking out for mottoes to adopt.

The two abbés and her son were pleasant company for the Marquise in the long, bright summer days. The Bien-Bon was well occupied with overseeing the building of the chapel, and as the Marquise watches the men running about the scaffoldings, she thinks how wise are the ways of Providence, in arranging that some men are willing to risk their lives in doing things for a few shillings which others would not do for a thousand pounds. The abbés and her son are always seeking the Marquise, and if at any time she is called away they think it strange that she should prefer talking business with a farmer to hearing a fable by La Fontaine. While her son reads, she works an altar-cloth ; but whenever she is alone, she puts her sewing aside, and reads or writes, or goes and talks business with the Abbé in his study. Mademoiselle du Plessis comes to see her much oftener than she is welcome, but she professes to be so devoted to the lady of Les Rochers that she is tolerated, and laughed at unmercifully by Charles de Sévigné. Of the latter the Marquise writes to her daughter—

"Your brother is a treasure of folly who does very well here. We have now and then a little serious conversation which might be of advantage to him, but his mind is rather too much like whipped cream; if it were not for this he would be amiable enough."

Another day she tells her daughter that her uncle the Abbé de Coulanges has made his will in her favour, and that even without counting on this she is worth about five hundred and thirty thousand francs! These were good and prosperous years for the Marquise; her tenants were able to pay their rents, Brittany was flourishing, and there was not even a hint of those lean black days that were to come upon the province all too soon.

But, notwithstanding the flourishing state of her affairs, the Marquise was not at all disposed to stay long at Les Rochers, for she looked with no little apprehension towards the coming of the Brittany States; at which she would be expected to dispense an almost boundless hospitality.

"I do not know what the States intend doing," she tells her daughter, "but I think I shall run away for fear of being ruined. It is a pretty thing to put myself to the expense of nearly a thousand crowns in dinners and suppers, and all for the honour of keeping a summer-house for M. and Madame de Chaulnes, M. de Rohan, M. de Lavardin, and half Brittany, who, without knowing anything of me, will honour me with their company for the sake of being in the fashion."

The following extract from a letter written to her daughter gives a good idea of how her days were spent in the cultured leisure and quiet of a country-house. We see her reading in Italian, listening with a kind of protest to the romantic novels of Calprenède, which her son insists on reading to her; talking to visitors, walking in her woods, and allowing a troop of Bohemians—gypsies we call them—to come and amuse the quality by their dancing. But everything recalls her daughter. Even among that roving band of vagrants she finds a girl who, to her mother-eyes, looks something like her daughter, the "little queen of Provence."

"LES ROCHERS, *June* 28, 1671

"We read Tasso with pleasure, and I am fairly proficient in the language, thanks to the excellent masters I have had. My son makes La Mousse read *Cléopatre*, and I listen to him whether I will or not, and am amused. My son is going to Lorraine; we shall be very dull in his absence. You know how it vexes me to see the breaking up of an agreeable party, and how delighted I am when I see a carriage driving off with people who have wearied me to death all day; upon which we might make the observation that bad company is more desirable than good. I recollect all the odd things we used to say when you were here, and all you said yourself, and all you did; the thought of you never leaves me; and then, again, I suddenly remember where you are, my imagination represents to me an immense space and a great distance; suddenly your castle bounds the prospect, and I am displeased at the walls that enclose your mall. Ours is surprisingly beautiful, and the young nursery is delightful. I take pleasure in rearing their little heads to the clouds; and frequently, without considering consequences or my own interests, cut down the tall trees because their shade is bad for my young ones. My son looks on at all these proceedings, but I do not allow him to interfere. Pilois continues to be a great favourite with me, and I prefer his conversation to that of many who have the title of chevalier in the Parlement of Rennes. I have grown rather more unceremonious than you, for the other day I let a carriageful of the Fouesnel family go home through a tremendous rain for want of a little pressing them with a good grace to stay; but I could not get the compliment to pass my lips! . . . I have just been writing to Vivonne about a captain of a troop of gypsies, whose confinement I have begged him to make as easy as possible, without detriment to the King's service. You must know that among the band of Bohemians I mentioned to you the other day, was a young girl who danced extremely well, and who put me very much in mind of you. I was pleased with her, and she begged me to write to Provence in favour of her grandfather. 'Where is he?' I asked. 'He is at Marseilles,' said she, with as much composure and unconcern as if she had said 'He is at Vincennes.' He was a man of singular merit, it appears, in his way; in short, I promised to write about him. I immediately thought of Vivonne, and I send you the letter I have written to him. If you are not on such terms with him as will allow me to jest, you may burn it; but if you are friendly with his corpulency, and my letter will save you the trouble of writing one, seal it and send it to him. I could not refuse this request to the poor girl, and to the best-danced minuet that I have seen since the days of Mademoiselle de Sévigné. She had just your air; with good teeth and fine eyes, and was about your height."

Madame de Grignan had quite recently written to her mother about Marseilles, where she had been received with a salute of cannon, and had been given great honours as the Vice-Governor's wife. A compliment had been paid to Madame de Sévigné, too, by giving her name as the watchword for one night. Madame de Grignan had written to her mother a most interesting account of the place; and with an intelligent observation that proved her to be kin, at least in some things, to her brilliant mother, she had described so movingly the terrible state of the galley-slaves, that Madame de Sévigné declared she felt great curiosity to come and see "this new hell" for herself. "Alas, that there should be men groaning night and day under the weight of their chains!" she exclaims. One of the dreadful sights that might have been witnessed in Old Paris, was the gangs of galley-slaves being driven in chains through the streets on their way to Marseilles. On one such occasion, the Marquise told her daughter that she had mingled with the crowd that surrounded them, and had spoken to one or two of the convicts, merely because they were going to breathe the air of Provence where her daughter lived. "But why not have come with them?" her daughter laughingly replies in answer.

Sometimes the Marquise and her son paid visits to their country neighbours, but not more frequently than politeness exacted, for she loved better than all else to be at Les Rochers. One day she went to return the visit to the Fouesnel family, and she tells her daughter, "Fouesnel is a delightful place; my son and I went there yesterday in a coach and six; nothing can be more enchanting; we seemed to fly. We made some little songs as we went along, which I send you." But by July her son is obliged to go to camp in Lorraine, and the Marquise writes to her daughter of the leave-taking, and of her hopes and fears on his account.

"My son set out yesterday, greatly concerned at parting with us. I tried to inspire him with every good, just, and noble sentiment that I could remember, and to confirm all the good qualities I had observed in him. He received my advice with all the sweetness imaginable, and with every mark of approbation; but you know the weakness of human nature. I leave him, therefore, in the hands of Providence, reserving to myself the comfort of having nothing with which to reproach myself on his account. He has such a fund of wit and humour that we shall miss him extremely. We are going to begin a moral treatise of Nicole's. If I were at Paris I would send it to you; I am sure you would admire it. We continue to read Tasso with pleasure. I am almost afraid to tell you that I have returned to *Cléopatre*, and, by good fortune, the short memory I have makes it still pleasing to me; I have a bad taste, you will say, but I cannot affect a prudery which is not natural to me. As I am not yet arrived at that time of life which forbids the reading of such works, I allow myself to be amused with them under the pretence that my son brought me into it. He used to read us some chapters of Rabelais, too, which were enough to make us die with laughing. In return, he seemed to take a good deal of pleasure in talking with me; and if he is to be believed, he will remember what I said to him. I know him well, and can often discern good sentiments through all the levity of his conversation. If he is dismissed this autumn we shall have him again."

The Marquise goes on to confide in her daughter concerning a subject which is giving her much thought for the moment. The States of Brittany were this year to be held at Vitré, only four miles away from Les Rochers, and the question that torments her is, shall she stay, or flee from Les Rochers and a heavy expense. All the gentlemen of Brittany, with their womenfolk, came to Vitré on these occasions for a month, and there was a bewildering succession of balls, comedies, and banquets in prospect. Every person in the town and neighbourhood was expected to show boundless hospitality; indeed, some were occasionally almost ruined by it. The Marquise, with a little of the hauteur of the great lady who frequents the best society in Paris, cannot tolerate the want of culture in provincial people, even in those of good birth and position. She frequently laughs at their pretences, their absurd mistakes when copying Parisian phrases or aping Parisian airs; and, with the true sentiment of the great lady in all ages, she likes to be a *châtelaine* in her country solitude, surrounded by her own dependants, or amongst the crowd at Court, who are all supposed, at least, to be well-bred, with a knowledge of the manners and usages of the polite world.

"I am very much perplexed about the States," she writes. "My first intention was to avoid them to save myself the expense. But you must know that while M. de Chaulnes is making the circuit of the province, his wife intends to remain at Vitré, where she is expected in ten or twelve days, which will be a fortnight before M. de Chaulnes arrives, and she has begged me not to set out till she has seen me. There is no getting out of this without breaking with them at once. I might, indeed, go to Vitré to avoid the annoyance of having them here, but I cannot bear the thought of passing a whole month in such noise and confusion. When I am not in Paris I should prefer to be wholly in the country."

Finally, after much consideration, the Marquise resolved to stay at Les Rochers for the States, and one wonders whether she wore the dress that she told her daughter she had bought to wear in Brittany. The Marquise is in one of her most whimsical and charming moods when she writes of this Paris purchase—

"I have bought some stuff like your last petticoat to make a morning-gown, and it is very beautiful. There is a shade of green in it, but violet predominates; in short, I could not resist the purchase. They would have had me line it with flame-colour, but this appeared to me inconsistent; for while the outside is expressive of frailty the inside would have signified impenitence, even obduracy, so I fixed on a white taffety. I have put myself to very little expense, as I hate Brittany, and shall be most economical till I come to Provence, that I may then support the position and dignity of the middle-aged wonder that you have represented me to be."

CHAPTER XXIV

The States of Brittany—A seventeenth-century town—The Duchesse de Chaulnes visits the Marquise at Les Rochers—A humorous criminal—A grand banquet at the Castle of Vitré—A doorway heightened to admit pyramids of fruit—Guests at Les Rochers—A collation in the garden

"IT will be July as long as it pleases God, and I believe the month of August will be longer still, for it will be the time of the Assembly of the States; and with all respect to the company, it will be a continual slavery to me to be obliged to join them at Vitré, or to live in constant fear of their coming here. It is embarrassing, as Madame de la Fayette says, and my mind is not in tune for it; but I must make the best of it and pass my time like the others."

So wrote Madame de Sévigné to her daughter at the end of July, with no very bright anticipations concerning the strenuous gaieties of the States, in which she would be forced to join without much inclination for such amusements. She was even in the beginning a little annoyed at being disturbed in her loved solitude at Les Rochers, and with a touch of the haughty exclusiveness of the *grande dame* she remarks to her daughter, "When I leave Paris and my friends, my poor merit, small as it is, has not yet reduced me to the necessity of hiding myself in a country town like a company of strolling players."

Fortunately, however, for us who read and enjoy her letters, she did go to the States, and they came to her; and she has left such a vivid and detailed account of what happened, that, carried along by her magic pen, we are transported back to the seventeenth century, among that gay provincial company of Bretons who danced, and drank, and flirted, and gambled day after day with primitive endurance, almost without cessation, for four or five weeks.

The States were held every two years, sometimes at Nantes,

sometimes at Dinan, sometimes at Vitré; and, for some reason, it was sixteen years since they had been held at the latter town. Though they were not a political power, and though they were not able to do much more than decide on enormous grants of money being made to the King, all good Bretons had a pride in this tremendous function as the remains of their former independence; it was the one reminder of their power as a separate kingdom from France, lost on the day that their good Duchess Anne of Brittany was united to Charles VI of France. The Assizes of the States of Brittany was a grand and imposing function. It was composed of all the Commissioners of the King; that is to say, the Governor, who at this time was the Duc de Chaulnes, the Lieutenant-General, the First President of Parlement, the Intendant, the Advocates-General, the Grand Master of the Waters and Forests, and the Receivers-General of Finance, in all about twenty-five people. Then came the great Church dignitaries to the number of twenty-two; those of the order of the nobility, about one hundred and seventy-four, with the Duc de Rohan at their head; and, finally, about seventy deputies of the people.

But these were only the nucleus of the enormous crowd. The Marquise, who was accustomed to big crushes in Paris, remarked to her daughter, "I thought all the stones in Vitré were metamorphosed into gentlemen; I never before saw such crowds assembled together." As many gentlemen of condition were lodged in the Castle as it was capable of holding; and guests, in those days, were not exacting. Some people on such occasions did not object to sleeping in big, almost communal, beds, which would accommodate what sounds to modern ears like a fabulous number of people; then every little hole and corner was utilised as a sleeping-room; everyone brought their own toilet necessaries, and numbers their own beds; and as for valets and men-servants of every description, they were simply dealt with *en masse*, and made themselves as comfortable as circumstances permitted, passing the short summer nights in barns or stables, or on the kitchen floor of an inn, absolutely indifferent as to where they slept off the fumes of the wine they passed their days in drinking.

Lodgings, it need hardly be said, were at a premium in the

town of Vitré; the visit of the States was a veritable mine of gold for the townspeople. By good, and most uncommon, fortune, a great part of Vitré still remains almost exactly as it was in the days when Madame de Sévigné drove over in 1671 to the grand entertainments given at the Castle. The chateau itself has been turned into a prison, but the Tour de Saint Laurent still remains, with its drawbridge and portcullis, by which one enters; its suites of rooms all beautifully polished and shining, and filled with treasures which are now curios, but which then formed part of the daily furniture of the Castle; fine brass fire-dogs, steel ratchets hanging in the chimney, damascened like swords in beautiful arabesque designs; quaint Breton pottery and magnificent tapestries; laces, miniatures, and enamels; with burnished arms and armour gleaming from every corner.

Descending from the Castle plain one enters the old Rue Poterie, and finds oneself at once in the heart of the seventeenth century. Out of those crazy old houses with the quaint roofs, and carved porches of brown timber, one would scarcely be surprised to see a Breton gentleman step forth "laced to the very eyes" in his wonderful native costume. Through the windows one gets a glimpse of Rembrandtesque interiors, beautiful warm brown shadows from which gleam white pillows belonging to the immense wooden family bed; or glints of copper vessels hanging above the wide hearth, or the lace and linen of Madame's cap as she is busied about her household tasks.

Nowhere in France is there a town with so many ancient houses, for its size, as Vitré. You pass an enormous outside wooden staircase, which winds round in easy flights like the marble staircases at Versailles; here there is a loggia with a miniature balustrade; a little farther on a big porch with a room above, the whole supported on weather-worn, roughly carved wooden pillars slowly crumbling to dust. The very people, too, have an antiquated air, as they sit outside their doors on the narrow pavement, and knit and gossip industriously, as if they, too, belonged in spirit to the same period as their dwellings.

Madame de Sévigné has peopled these old streets, and the Castle plain, with a whole company of her Breton friends and neighbours. There is first, as is fitting, the President of the

States, the Duc de Chaulnes, and Madame la Duchesse his wife, two charming people, whom Madame de Sévigné had known only slightly in Paris, but who from this time onward were among her most intimate and admiring friends. Mademoiselle de Murinais, who was staying with them, a tall beauty of twenty-two, speaking Italian like a native, who had just returned from Italy with the de Chaulnes. There was the Marquis de Lavardin too, the son of one of Madame de Sévigné's Parisian friends; he also was a great official at this gathering, next, in fact, to the Governor. Then there was M. d'Harouys, a generous and hospitable man, the treasurer to the Estates; he was a connection of her cousin, Emmanuel de Coulanges, and a valued friend of the Marquise. The Duchesse de Rohan was also there, the proud and haughty dame who, nearly twenty years before, had behaved with such arrogance in the affair between her husband and Tonquedec in the *ruelle* of the Marquise. That same Tonquedec, as a patriotic Breton, was at the States; and it is pleasant to find that Madame de Sévigné, instead of the utter weariness she expected to endure while the States lasted, found herself so fêted and welcomed whenever she appeared, that she grew to think even some of the Breton country gentlemen quite tolerable people, though they had never been to Court, or even to Paris. The most amusing person at the States, to the Marquise, was Pomenars, who had frequently to appear before the courts for crimes—actual crimes. The Comte de Créance was prosecuting him for the abduction of his sister, and sincerely hoped to see him hanged; he was tried for coining false money, and, it is said, he paid the costs and fees in the spurious coin of his own manufacture. He was altogether such a witty, absurd, and ridiculous felon, that Madame de Sévigné can never write to her daughter about him without laughing; and the oddest and most inconceivable part of all is, that the Marquise and Madame de Chaulnes, both ladies of high birth and position, could countenance such an unmitigated rogue, could accept him as an equal, and greet him as a welcome guest among the best society at the States. But in those days people of good birth, like the King, could do no wrong. There was at least an absolutely different standard of conduct for people who were nobly born and for those who were only of the bourgeoisie or peasantry. Madame de Sévigné sends her daughter an account of the first visit of the Duchesse de Chaulnes, a lady who was charming and well educated, and on occasion somewhat unconventional.

"LES ROCHERS, *July* 26, 1671

"Yesterday, as I was sitting alone in my room with a book in my hand, I saw my door opened by a tall, good-looking woman, who was almost choking with laughter; behind her was a man, who was laughing even more than she was; he was followed by a young lady with a good figure, who was laughing also; and seeing them all in this merry humour, I laughed with them, without knowing why, or recognising who they were. Though I was expecting Madame de Chaulnes, who is to spend two days with me, I could not believe that it was her ladyship. She, however, it was; and she had brought Pomenars, who, on arriving at Vitré, had put it into her head to surprise me in this fashion. The Murinette beauty was of the party, and Pomenars was in such high spirits that he would have forced a smile from sorrow itself. At first they played at battledore and shuttlecock; and Madame de Chaulnes, I find, plays it like you. Then we had a slight repast, and afterwards we took a walk, during which we talked of you. I told Pomenars that you were very much interested in his affairs, and that you had said to me in your letters that if he had nothing more to fear than the present affair, you would be under no apprehension for him. . . . We kept up this jest a long time. In short, I never saw anyone so mad as Pomenars; his gaiety increases with his crimes, and if one charge more is brought against him he will certainly die with joy."

But late that same evening Pomenars went to Madame de Sévigné's room and had a little quiet conversation with her. "Pomenars has just left my room," she writes; "we have been talking over his affairs very seriously: they are questions of life and death. The Comte de Créance is resolved to have his head at all events, but Pomenars will not submit to this. Such is the state of things between them. . . . He does not take a single step which is not likely to be his last; and every time I bid him good-bye I do not know whether it will not be for the last time."

On Sunday, the 2nd of August, the Duc de Chaulnes made an imposing entry into the town, attended in the most solemn state by all his fellow-officials in their gorgeous robes of office, and welcomed by cannon, trumpeters, heralds, and church bells, in one confusing and deafening roar. A few days after Madame de Sévigné writes to give an account of what part she took in the opening of the States.

"LES ROCHERS, *August* 5, 1671

". . . And now I will give you news of the States, as a reward for being a Breton. M. de Chaulnes made his entry on Sunday evening, with all the noise that Vitré could supply. On Monday morning he sent me a letter by a gentleman, which I answered by going to dine with him. There were two tables in the same room, forty covers at each table; M. de Chaulnes presided at one, and Madame at the other, which made a fair-sized dinner-party. The good cheer was excessive; whole dishes of roast meat were carried away untouched, and the doors were obliged to be made higher to admit the pyramids of fruit. Our forefathers had certainly no idea of these articles, for they imagined that if a door was high enough for them to enter it was sufficient. A pyramid was about to be taken in (one of those, for instance, that oblige you to write notes from one end of the table to the other; but that in this case was no inconvenience; on the contrary, one is very well pleased at not seeing what they hide), —this pyramid, with about twenty pieces of china on it, was so completely overturned at the door, that the noise it made silenced the violins, hautbois, and trumpets. After dinner Messieurs de Locmaria and de Coëtlogon danced some marvellous *passe-pied* and minuets with two Breton ladies in a style that was far beyond our best dancers at Court; they danced their Bohemian and Bas Breton steps so lightly and precisely that I was quite charmed. I thought of you continually, and had so tender a recollection of your dancing that this pleasure became a grief to me. I am sure you would have been enchanted with Locmaria's dancing; the violins and *passe-pied* at Court are absurd in comparison; it is really extraordinary how they make a hundred different steps and always keep such excellent time; I never saw any man perform this kind of dance so well as Locmaria.

"After this little ball was finished, we saw arriving together in a crowd all the gentlemen who were to open the States the next morning: Monsieur the first President, the procurators and advocates-general of Parlement, eight bishops, Messieurs de Molac, la Coste, and the elder Coëtlogon; M. Boucherat from Paris, fifty Bas Bretons laced and gilded up to the eyes, and a hundred of the commons. Madame de Rohan and her son, and M. de Lavardin, were expected that evening, at which I was much astonished. I did not see the latter, for I was determined to return here to sleep after having been to the Tour de Sévigné to see M. d'Harouys and Messieurs Fourché and Chésières, who had just arrived. M. d'Harouys will write to you; he is delighted with your attentions; he received two letters from you at Nantes, for which I am even more obliged to you than he is. His house is going to be the Louvre of the States; there will be such play, such good cheer, such liberty day and night, that everyone will be attracted to him. I had never seen the States before; it is a very pretty sight; I do not believe that the States of any other province have a grander appearance than this. This province is full of nobility, and none of them are at Court or in camp except our little cornet, who may rejoin them before long. I shall go soon to see Madame de Rohan; I should quickly have a number of people here if I did not go to see them at Vitré. There was great rejoicing to see me at the States, as I never was there before; but I was not at the opening ceremony, for it was too early in the morning. The Assembly will not stay long; there is nothing to do but to ask what are the King's commands; no reply is made, and the affair is finished. As for the Governor, he secures, but I do not know how, more than forty thousand crowns. A number of other presents, of pensions, of repairs of highways and towns, fifteen or twenty big tables, continual play, balls without number, comedies three times a week, and a great deal of display and magnificence: these constitute the States. I have forgotten three or four hundred pipes of wine which are drunk there; but if I forget this trifling article, others do not, I assure you, for with them it is the first consideration. These, my dear, are what you may call tales to make you sleep standing, but they run to the end of your pen when you are in Brittany, and there is nothing else to say."

The Marquise was very well entertained when she drove over from Les Rochers to Vitré to see the fine company that swarmed in the town, but she was determined to keep visitors from coming to see her at Les Rochers as long as was possible. The Duc de Chaulnes, with the true spirit of friendship and self-sacrifice, kept the States sitting twice a day on purpose to keep the gentlemen from riding or driving the short four-and-a-half miles to Les Rochers; but whenever Madame de Sévigné appeared among them at the Castle she was received with the utmost cordiality and enthusiasm. "I am ashamed to tell you what honour they pay me at the States," she writes, "it is absolutely ridiculous."

They tried their hardest to induce her to sleep at Vitré, but this she resolutely refused to do; their entreaties had no weight when she thought of the luminous green solitudes of her woods and allées, doubly delightful in the hot August weather; of the tranquil calm of her own home after the noisy racket of the "dirty little town"; of the freedom and blessed silence which awaited her after the fatigue of talking and being amiable to a dozen people at once.

But it was not in the friendly human nature of the Breton gentlemen to have so charming a neighbour less than five miles away, without contriving somehow to see her amid her beautiful gardens and woods; and as there were no States to be held on Sunday, even her thoughtful friend the Duc de Chaulnes, could keep them away no longer—indeed, it was he who headed the procession there himself. The Marquise gives a gay account of their visit, incidently revealing on what a formidable scale hospitality was exercised among the nobility of Brittany two or three hundred years ago. The letter describing it to her daughter is dated from Vitré, to which town she had been compelled to escape.

"VITRÉ, *Wednesday, August* 12, 1671

"At last, my dear child, I am in the midst of the States, otherwise the States would have been in the midst of Les

Rochers. Last Sunday, just as I had sealed my letters, I saw four coaches-and-six drive into my court-yard, with fifty mounted guards, several led horses, and several pages on horseback. These were M. de Chaulnes, M. de Rohan, M. de Lavardin, Messieurs de Coëtlogon, de Locmaria, the Barons de Guais, the Bishop of Rennes, the Bishop of Saint-Malo, the Messieurs d'Argouges, and eight or ten more whom I did not know. I forgot M. d'Harouys, who is not worth mentioning. I received them all, and a great many compliments were paid on both sides. Finally, after a walk with which they were very well pleased, a very good and elegant repast appeared at one end of the mall, and above all there was Burgundy as plentiful as the water of Forges. They declared it must be the work of enchantment. M. de Chaulnes pressed me to go to Vitré, and I therefore arrived here on Monday night. Madame de Chaulnes entertained me at supper, with the comedy of *Tartuffe* after it, not badly played for a strolling company; and then we had a ball, at which the *passe-pied* and minuet almost made me weep: they brought you so vividly to my recollection that I could scarcely resist the impulse, and was obliged to do something to divert my thoughts. They talk to me of you very frequently here, and they do not have to wait long for an answer; for I am generally thinking of you at the time, so that I sometimes fancy they can see my thoughts through my bodice.

"Yesterday I received all Brittany at my Tour de Sévigné. I was at the play again; it was *Andromaque*, which made me cry more than six tears; quite enough for strolling players! In the evening we had supper, and then a ball. I wish you could see the elegance of M. de Locmaria, and in what style he takes off and puts on his hat, with what lightness! what precision! Upon my word he could excel all our courtiers and put them to shame. He has 60,000 livres a year, and has just come from the Academy; he is all that is handsome and agreeable, and would gladly have you for a wife. For the rest, do not think that your health is not constantly drunk here; the obligation, indeed, is not great, but such as it is you owe it every day to half Brittany. They begin with me, and then Madame de Grignan comes, of course. The civilities they show me are so ridiculous, and the women of this country are so foolish, that you might suppose I was the only lady of quality in the town, though it is full of them. . . . My Abbé goes on with his building, and cannot be persuaded to stay at Vitré; he sometimes comes, however, and dines with us. . . .

"Now, thank God, you are very well instructed in all that relates to your good country. But all this time I have had no letter from you, and consequently nothing to answer, so I must naturally talk to you of what I see and hear. Pomenars is a most extraordinary creature ; there is no man to whom I more willingly wish two heads, for he will never be able to carry his own safely away. For my part, my daughter, I long to see the end of the week, that I may repay all the civilities I have received from everybody in a proper manner, and then retire to enjoy myself at Les Rochers."

CHAPTER XXV

The "Fête de Marie" at Vitré—A drinking province—The Marquise takes refuge at Les Rochers—An exhausted hostess—Madame de Sévigné is escorted back to Vitré by the Governor's guards

BUT Madame de Sévigné could not escape from Vitré to her dear Les Rochers as easily as she had hoped. The Duc and Duchesse de Chaulnes were most unwilling to let their charming guest depart, and they treated her with much distinction, and did everything they could think of to make her prolong her visit. "But for this," she says, "you can well understand that I should hardly stay at Vitré, where I have no business. The comedians have amused us, the dancers have diverted us, and our walks and drives have supplied the place of Les Rochers. But to-morrow I shall go to Les Rochers, where I shall be enchanted to see no more fêtes, and to be a little to myself. I am dying of hunger in the midst of all their dainties, and the other day I actually proposed to Pomenars to order a leg of mutton to be prepared for us at midnight at the Tour de Sévigné after leaving Madame de Chaulnes. In short, whether it is from hunger or disgust, I long to be once more in my mall, from whence I shall not stir for eight or ten days. Our Abbé, la Mousse, and Marphise are in great need of my presence; the two first, indeed, come here and dine sometimes. Madame la Gouvernante de Provence is often talked of; for you must know that it is by this title that M. de Chaulnes always calls you when he drinks your health."

Besides the ordinary business—and pleasure—of the States, the Day of the Assumption, the grand Fête de Marie, was on the 15th of August, and one can understand that with such an immense company of decorative people to hand—bishops, lesser clergy, Governor, officers of all grades, and in a bewildering variety of costumes—*nous fîmes de grandes dévotions*, as the

Marquise told her daughter. What a sight would have been that long, gorgeous procession filing through the narrow, quaint old streets with brown, over-lapping storeys, up the massive stone steps and into the magnificent church of Notre Dame!

At last, however, Madame de Sévigné did manage to escape from the pressing attentions of the Governor and his wife, and from the overwhelming gaieties of Vitré. Her next letter is dated from Les Rochers, and she gives a vivid picture of what happened the day before she left, and makes a passing, but very amusing, reference to some hanging sleeves of a Provençal gentleman of which her daughter had given her a description.

"LES ROCHERS, *Wednesday, August* 19, 1671

". . . I have seen sleeves like those of your chevalier. Ah! what a charming picture they make, dancing in a plate of soup or sweeping over a salad bowl! But though they draw everything with them, I question whether they would draw me; in spite of my weakness for fashion, I have a great aversion to slovenliness. Vitré would be an excellent place for him; I have never seen such profusion. There is not a table at Court that could be compared with the least of the twelve or fifteen that are constantly kept up here; and, indeed, this is necessary, for there are three hundred people to be provided for who have nowhere else to eat. I left this good town on Monday, after having dined with Madame de Chaulnes, and I gave your compliments to her and to Mademoiselle de Murinais. . . .

"All Brittany was drunk that day. We dined apart. Forty gentlemen dined in a lower room, each of whom drank forty toasts; the King was the first, and then the glasses were broken. All this was done under the pretext of extreme joy and gratitude for the hundred thousand crowns which the King had returned to them from the free gift the province had made him, wishing to reward them for having so cheerfully complied with his request. There is now, therefore, only two millions, two hundred thousand livres to pay, instead of five hundred thousand. The King, too, has written a letter with his own hand, with a thousand kind wishes for his good province of Brittany. This letter the Governor read to the assembled

States (a copy of it was registered), and they shouted *Vive le Roi* to the skies, and immediately fell to drinking; and drink they did, God knows! M. de Chaulnes did not, on this grand occasion, forget the health of la Gouvernante de Provence; and a Breton gentleman, wishing to toast you by name, and not remembering it correctly, got up, and said in a loud voice, 'Here's to the health of Madame de *Carignan*!' This ridiculous mistake made MM. de Chaulnes and d'Harouys laugh till the tears came. The Bretons drank it, thinking it was all right, and for a week to come you will be Madame de *Carignan*; some called you the Comtesse de *Carignan*, and this was the state in which I left them.

"I have shown Pomenars what you say of him. He means to write to you, and while awaiting his letter, let me assure you that he is so bold and hardened that every day he makes the First President, who is his enemy, leave the room. He makes the Procureur-Général go also; but that is nothing, it is just like Bussy over again. . . . There was a pretty ball on Sunday. We saw a girl of Lower Brittany, who, they assured us, carried off the honours. My faith! she was the most ridiculous creature, who threw herself into such attitudes that we burst out laughing; but there were others, both men and women, who danced exquisitely.

"If you ask me how I like being at Les Rochers after all this noise, I shall tell you that I am transported with joy. I shall stay here at least eight days in spite of all their endeavours to get me back again. I want rest more than I can tell you; I want to sleep, I want to eat (for I am starved at all these fêtes); I want the fresh air; I want silence, for I was attacked on all sides and my lungs are almost worn out with talking. In short, my dear, I found my Abbé, my Mousse, my dog, my mall, my Pilois, and my masons; and all these are the only things which will do me good in the state in which I am at present. When I begin to be tired of them I will take another trip to Vitré. Among that immense crowd of Bretons there are some who have a good share of wit; there are some, even, who are worthy of talking to me of you. . . ."

The Marquise, as we may see, was inexpressibly glad to be

back again to her tranquil retreat, which she infinitely preferred to all the noise and pageantry of Vitré. On the 23rd of August she says to her daughter: "I have been here a week in a tranquillity, which has cured me of a frightful cold; I drank nothing but water; I have talked very little, I have left off suppers, and by these means, without having shortened my walks, I am quite well again."

It was scarcely surprising that several people among such a numerous company should be ill. The late hours, the excessive drinking, the continual excitement, and the necessarily cramped and unwholesome accommodation, would be sufficient to account for many disorders. One has only to glance at the narrow streets that remain of old Vitré, to guess what the atmosphere would be like more than two hundred years ago, when sanitation was an undiscovered science; when refuse of every description was thrown from the windows into the street; when any attempt to interfere with everyone's right to be a nuisance to his neighbour was regarded as an unheard-of impertinence.

Madame de Sévigné was fortunate to escape with merely a cold. Towards the conclusion of the States, she is constantly mentioning one or another of their friends who have been taken ill. Now it is Chésières, "who is completely cured by the noise of the backgammon table at M. d'Harouys'." Then M. de Chaulnes, just as he was stepping into his carriage to go to a dinner that M. d'Harouys was giving in his honour, was suddenly taken with shivering and fainting, the unpleasant preliminaries of an attack of fever and ague. Happily he recovered from this; but the Bishop of Léon, a great friend of the Marquise, had an attack of fever also, and, after lingering for some time between life and death, late in September "set out for a more pleasant country than this," as the Marquise told her daughter.

Madame de Sévigné describes very well the utter weariness and exhaustion of Madame de Chaulnes, who, as the Governor's wife, had not been able to flee from the gaieties of the States for a period of healing serenity at Les Rochers.

"Madame de Chaulnes, Mademoiselle de Murinais, Madame Fourché, and a fine young girl from Nantes, came here last Thursday. Madame de Chaulnes told me, as she came into my room, that she could no longer exist without seeing me; that she had the weight of all Brittany upon her shoulders, and that, in short, she would die of fatigue. She then threw herself upon my bed; we sat round her, and in one minute she was fast asleep from sheer fatigue, though we continued talking all the time. At last she woke, delighted with the charming liberty we enjoy at Les Rochers. We then took a walk, during which she and I seated ourselves in the heart of the wood, and while the others were playing at mall, I made her tell me all about Rome and how she came to marry M. de Chaulnes, for I always love to seek for something by way of amusement. In the midst of our talk there came on a treacherous shower, like the one we once had at Livry, so that we were nearly drowned. The water ran from our clothes in streams; it came through the trees in a moment, and the next minute we were wet through to the skin. We all ran as fast as we could, screaming, slipping, falling; but at last we reached the house, and a great fire was made, and we changed all our clothes, I providing everything; we dried our shoes, and were ready to die with laughter all the time. And this is how the Gouvernante of Brittany was treated in her own province. After this we had a good meal, and then the poor woman left us, more worried, I daresay, at the part she had to play when she got back to Vitré than at the affront she had received here. She made me promise to relate this adventure to you, and to go to-morrow to assist her in entertaining the States, which will finish in about a week. . . ."

The Marquise was not long permitted to enjoy the serenity of her woods and gardens. On the Sunday following this visit, M. de Chaulnes despatched his company of mounted guards to Les Rochers with a note to tell Madame de Sévigné that she was wanted on His Majesty's service, and that Madame de Chaulnes expected her to supper. Little as the Marquise desired to go, she did not like to refuse the amiable and friendly Duchess, so, though it was getting rather late, she ordered her carriage, and was soon driving towards Vitré escorted by the Governor's guards.

It is amusing to find that Madame de Sévigné, with all her

tact and *savoir faire*, occasionally made the same social mistakes that harass the lives of less fortunate individuals.

"I must tell you of an absurd mistake I made the other day," she writes to her daughter. "I was at M. de Chaulnes' house, and I saw a man standing at the end of the room whom I believed to be the *maître d'hôtel*. I went up to him and said, My good sir, do let us have dinner; it is one o'clock, and I am fit to die with hunger.' 'Madame,' he said, looking gravely at me, 'I should be very happy to give you a dinner at my house; my name is Pécaudière, and I live only two leagues from Landerneau.' My child, it was a gentleman of Lower Brittany, and you may imagine how foolish I felt at the discovery; I cannot help laughing even while I write it."

The States were gradually drawing to a conclusion, as may be seen from Madame de Sévigné's letters. We get a glimpse of the young Duc de Rohan paying conspicuous attention to a beauty of Lower Brittany, who dances beautifully, and who entirely neglects her betrothed to listen to the flattering nothings of the young nobleman, in spite of her mother's evident frowns and disapproval. Monsieur Locmaria has lost none of his fascination; his dancing, his figure, his face, his manners are all captivating; and she tells her daughter that the "Murinette beauty," that is to say Mademoiselle Murinais, would accept him willingly, but that he has not the same inclination for her. Pomenars has grown bolder than ever, and sends word to Madame de Grignan that he is sure he will not be hanged now because he has escaped so long. We catch, too, a glimpse of the tender heart of the brilliant mistress of Les Rochers, who is always ready with a jest, always ready to laugh at the jests of others, whose spirits are always bright and buoyant in company. "I am ready to die sometimes," she tells her daughter, "for want of giving vent to my tears at a ball where I am reminded of you; and sometimes I actually enjoy my tears unobserved. There are some airs and dances that almost always produce that effect on me. Our States may sing and dance and drink as long as they please, but your dear picture finds its way through all, and fixes itself in my heart as on its proper throne."

The Marquise is drily sarcastic over the large sums of

money voted by the Breton gentlemen, in addition to that already promised to the King. "They must think they are going to die, and are disposing of all their effects," whispered a Breton gentleman in her ear, at one of these generous and enthusiastic moments; and the Marquise cordially agreed. She knew that all this money would have to be raised somehow, and indeed, only a few years later, Brittany was so impoverished by its "free gifts" to the King, that the province was well-nigh bankrupt.

"The contract our province made with the King was signed last Friday, but before that we had given two thousand louis-d'or to Madame de Chaulnes, besides many other presents. It is not that we are so rich here; but we have courage, we are very obliging, and between twelve and one at noon we can never refuse anything to our friends. That is the fortunate moment; the odours of your orange-flowers do not produce such fine effects. I do not know how you are at present, but your health is drunk here every day by more than a hundred gentlemen who never saw you in their lives, and in all probability never will. . . .

"Provincial splendour appears here in all its glory, but the other day M. de Grignan's post was admired and envied by everyone for being without this parade. . . . While the rage for making presents prevailed, we had a desire to propose to the States to give ten thousand crowns to M. and Madame de Grignan. M. and Madame de Chaulnes declared that they would listen to the proposal; the others that they would actually make the present. Finally, we agreed to have it whispered about, to make a few of the Bas Bretons murmur, to soften them down at table, and make them promise to propose it."

But, needless to say, this proposal was never made; the States had promised all they could perform to the great officials of Brittany. It is amusing to find that as the States drew near the end the Marquise told her daughter that she did not dare to keep at Les Rochers any longer, as the way there was too well known. On the last Sunday in August, a day of leisure, no less than five carriages-and-six came to give her a surprise visit. However, a week after this, on September 6, the Marquise was very happy to be able to write to her daughter of the actual conclusion of the Assembly.

"'The best of company must part,' said M. de Chaulnes, on dismissing the Bretons to their homes. The States broke up about midnight. I was present, with Madame de Chaulnes and some other ladies. It was a very fine, very grand, and very magnificent assembly. M. de Chaulnes spoke to everybody with great dignity, and expressed himself extremely well. After dinner we all go to our own places. I shall be rejoiced to find myself again at Les Rochers. I have had an opportunity of obliging several people; I have made a deputy and a pensioner; I have spoken for several unfortunate folk, but of myself not a word, for I cannot ask without a reason."

CHAPTER XXVI

Wolves in the woods at Les Rochers—The birth of a grandson—The Marquise and her household return to Paris—A warm welcome given to the mère-beauté—A charming society—A brilliant group of writers

THE Marquise was so overjoyed to leave Vitré, to be able at last to bid good-bye to her pleasant friends, and to the crowds of Breton ladies and gentlemen whose acquaintance she had made during the States, that she tells her daughter—

"I am going back to Les Rochers, so delighted to go that I am almost ashamed of being so tranquil in your absence."

She had really enjoyed the festivities, however, and it is pleasant to find that a closer acquaintance with the people of her own province—by marriage—had given her a cordial liking and respect for their good qualities.

"I like your Bretons very much," she says; "they smell a little of wine, it is true, but your orange-flower perfumes do not hide such good hearts."

The rest of the month of September was passed in the serene solitude of Les Rochers, which the Marquise had so yearned for in the midst of the entertainments of the States. Day after day she wandered in her mall, her labyrinth, her walks and woods; sometimes taking a book, sometimes "ploughing the mall with her eyes," or reading and re-reading her daughter's letters. She occasionally varied these occupations by going to see how the chapel, in which the Bien-Bon was so interested, was progressing, or she talked business with her tenants, or discoursed on religion and philosophy with her two abbés.

In October she mentions the nut-gathering; a sober harvest enough, she thinks, in comparison with the lovely fruits and flowers of her daughter's little kingdom.

"I know Provence only by its pomegranates, its orange-trees, and its jessamines," she writes; "for that is how it is described to me; but for us, chestnuts are our greatest ornament. The other day I had three or four baskets full of them round me; some I boiled, some I roasted, and with others I filled my pockets; they are served up at table, they are trodden underfoot; this is Brittany in all its glory."

We have another most piquant glimpse of this beautiful and stately *châtelaine* as she wanders in her woods, under the alluring rays of the October moon. She loves her woods and gardens with a passion that causes her to seek them every spare hour of the day when the weather is fine; she watches the young trees growing, with an almost maternal solicitude; and when Pilois, her chief gardener, and his men are planting, she sometimes holds up the saplings for the sheer pleasure of helping at so congenial an occupation. Even in the evenings, moonlight in her woods is so seductive that, to the alarm of her household, she stays there till late at night. But she takes precautions—

"Apropos my woods are infested with wolves; I have two or three guards to follow me every night with their muskets upon their shoulders; Beaulieu is their captain, and for these two days past we have honoured the moonlight with our presence between eleven and twelve at night. The night before last I saw a black man coming towards me; I thought of the Augur of whom you told me, but, on approaching, it proved to be la Mousse. A little farther on we saw a white body extended along the ground; we came up to this quite boldly, and, behold! it was a tree I had had cut down a week ago. These are extraordinary adventures!"

Finally, on November 29, she received the news for which she had been waiting so long at Les Rochers, with deep anxieties and silent tears, with continual prayers of her own, as well as daily masses at church—the safe delivery of her daughter. Everyone concerned was especially delighted, because this time it was a son; and the Marquise, in the excess of her emotion, wept for joy, and immediately went to have as many masses said by way of thanksgiving, as she had ordered before when hoping to ensure the safety of her daughter. Her first impulse was one of devout thankfulness.

"I am now so entirely happy," she writes, "that I cannot

help returning thanks to God without ceasing for the peace of mind which I did not expect so soon. I have received letters of congratulation, without number and without end, from Paris and Brittany, and the baby's health has been drunk for miles around. I have distributed money for drink, and have feasted my people on the occasion, exactly as if it were Twelfth-night. But nothing gave me greater pleasure than the compliment I received from Pilois, who came this morning with his spade upon his back, and said to me, 'Madame, I have come to tell you how heartily glad I am to hear that Madame la Comtesse has a fine boy.' That, to me, is worth all the fine speeches in the world. . . . Adieu, divine Comtesse; I kiss the little child whom I love tenderly, but not so well as Madame his mother; it will be a long time before he attains to that degree of affection."

After having stayed nearly seven months at Les Rochers, Madame de Sévigné set out for Paris on December 9, with the Bien-Bon, the Abbé de la Mousse, her waiting-women, and her pet dog Marphise. They had four horses to each carriage, and though they "flew like the wind" they were nine days on the road, including a short stay at Malicorne. The first thing she did on reaching Paris was to write again to the daughter who was never long absent from her thoughts. She gives a vivid picture of her meeting with her friends and relatives, particularly with Emmanuel de Coulanges, her cousin, who while staying at Lyons had gone for a short visit to Madame de Grignan; indeed, the part that relates to him is an extraordinary impressionist picture of the emotions.

"PARIS, *Friday, December* 18, 1671

"I have just arrived, my dear child, and am at my aunt's house, surrounded, embraced, and questioned by all my family and hers; but I have left them all, resolved to say good-day to you as well as to other people. M. de Coulanges is waiting to take me home with him, where he says I shall stay because one of Madame de Bonneuil's sons has the small-pox. . . . Suppose me now arrived at M. de Coulanges', whom I adore because he is always talking to me of you; but can you guess what happens? Why, I cry, and my heart is so strangely oppressed that I make a sign with my hand for him to be silent, and silent he is. My eyes are red, and we speak quickly of other things, on the condition, however, that one day I shall give myself up entirely to talking of you, to the exclusion of everything else. He tells me that when he saw you, you shut your eyes and said you were in my room; yes, certainly you were in Paris, for there was M. de Coulanges! He acted this very charmingly, and I am delighted to find that you have still a little foolishness left, for I was terribly afraid lest you should always be Madame la Gouvernante. . . . "

Then the amiable, witty, frivolous Emmanuel de Coulanges —the cousin, eight years younger than the Marquise, whom she remembers as a baby, when she, a little orphan, was staying with his mother at Sucy—takes up the pen to write to Madame de Grignan, and from his note we gather something of the exquisite beauty of the young Comtesse, who is now about twenty-five, and of the gracious charm and affection of her whom he generally calls *mère-beauté*.

"I shut my eyes, and on opening them again, I see that *mère-beauté* who is your delight and mine; and this assures me that I am at Paris. I am going to entertain her with all your perfections. Do you know that I am more bewitched with you than ever, and that I am afraid I shall take the Chevalier de Breteuil's place? I know that this would not please M. de Grignan, and it is the only thing that keeps me from so great an undertaking. But in truth, Madame la Comtesse, you are a master-piece of Nature, and it is thus I speak of you whenever I mention you. I was yesterday at M. de la Rochefoucauld's, where I met M. de Longueville [the Comte de Saint-Paul, who had recently taken the title of the Duc de Longueville when his elder brother entered the Church], and we talked of nothing but Provence and you. Adieu, my charming Comtesse; I can see your room, I am looking at that man in the tapestry who is opening his breast; believe me, if you could see mine at this moment, you would see my heart as you see his, a heart which is yours, which languishes for you; but do not tell this to M. de Grignan. Your daughter is a little brown beauty; she is very pretty; there, she is kissing me and prattling to me, but she never cries. She is beautiful, but I do not love her so well as I love you. There is no such thing as talking to your *mère-beauté* about you; the great tears fall from her eyes. *Mon Dieu!* what a mother!"

The little Blanche d'Adhémar, now about a year old, is frequently mentioned by the Marquise, whose graphic pen-sketches to the Comtesse (who had not seen her daughter since she was a few months old) bring the baby vividly before us. Sometimes she says she can hardly leave the child's bedside, even to write to its mother, because of its sweet and fascinating baby-ways; at other times we see her, by means of the magic pen of the Marquise, chattering baby-talk to her mother's picture; and in May, when Blanche is just about a year and a half old, Madame de Sévigné gives a delightful portrait of her tiny granddaughter.

"You tell me," she writes to the Comtesse, "that your son's beauty diminishes, and that his merit increases. I am sorry for the loss of his beauty, and I am rejoiced to find that he loves wine; this is a little spice of Brittany and Burgundy together, which will produce a charming effect with the prudence of the Grignans. As for your daughter, she is just the reverse; her beauty increases and her merit lessens. I assure you she is very pretty, but as obstinate as a demon; she has her little will, and intentions, with which she diverts me extremely. She has a beautiful complexion, blue eyes, black hair, a nose that is neither handsome nor ugly; her chin, her cheeks, and the contours of her face are faultless. I shall say nothing of her mouth, it will do very well; she has a very sweet voice, and Madame de Coulanges thinks it suits her mouth."

The Marquise sends yet another delightful little picture of baby Blanche to her mother in Provence. On Monday, 23rd of May, she writes to Madame de Grignan—

"... Yesterday I dined at the la Troches' with the Abbé Arnauld and Madame de Valentine. After dinner we had le Camus, his son, and Ytier, and together they gave us a charming little concert. After that Mademoiselle de Grignan arrived with her equerry Beaulieu, her governess Hélène, her waiting-woman Marie, her little page Jacquot her nurse's son, and her nurse Mère Jeanne, dressed in her Sunday clothes;

she is the most amiable country-woman I have ever seen. This little procession made a fine appearance. We sent them into the garden, and we all watched them with much pleasure; I was much charmed with her little household. . . ."

Poor little Blanche d'Adhémar! These early years that she passed with her loving grandmother were probably the most sunny days of her life. There is no actual record of the date when she was taken to Provence by her mother, but we gather from the *Letters* that it was soon after her fifth birthday. M. de Grignan then expresses his satisfaction with his little daughter, and shortly after she was placed in the convent at Aix, founded by her ancestress Sainte-Chantal. Fleeting mention is now and again made of her in Madame de Sévigné's letters. We gather that the child was sometimes jealous, sometimes a little rebellious; sometimes chafing at being away from home where her brother and sister were so happy. Occasionally the Marquise pleads for her, but evidently the Comtesse de Grignan had never felt much affection for her eldest-born, and she had no scruple in devoting her to a religious life. One child at least, in good Catholic families, was often "given to God"; and it mattered not at all that her daughter Blanche did not evince any "vocation," that the Rabutin blood in her young veins desired ardently to be released into the world; it was necessary, so the Comtesse thought, that one child at least should be economically provided for, and as the baby Pauline promised to have beauty as her dower, the unfortunate little Blanche, who was plainer, was chosen for the sacrifice.

Back again in Paris among her friends, the Marquise gives many most interesting glimpses into the charming and varied society among which she spent her days. The friend whom she most frequently visits is Madame de la Fayette, by whom she is sincerely loved and always cordially welcomed. Here, the Marquise tells her daughter, is the prettiest little garden in Paris, where they sit and breathe the perfume of the flowers, and enjoy the lovely spring evenings, because Madame de la Fayette is so delicate that she cannot even venture into a carriage. Madame de la Fayette is visited every day by the cynical Duc de la Rochefoucauld, who is a martyr to gout, but who always contrives to limp or drive to see his friend, where they both sit and talk so sadly, or groan over their sufferings, till, the Marquise de Sévigné tells her daughter afterwards, "Madame de la Fayette is always ailing, M. de la Rochefoucauld is always lame, and we sometimes talk so dismally, till it seems that there is nothing to be done but to bury us."

Very often, too, the Marquise goes to the house of the Duc de la Rochefoucauld, which is also in the Faubourg Saint-Germain, and though the Duke does not hold a salon, he frequently arranges for dramatists and authors to read or act their new pieces to a select company of his friends. What a group of authors were then amusing Paris! The brilliant Molière, whose glance noted every absurdity, whose every play was a satire on some existing abuse; Racine, Corneille, La Fontaine, whose names, after the test of centuries, proudly hold their places among the greatest in France! One day the Marquise happened to be at the Duke's house when Corneille was giving one of his plays, and, as was her usual custom, she writes her daughter an account of it.

"The other day at M. de la Rochefoucauld's, Corneille read one of his comedies, which showed us what he once had been. I wish you had been with me that afternoon, I am sure you would not have been wearied or indifferent; indeed, you would have dropped a tear or two, since I myself shed twenty. The Duke was behind the scenes, and Pomenars was above with the lackeys, wrapped in his cloak up to the eyes for fear of the Comte de Créance, who is resolved to have him hanged at all costs. The *beaux* were all upon the stage; the Marquis de Villeroi was in a masquerade dress, the Comte de Guiche was as obscure as his own wit, and all the rest were in cloaks like so many banditti."

The Duc de la Rochefoucauld frequently sent messages to Madame de Grignan, and on one occasion he sent her his famous *Maximes*. "Here are M. de la Rochefoucauld's *Maximes*, revised and corrected with additions; it is a present to you from himself," writes the Marquise. "Some of them are exquisite; but there are others that, to my shame, I cannot understand at all. God knows whether you will."

But the Marquise does not confine herself to visiting these two friends. We must not overlook the fact that she sometimes goes to visit the sick, who, she says, are as full of sorrow and vexation as herself when she remembers her separation from her daughter. There is Madame Scarron too, "who sups with us almost every evening, and is the most agreeable companion imaginable. She knows perfectly well how to please me, by talking to me of you. She admires you greatly."

Cardinal de Retz, too, has returned to Paris, and is now the Abbé of Saint-Denis. The Marquise has a great affection for this relative, and often mentions him in her letters. "We do all we can to amuse our dear Cardinal," she says. "Corneille has read him one of his comedies, which is soon to be produced, and which recalls the fine works he has written. On Saturday, Molière is to read him *Trissotin* [*les Femmes Savantes*], which is a very amusing comedy; and Despréaux will read him his *Lutrin* and his *Poétique*; this is all we can do for him. He loves you with all his heart, and often speaks of you; and we are not so ready to finish your praises as we are to begin them."

It was always the same; wherever she went she was sure to talk of her daughter, and, in that agreeable, charming society, which she herself said "was the kindest in the world," they did not fail to mention the subject that concerned her most, even though they might not be so interested in Madame de Grignan as was her mother. "Everybody talks to me of my daughter," innocently declared the Marquise.

"Do you see that good woman?" said her cousin Emmanuel de Coulanges one day. "She is for ever in the presence of her daughter!"

Besides talking of her daughter, and writing to her almost every day, she delighted in sending her presents. Sometimes it is a parcel of books; sometimes a fan, which she thinks charming because it is decorated with a group of little chimney-sweeps instead of the fashionable cupids; or it is a pair of *pincettes* for M. de Grignan's "incomparable beard." But she loves to adorn her beautiful daughter, and once she sends her a lovely pearl necklace, which always appears in Madame de Grignan's portraits after this date.

"I forbid you, my dear child," she writes, "to send me your portrait. If you are looking pretty, have it painted, but keep the delightful present for me till I come to see you, for I should be very sorry to leave it here. In the meantime, accept one from me that surpasses all presents, past and to come; this is not saying too much, my child, for it is a pearl necklace worth twelve thousand crowns. It is a large sum, but not greater than my love and goodwill towards you. Examine it well, weigh it, see how beautifully it is set, and then tell me your opinion of it. It is the finest I ever saw; it belonged to our late neighbour, the Venetian ambassador, who is dead; and it has been greatly admired here."

Through all the letters she rings the changes on the same theme, her intense longing to visit her daughter; to see her in her own home, in the new and strange surroundings of Southern France. But her aunt, Madame de la Trousse, who had watched over her with constant care and affection since the first days of her widowhood, was ill, and her love and duty would not allow her to leave her, even though she had the utmost care and attention from her daughters, Mademoiselle de la Trousse and Mademoiselle de Méri. Of the Marquis de la Trousse, who had not been a very loving son, but who now expressed affection for his mother, she says: "I do not place much value on such deathbed affections, and I would not thank those who only began to love me then. My child, we must love during life, as you do so well; we must make the existence of those we care for calm and happy, not fill it with bitterness and grief. It is too late to change at the point of death."

Madame de Sévigné was kept for months in a state of uncertainty. Sometimes her aunt, who was suffering from dropsy, rallied a little, and the doctors said she might linger for some time; then the Marquise would think that she and the Bien-Bon might leave her, and perhaps even find her recovered on their return. Following this, Madame de la Trousse grew so much worse that her death seemed only a question of hours; but, though sorely tempted, the Marquise always kept her post, and through the long, bright spring days sat by the bedside of her aunt—whose terrible sufferings she described most movingly to her daughter—and only left her for short periods while she paid brief visits to her ailing friend the Marquise de la Fayette. At length, on the last day of June, the Marquise de la Trousse died, and Madame de Sévigné was free to think of her visit to her daughter in Provence.

CHAPTER XXVII

The Marquise visits her daughter in Provence—Madame de Sévigné at Marseilles—Her return to Paris—A midnight walk with Madame de Scarron—The death of Turenne

THE Marquise de la Trousse died on the 30th of June 1672, and by the 13th of July Madame de Sévigné, who for months previously had been making preparations for her visit to Provence, was able to set out on the journey, accompanied by the Bien-Bon and the Abbé de la Mousse. They arrived at Grignan in the beginning of August, and the Marquise spent the whole of the following year with her daughter. We hear very little of this visit, because most of the letters that the Marquise sent to her friends in Paris and elsewhere have been lost, but we gather from one or two notes to her daughter that she visited Marseilles with M. de Grignan, and was delighted with the reception accorded to the Governor of Provence. With her usual keen interest in everything novel or strange, she immediately wrote to her daughter, who was at Grignan, with a charming vivacity, her impressions of the place and people.

"I sit down to write to you between a visit from Madame the Intendant's wife and a very fine harangue. I am now expecting a present, and the present expects my pistole. I am charmed with the singular beauty of this town. Yesterday was a glorious day, and the place from which I could see the sea, the bastions, the mountains, and the town, is a most remarkable spot. . . . The crowd of chevaliers who came to see M. de Grignan on his arrival—some with names that are familiar, like Saint-Hérem, others unknown adventurers with swords and fine hats—gave a suggestion of war and romance, of embarkations and adventures, of chains and irons, of slavery, of captives and captivity; and all this, to one who loves romance as I do, is inexpressibly delightful."

It was probably on this same journey that she was detained at Lambesc, from whence she wrote to her daughter, with her own inimitable charm, of the difficulties that beset travellers in Provence.

"LAMBESC, 10 *o'clock Tuesday morning*
"*December* 20, 1672

"When we reckon without Providence, my dear daughter, we are often obliged to reckon twice. I was all ready dressed by eight o'clock; I had drank my coffee, heard mass, bidden good-bye to everybody, the little mules were loaded, and the tinkling of their bells reminded me that it was time to get into my litter; my room was full of people, who begged me not to set out because of the heavy rains of the last few days, and because it had rained without cessation the whole of yesterday and this morning. But I resisted all their arguments, determined to keep the promise I made you in my letter of yesterday, of being with you on Thursday, when suddenly in came M. de Grignan in his dressing-gown, and talked to me so seriously of the rashness of my undertaking—saying that the muleteer would not be able to follow my litter, that my mules would fall into the ditches, that my people would be too fatigued to be able to assist me—that I at once changed my mind and yielded to his wise remonstrances . . . and now I shall depart when it pleases Heaven and M. de Grignan, who governs me entirely."

While staying in Provence, Madame de Sévigné was kept well posted with what was going on at Court by her friends Madame de la Fayette and Madame de Coulanges. The Marquise on one occasion scolded Madame de la Fayette for not writing oftener, and that ailing lady, who always "enjoyed" miserable health, wrote back, "You love writing to everyone; I hate it just as much, and if I had a lover who expected a letter every day I should certainly break with him."

Madame de Coulanges tells her how her letters are appreciated by everyone who has the privilege of reading them, and it is pleasant to us, who are so charmed with them to-day, to find that even during her lifetime this delightful writer was not without honour in her own country.

"But I must not forget what happened this morning," writes

Madame de Coulanges. "A footman from Madame de Thianges [sister to Madame de Montespan] wanted to speak to me. I ordered him to be shown in, and this is what he said. 'Madame, I have come from Madame de Thianges, who begs you to send her the letter about the Horse, and the one about the Meadow, from Madame de Sévigné.' I told the lackey that I would take them myself to his mistress, and so I got rid of him. Your letters have the reputation they deserve, as you see; it is certain that they are delightful, and you are as delightful as your letters."

During the time that the Marquise was staying in Provence, Madame de Grignan's youngest daughter, Pauline, was born. On October the 5th, 1673, Madame de Sévigné left her daughter with much grief, especially as the latter was not in good health. On the way home she stayed for a short while at Bourbilly, her castle in Burgundy, and arrived in Paris on All Saints Day. She was welcomed by numbers of her friends: Madame de la Fayette, the Duc de la Rochefoucauld, Madame de Scarron, who was steadily and stealthily rising in favour at Court, the Archbishop of Rheims, the Abbé de Grignan, d'Hacqueville, the Abbé Têtu, and a host of others, all eager to welcome the charming Marquise to their society after her long absence. The next morning, as early as nine o'clock, M. de la Garde, the Abbé de Grignan, Brancas, and d'Hacqueville crowded into her room to have a little private conversation, for at this period Madame de Sévigné was much occupied in Paris with supporting the interests of M. de Grignan, as the Bishop of Marseilles, his old enemy, was secretly working against him.

Madame de Sévigné in giving her daughter the news that would be sure to interest her, did not forget Madame de Scarron, whom they had both known in the days of her poverty and obscurity. During Madame de Sévigné's absence she had been promoted, and instead of existing on a small pension in an *appartement* in the Marais, she was now governess to the children of the King and Madame de Montespan, and lived in the utmost privacy in a beautiful house on the confines of Paris. The Marquise gives her daughter an account of a perfectly safe midnight walk through the streets of Paris, for by this time—in fact since the year 1666—Paris was lighted with candle lanterns suspended in the middle of the street, except on moonlight nights, of course! On December 4 she writes—

"We supped yesterday with Madame Scarron and the Abbé Têtu at Madame de Coulanges'. We talked a great deal, and you were not forgotten. We took it into our heads to accompany Madame de Scarron home at midnight to the farthest end of the Faubourg Saint-Germain, past Madame de la Fayette's, almost as far as Vaugirard in the country. She lives in a fine and beautiful house, where no one is allowed to enter. She has a large garden, handsome apartments, servants, a carriage and horses, and she dresses neatly but richly, like a woman who has passed all her life with people of rank. She is amiable, pretty, good, and free from affectation; one can converse very pleasantly with her. We returned gaily by the light of the lanterns, and in no danger from thieves."

About two months after this, however, to Madame de Sévigné's great satisfaction, she wrote no more letters to her daughter for a whole year, for Madame de Grignan came to Paris on a long visit to her mother; and it was then, no doubt, that she renewed her interest in the people about the Court, for after her return to Provence in May 1675, the Marquise writes more frequently than ever about the happenings at Versailles and at Saint-Germain. But it is particularly noticeable that at this period Madame de Sévigné writes with especial caution whenever she mentions her friends who have any interest at Court. "It is sometimes necessary to write in cypher," she tells her daughter, for letters were frequently opened as they passed through the post. She also speaks in terms of eulogy of the King whenever she has occasion to mention him; for Louis XIV was ruling with a strong hand; rewarding and punishing with such autocratic power, that all his subjects feared him, and few, very few, dared to be as outspoken as the brusque Marquis de Montausier, who one day remarked angrily, "No one but mistresses and ministers has any influence nowadays!" We therefore find that Madame de la Fayette, who had considerable political influence in a quiet way, in connection with the Princess of Savoy, is sometimes mentioned as the *Mist*, Madame de Coulanges is the *Leaf*—a term well suited to her airy and frivolous character—Madame de Montespan is *Quantova*, M.

de Pomponne is the *Rain*, while the *Torrent* and the *Dew* are names for persons who have not been very clearly identified.

Soon after Madame de Grignan's return to Provence, an event occurred at the seat of war which seems to have affected Madame de Sévigné with a deep personal grief, the death of the Maréchal de Turenne. It would be particularly interesting to know what degree of intimacy existed between the Marquise and the great hero; we know they were personal friends, for Madame de Sévigné mentioned to her daughter one day that she had been to visit him with Madame de la Fayette. It is somewhat curious that of Foucquet, and of the brave Maréchal, Madame de Sévigné has left the most touching and interesting records; especially noticeable because both these men, as we know from Bussy's letters, during the earlier, more brilliant days of her widowhood, would fain have become her lovers. Their intentions — neither of them honourable — seem not to have shocked the Marquise in the least degree, though when her more severe daughter wrote with expressions of horror on the subject of adultery, she cordially agreed with her. The truth is that Madame de Sévigné, to use a common phrase, "took her world as she found it," and her world thought it a light, almost venial sin to break the seventh commandment. It was this easy and graceful adaptability of mood and temper that made Madame de Sévigné such a charming companion. "If I had a little more warmth in my disposition I should be angry," she wrote on one occasion, and it was probably the decision and emphasis—not always agreeable!—in Madame de Grignan's character that caused Ninon to declare that she had all the *sel* of the family.

M. de Turenne was killed in July 1675, and all Paris was shocked and grieved when the news reached the city. Madame de Sévigné tells the sad circumstance to her friends, and continually mentions incidents of his life, and always with loving and admiring affection. There is something singularly good and attractive in his portrait, a look of far-seeing wisdom and human sympathy combined, which distinguishes him from the other nobles of his day; indeed, most of his actions were totally unlike those of his compeers, especially in matters relating to the poor soldiers under his command. As the Marquise relates,

MARÉCHAL TURENNE.

he clothed a whole regiment at his own expense; and on another occasion he sold his plate that his soldiers might be fed. Madame de Sévigné uses a very happy phrase in mentioning his death to her cousin Bussy, which informs us at the same time that she was a fatalist.

"You are an excellent almanac," she writes to Bussy, "you predicted like one of the profession all that happened in Germany; but you did not foresee the death of M. de Turenne, nor the cannon-ball, shot at random, which singled him out of ten or twelve others. But I, who see the hand of Providence in everything, I see that cannon loaded from all eternity. I see that everything combined to lead him to that fatal spot; and I do not consider it very terrible for him, supposing him in a fit state of mind to die. What more could he have desired? He died in the midst of glory."

As the Marquise was on intimate terms with Cardinal Bouillon, his nephew, and Madame d'Elbœuf, his niece, she was invited by them to meet some of the gentlemen and soldiers who had witnessed his death, and the day after she writes a most touching account of the meeting to her daughter, giving, at the same time, a detailed description of the hero's death.

"PARIS, *Wednesday, August* 28, 1675

" In truth, my daughter, I am going to write to you yet once again of M. de Turenne. Madame d'Elbœuf, who is staying for a few days with the Cardinal de Bouillon [her brother], invited me to dine with them yesterday to talk of their sad loss. Madame de la Fayette was there also, and we did what we proposed to do, till there was not a dry eye among us. Madame d'Elbœuf had a portrait, exquisitely painted, of the hero, whose people all arrived at eleven o'clock. They were already clothed in mourning, and all were bathed in tears; three gentlemen came in who were fit to die with grief at the sight of the picture; they could not utter a word, and their cries pierced one to the heart. His valets, his lackeys, his pages and trumpeters, were all in tears, and made everyone weep to see them. The first who was able to speak answered our sad questions; we made him tell us the manner of his death. M. de Turenne wished to confess, and when he retired for that purpose, he gave his orders for the evening, and intended to communicate the next day, which was Sunday. He thought about giving battle, and mounted his horse at two o'clock on Saturday, after he had eaten his dinner. He had several people with him, but he left them all at about thirty paces from the height where he intended to go, and said to young d'Elbœuf, 'Nephew, stay you there; you keep so close to me that I shall be recognised.' M. d'Hamilton, who was near the place where he was passing, said to him—

"'Monsieur, come this way; the enemy is directing the fire to the spot where you are!'

"'I will do as you say,' replied M. de Turenne, 'I do not wish to be killed to-day. This place will do admirably.'

"He turned his horse, and perceived Saint-Hilaire, who, coming up to him with his hat in his hand, said—

"'Will you look at that battery I have placed over there, Monsieur?'

"The Maréchal turned back, and, without having time to stop his horse, his arm and part of his body were torn to pieces by the same ball that carried away Saint-Hilaire's arm, and the hand in which he held his hat. That gentleman, who was looking at him attentively, did not see him fall, for the horse ran away with M. de Turenne to the spot where he had left young d'Elbœuf; he was then leaning with his face over the pommel of the saddle. At this moment the horse stopped, and he fell into the arms of his people; twice he opened his eyes wide, and moved his lips, and then remained silent for ever. Only to think that he was dead; that part of his heart was carried away!

"His people burst into tears and loud cries, but M. d'Hamilton quieted them, and took young d'Elbœuf away from his uncle's body, where he had thrown himself, almost fainting with grief. A cloak was placed over the body, which was carried to the shelter of a hedge, where they kept watch over it in silence, till a carriage was brought to convey it to the tent. There it was met by M. de Lorges, M. de Roye, and several others, who were almost dead with grief; but they were obliged to control themselves, and to think of the great responsibility that had fallen upon them.

"A military service was held in the camp, where tears and

cries made truest mourning; all the officers had crape scarves, all the drums were covered with crape also, and they beat only a single stroke; the soldiers marched with their pikes trailing and their muskets reversed, but the cries of a whole army cannot be described without emotion. . . .

"When the body was removed from the camp to be brought to Paris, the weeping and lamentations were renewed; and in every place through which it passed there was nothing but grief and mourning. At Langres, however, they did more than this: the sad procession was met by more than two hundred of the chief inhabitants, clothed in mourning; these were followed by the people, and all the clergy in their vestments, who held a solemn service in the town. A voluntary contribution was immediately made to defray this expense, which amounted to five thousand francs. What do you say to these marks of natural affection founded upon an extraordinary merit?

"He is to be brought to Saint-Denis this evening or tomorrow; his people are all gone to meet the body at a place about two leagues distant, from whence they will escort it to a chapel where it will be placed for the present. There will be a service at Saint-Denis, and afterwards one at Notre Dame, which will be very solemn.

"What do you think of our entertainment at the Cardinal's house? We dined, as you may imagine, sadly enough, and till four o'clock we did nothing but sigh. . . ."

Two days after writing this, the Marquise went with Madame d'Elbœuf and the Cardinal to the service at Saint-Denis, of which she writes a sad and moving account to her daughter. Perhaps the most noticeable difference in the mourning of that day and this, was the utter lack of restraint among relatives, friends, servants, and people of every degree. At this service Madame d'Elbœuf "filled the chapel with her cries"; nor is this occasion singular, for Madame de Sévigné relates that at the death of the Princesse de Conti, all her ladies-in-waiting gave themselves up to grief in the most extravagant fashion, some of it, as she noted, most evidently in use for the occasion.

Shortly after the funeral service at Saint-Denis, Madame de

Sévigné left Paris to spend the autumn in Brittany, against the wishes and advice of all her friends, for Brittany was in revolt against authority; castles were pillaged, seigneurs were hanged, raids were made on government offices, the Governor was stoned, and the whole country was in inexpressible confusion and uproar. Indeed, said the Marquise, the whole province held the Governor, her good friend the Duc de Chaulnes, in unspeakable hatred. The poor ignorant Bretons, who did not know a word of any other language except their own patois, naturally enough blamed their Governor for the crushing taxes under which they groaned, and especially for a new tax on tobacco, which was the immediate cause of the rising. But Madame de Sévigné, more enlightened, knew that these taxes had year after year been augmented till they had grown unbearable, not by the Governor, but by the King, whose journeys, whose magnificent entertainments, whose palaces, whose vices of gambling and adultery, whose extravagance, in short, was a bottomless pit of expenditure, into which the funds of the nation continually disappeared. Brittany was ruined, said the Marquise. Of the "gift"—a gracious name for taxes—to be given to the King that year, they were nine hundred thousand francs short; and this general poverty and distress had a marked influence on Madame de Sévigné's own fortune. "The Abbé is continually counting," she told her daughter, "but we are not a penny the richer for all his reckoning." Tenants could not pay their rents, but the landlords had to find the money somehow, and the Marquise expresses her own indignation very forcibly. "Our gift to the King is increased, and I thought I should have beaten the honest Boucherat when I saw the augmentation . . . I do not see how we are to pay half of it. Rennes is like a desert; the punishments and taxes are unmerciful; I might write from this time till to-morrow if I were to repeat the tragic stories that I hear."

Some of the tragic stories she did relate, and she has sometimes been accused of indifference in speaking of the sufferings of the peasantry. But it is impossible not to understand the indignation which breaks out now and again, as she writes of the outrageous punishments that are being inflicted. "You perceive," she tells her daughter, "that I have grown quite

Bretonne, but you will understand that it is because of the air we breathe, and also due to something else, for everyone is affected. . . . Do you wish to know the news from Rennes? They have levied a tax of one hundred thousand crowns to be paid by the bourgeois, and if this is not done in twenty-four hours it will be doubled, and the soldiers will extort the payment. They have banished all the inhabitants of one big street, and have forbidden all the townspeople to receive them under pain of death; and one may see all those miserable creatures, old men, women who have been torn from a sick-bed, and young children, wandering in tears outside the town, not knowing where to go, or how they will find food, or where to sleep. The day before yesterday a pedlar was broken on the wheel; he had begun the dance with the pillage of the stamp-office. Sixty of the bourgeois have been arrested, and to-morrow they will begin the hangings. M. de Chaulnes has been received like the King, but it is only fear that has made them change their tone; and M. de Chaulnes does not forget all the shocking things they have said about him, of which the sweetest and most familiar was *gros cochon*, without counting the stones thrown at his windows and into his garden, and the threats, which God alone prevented from being put into execution."

The hangings did indeed go on, and what disgust and irony is in the letter of the Marquise in which she replies to her daughter's comments on affairs in Brittany. "You speak very pleasantly of our miseries. But we are no longer so much broken on the wheel as we were. Only one a week now, just to keep justice in practice. It is true, too, that mere hanging now seems a refreshing process. I have quite a new idea of justice since I have come here. Your galley-slaves seem to me to be a company of honest folk who have retired from the world to lead a peaceful life."

But the life at the chateau went on as usual, though few visits were paid or received, a melancholy contrast to her previous stay at Les Rochers in 1671, when day after day she was able to send to her daughter the chronicle of the feasting and gaieties of the States. In December, however, she had the pleasure of welcoming her son Charles, who had been campaigning in

Turenne's army, and who was now trying to get rid of his cornetcy. He had had no promotion for five years, and in disgust he wrote to his sister: "I am still a cornet, always a cornet, and shall be a cornet when my hair is grey."

His mother expected him at Les Rochers for some weeks before he appeared, but he was paying attention to a pretty abbess, and their first meeting, as described to her daughter, is so characteristic of both mother and son, that it deserves quotation. On December 4, 1675, she writes—

"As I was returning from my walk yesterday, I found *frater* at the end of the mall, who fell on his knees as soon as he saw me, feeling so culpable for having been singing matins for three weeks underground, that he thought he dared not approach me in any other fashion. I had resolved to scold him well, but I never know how to be angry with him; and I was heartily glad to see him, for you know how entertaining he is. He embraced me a thousand times, and gave me the worst reasons in the world, which, however, I accepted as perfectly good. We talk, we walk, we read, and so wear away the year, or at least what is left of it. We are determined to dispose of our wretched cornetcy as well as we can, if the King permit. . . ."

The only neighbour at this time, except the irritating Mademoiselle du Plessis, was the Princesse de Tarente, who lived at Vitré; who, said Madame de Sévigné, was very well in the country, though she should not enjoy her company greatly at Paris. It was from the Princesse that the Marquise had a charming little dog, of which she writes most whimsically to her daughter—

"Aux Rochers, *November* 13, 1675

". . . You are surprised to hear that I have a little dog; this is how it happened. One day I was calling a little dog which belongs to a lady who lives at the end of the park. Madame de Tarente said to me: 'What! do you like dogs? I will send you one of the prettiest you have ever seen.' I thanked her, and said that I had made a resolution never again to indulge myself in an affection of that kind; so the subject was dropped, and I thought no more of it. A few days after, I saw a footman bring a little dog-kennel, all decorated with ribbons, and out of this pretty kennel jumped a little perfumed dog, quite extraordinarily beautiful, with ears, coat, and sweet breath, like a little sylph, the fairest of the fair. I was never more surprised nor more embarrassed. I would have returned it, but the servant would not take it back; though the chambermaid who had reared it was fit to die with grief for the loss of it. It is Marie who is so fond of it; he sleeps in his kennel in Beaulieu's room, and eats nothing but bread. I try not to become too attached to it, but it begins to like me, and I am afraid I shall succumb to its affection. This is the story, which I beg you not to tell to Marphise [her pet dog] at Paris, for I dread her reproaches. But it is the cleanliest little animal you ever saw; its name is Fidèle, a name, I believe, that the lovers of the Princess have never deserved, though they have been of some importance. Some day I will amuse you with her adventures. Her style, it is true, is full of faintings, and I do not think she has had sufficient leisure to love her daughter, not at least as I love mine. More than one heart would be necessary to love so many things at once, and I perceive every day that the great fish eat up all the little ones. If you are, as you say, my preservative, I am very much obliged to you, and I cannot too highly prize the love I have for you. I do not know from what dangers it has guarded me, but if it were from fire or from water, it could not be dearer to me than it is."

CHAPTER XXVIII

The Marquise has an attack of rheumatic fever—She is tenderly nursed by her son and the Bien-Bon—Rival beauties at the Carmelites—The Marquise goes to Vichy for the waters—A coquette at the Baths two hundred years ago—Appalling remedies prescribed by physicians—The hanging of a countess

SOME of the most delightful pictures the Marquise gives of herself at Les Rochers, are those in which she describes her wanderings along her sunny walks or her musings in the shady allées. "I am always out of doors, like a wild man of the woods," she tells her daughter. "My health and vivacity depend so much on the weather, that in order to know how I am you have only to consult the stars." In November, again, she says—

"Our Saint Martin's summer still continues, and I take long walks; and as I do not use an easy-chair I repose my *corporea salma* at length in these avenues, where I spend whole days alone, attended by a single servant, and I do not return till almost night, when fire and candles make my room cheerful. I hate the twilight when I have no one to talk with; I would far rather be alone in the woods than alone in a room; this is what is called jumping into the water to get out of the rain, but I enjoy my solitude better than the weariness of an arm-chair. Do not be afraid of the night dews for me, my child, there are none in these old avenues; they are like galleries; fear nothing but heavy rains, for from them I am forced to flee indoors, and I can do nothing which does not injure my eyes. It is to preserve my sight that I brave what you call the night dews; but you need not fear for my health, it is perfectly good."

The Marquise had always delighted in going out in all weathers. In rain, in sunshine, in bitter frosts, she would be in the park and gardens when she was in Brittany, full of confidence in her magnificent health and constitution, which for nearly fifty years had scarcely caused her a day's uneasiness. But perhaps the Marquise did not pay the deference of precaution that time inexorably exacts, even from the most robust, for, some two months after that enjoyable Saint Martin's little summer, she one day found herself with a stiff neck and unable to move all her right side. Her son Charles, in much concern, brought a doctor from Vitré, who pronounced it to be an attack of rheumatic fever.

The affection that her children, the Abbé, the household, everyone, in fact, who came in close contact with this lovable woman, felt for her, was displayed at this crisis in every possible way; but the dominant thought was how to prevent Madame de Grignan from being alarmed, so that she in turn might not alarm her mother by her grief. It was at this time that Charles de Sévigné showed the most amiable and charming side of his character, his true affection for his sister, his loving thoughtfulness for his mother; indeed, as a son his tender devotion and graceful social gifts made him almost perfect; it was only as a man that he showed himself light-minded, weak, and frivolous, and lacking in the energy and ambition that would have delighted his mother, and which were necessary for him to make, or even fitly to hold, his place in the world.

On January 21, 1676, he writes to assure his sister—

" Begin, if you please, my dear little sister, by firmly believing everything that the good Abbé and I shall tell you to-day, and pray do not be alarmed if by chance you do not see my mother's handwriting. The swelling in her hands is still so much that we do not think it advisable to let them be exposed to the air, and another reason is that, since yesterday, which was the ninth day of the disease, the inflamed parts have begun to perspire. Do not imagine that we have not taken the utmost care of her, or that any precaution has been neglected. There is a very good physician at Vitré, who has bled her in the foot with perfect success; she is taken care of here as well as she could have been in Paris, and, what is even better, she herself thinks so. For the first illness she has ever had in her life it has been most severe and painful, but as it is almost a necessity to have some ailment this year, it is infinitely better for her to have had this rheumatism than inflammation of the lungs, which has been so prevalent. In short, every day we have some consolation in our sorrow, and we feel almost greater pleasure in seeing our mother's two hands packed up in cloths, and herself unable to stand, than we felt when we saw her walking and singing in our avenues from morning till night."

Not a word of his mother's delirium; scarcely a hint of the terrible pains by which the poor Marquise was racked; the report was designedly as favourable as possible, so that the Comtesse de Grignan, who loved her mother so dearly, should not be disturbed more than was absolutely necessary. The Comtesse had, at the time of Madame de Sévigné's illness, prematurely given birth to her youngest child, a little boy who died in 1677.

The Bien-Bon and his nephew Charles were so anxious on account of the two invalids, that they could not always agree as to the best method of lessening Madame de Grignan's fears for her mother. The Abbé declared that a few lines in the Marquise's handwriting, no matter how bad it might be, was necessary to reassure her daughter; "while I maintain," wrote the young Baron to his sister, "that it would be much more likely to frighten you, and that you will have done us the honour to believe what we have reported to you about her health, . . . you never could suspect me of being so callous as to write in a jesting strain at a time when I was threatened with the most dreadful calamity."

Mademoiselle du Plessis, too, the young lady who so annoys the Marquise by her persistent flattery of imitation, shows herself jealously anxious to do something to help the invalid, though in everything she attempts, according to Charles Sévigné, she makes ludicrous mistakes even in her best-intentioned efforts. There is a "little person," too, the daughter of a neighbouring lady, who is about fourteen, and so devoted to the Marquise that she weeps forlornly during her illness, and who, as soon as her help is required, makes herself useful in the sick-room, and as an amanuensis when the Baron is not there to write at his mother's dictation.

The object of all this care and affection found her illness a severe trial. After two months of pain she partially recovered, though her hands were still very swollen, and she was not able to write to her daughter for some time. Even when she was allowed to go into the gardens again, she was "ready to cry" at being obliged to leave her dear woods at five o'clock instead of wandering in them till nearly midnight, and she felt the humiliation keenly.

"Of all the maladies that could have befallen me," she tells her daughter, "I have had the least dangerous but the most painful, and the one most calculated to correct my pride, and to make me humble and apprehensive; for I would now run a hundred leagues to avoid such agony. But you, my dear child, who have suffered so much, and with so much courage, your resolution and endurance are greater far than mine; may your noble soul long remain united to your lovely body!"

The Marquise was able to return to Paris by the 8th of April, and the air did her good almost immediately; there was no air, she always declared, that suited her so well as that of the Île de France! But she was already thinking of taking the waters at Vichy or Bourbon, and she finally decided on Vichy. Her son had rejoined his regiment; and it was something of a wrench to leave the Bien-Bon alone, but the health of the Marquise was just then the first consideration, and in May she set out for Vichy in her big carriage, so as to be quite comfortable. As it happened, Madame de Montespan was just in front of her, on the way to Bourbon, and she gives a vivid little pen-picture of the lady's progress to her daughter, who, remembering the days when she had danced with Mademoiselle de Mortemart, would have a special interest in the doings of the haughty beauty.

"We closely follow the footsteps of Madame de Montespan," wrote the Marquise; "and at every place we are told what she said, what she did, what she ate and how she slept. She is in a carriage with six horses, and the little Thianges is with her; another carriage follows, drawn by the same number of horses, with six of her women in it; she has two sumpter waggons, six mules, and ten or twelve cavaliers on horseback, without reckoning her officers; her train consists of about forty-five people. She always finds her room and bed ready, and on her arrival she retires, and eats heartily. She gives away a good deal in charity, and throws a good many louis d'or about with a very good grace. She receives a courier from the army every day."

Only a week or two before this the Marquise had mentioned another little incident of which Madame de Montespan was the heroine; a meeting between two rivals, that, to those who know their history, covers a whole world of bitter humiliation and chagrin on one side, and on the other the ungenerous triumph of victorious beauty. It reminds one of the pregnant little speech of Louise de la Vallière, when she was thinking of entering the convent where she was now Sister Louise de la Miséricorde. "If at any time I think the hardships of the religious life too great to bear, I shall only have to remember what those two [the King and Madame de Montespan] have made me suffer!"

That the Queen should form one of the trio who met at the convent, gives an almost Oriental touch to the grotesque and infamous absurdity.

"The Queen has been twice to the Carmelites with Madame de Montespan. The latter took it into her head to have a lottery, and collected everything that could be useful to the nuns; which caused great amusement and interest in the convent. She talked a long time with Sister Louise de la Miséricorde, and asked her whether it was true that she was as happy there as people had said. 'No,' she replied, 'I am not happy, but I am contented.' Quanto spoke a great deal of the brother of Monsieur, and asked her if she had no message to send to him, and what she should say to him on her account. The other replied in the sweetest tone and manner possible, though perhaps she was a little piqued at the question, 'Whatever you please, Madame, whatever you please.' Imagine this being said with all the grace, wit, and modesty that you will remember.

"After this Quanto [Madame de Montespan] wished for something to eat, and she gave the Sisters four pistoles to purchase what was necessary for a sauce which she prepared herself, and ate with an excellent appetite. I tell you this exactly as it happened, without the least paraphrase."

But the Marquise has arrived at Vichy, where there are other

THE MARQUISE DE MAINTENON

THE MARQUISE DE MONTESPAN

scenes for her to describe; a romantic countryside, where she thinks the shepherds and shepherdesses of the novels of d'Urfé might be found if they were searched for; lads and lasses who dance in the evening; languishing beauties at the baths; old age hoping to find the sulphur springs the fountain of youth. In her own inimitable way she gives the vivid pen-pictures one after another, all taken down with a marvellous impressionism that preserves the society and surroundings of Vichy with the faithfulness of a photograph and the added grace of the selective artist-mind.

"*Wednesday, May* 20, 1676

"Well, I have taken the waters this morning, my dear, and how disagreeable they are! We go at six o'clock to the spring; everybody is there, and one drinks and makes wry faces, for, just imagine! the water is boiling hot and tastes strongly of saltpetre! We walk backwards and forwards, we come, we go, we promenade, we go to mass, we speak without hesitation of the effect of the waters. All this we do till noon. Then we dine, and after dinner we pay visits. To-day they came to see me. Madame de Brissac played at *ombre* with Saint-Hérem and Plancy; the Canoness and I read Ariosto; she is fond of Italian, and seems to like me very much; some girls of the neighbourhood came with a flute, and danced a *bourrée* delightfully. At five o'clock we take a walk in a delightful country, at seven we eat a light supper, and at ten we go to bed."

A few days later she continues the description—
"To-day I began the pump operation, and it is not a bad foretaste of purgatory. The patient is quite naked, in a little underground room where there is a tube of hot water which a woman directs wherever you wish. Behind a curtain is a person who sustains your courage for half an hour. A physician of Ganat fell to my lot; a very worthy man, who is neither a quack nor a bigot; I shall keep him though it cost me my cap, for the doctors here are unbearable, and this man amuses me; he has wit and honesty, and knows the world. He talked to me the whole time I was under torture. Just think of a spout of water

pouring over one or other of your poor limbs! It is first applied to every part of the body to rouse the spirits, and then to the affected joints; but when it comes to the nape of the neck, the heat produces such a surprise that it is impossible to describe it. However, it is necessary to suffer, and we do suffer, but we are not quite scalded to death; and we are then put into a warm bed, where we perspire profusely, and in this way we are cured. It is like taking a new lease of life and health, and if I could only see and embrace you once more, with a heart overflowing with tenderness and joy, you would perhaps again call me your *bellissima madre*, and I should not give up the title of *mère-beauté* with which M. de Coulanges has honoured me."

At Vichy Madame de Sévigné sees daily yet another of those charming beauties who some ten years before had danced in the famous *ballet royal* with her daughter. The Duchesse de Brissac was then Mademoiselle de Saint-Simon, and in the intervening years she had evidently learned how to use her beautiful eyes, and to display to the greatest advantage all her indisputable charms. Seeing this young beauty of the Baths, with her train of followers, the Marquise expressed a light regret that her daughter took no pains "to retain her power of making conquests," but at the same time she is amused and scornful at Madame de Brissac's transparent artifices to attract admiration.

"Madame de Brissac was ill to-day, and remained in bed, with her hair dressed so beautifully, and looking so handsome, that she was fit to turn everybody's head. I wish you could have seen how prettily she managed her sufferings, her eyes, her arms, and her cries, with her hands lying helplessly on the quilt, and looking for the sympathy she expected from all the bystanders. I was quite overcome with tenderness and admiration as I watched this little performance, and thought it so excellent that my evident attention must have given much satisfaction. Just think, this scene was played entirely on account of the Abbé Bayard, Saint-Hérem, Montjeu, and Plancy! My child, when I remember with what simplicity you are ill, and the calmness in your pretty face, you seem to me a mere bungler! What a difference! I found it very amusing."

Almost every day the Marquise writes to her daughter of

the society she is in. She describes Madame de Péquigny, the mother of the Duc de Chaulnes, an old lady of seventy-three, who is persuaded by her physicians that if she takes exactly the same remedies as Madame de Sévigné she will recover in the same way. At which the other doctors laugh, and the Marquise, conscious of being twenty years younger than Madame de Péquigny, laughs also.

The invalids dine informally at each other's houses, they gamble a little, and Madame de Sévigné often reads Italian; but what is most charming to the Marquise is the dancing, over which she is quite enthusiastic.

"My knees are quite cured," she tells her daughter, "and if I could only close my hands I should be perfectly well. . . . What most vexes me is that you cannot see the *bourrées* of this country; it is the most astonishing sight. The peasants, both men and women, keep time as truly as you do, with such lightness and agility that I am enchanted with them. I have a little band of music every evening which costs a mere trifle, and it is an absolute joy to see the last of the shepherds and shepherdesses of Lignon dancing in these lovely groves and meadows. It is impossible not to wish you were here, wise as you are, to witness these charming follies."

Then she gives one other brilliant little glimpse of Madame de Montespan, who is just going away from the neighbourhood to join the King.

"Madame de Montespan set out last Thursday from Moulins, in a boat which was beautifully painted and gilded, and decorated with crimson damask. It had been prepared for her by the Intendant, who had caused it to be ornamented with a great number of devices, and the colours of France and Navarre. Nothing could have been more splendid, and it could not have cost him less than a thousand crowns; but he was amply repaid by a letter which the fair one wrote to the King on the occasion, filled with a description of its magnificence. She would not be seen by the women, but the men got a glimpse of her under the shadow of the Intendant. She is gone down the Allier to meet the Loire at Nevers, which is to have the honour of conveying her to Tours."

Some days after this, the Marquise, who was very satisfied

with the effect of the waters of Vichy, returned to Paris by way of Vaux, where she expected to have a "couple of fresh eggs," as she says, and to see the beautiful fountains play. Foucquet's son, however, had heard of her intended visit, and had prepared a fine repast, but the fountains were broken and silent; "exactly the contrary to what I expected," she remarks. In trying to cure the remains of her rheumatism, the Marquise has revealed a good many of the absurd practices of the doctors of the day, who were all more or less charlatans, sometimes more ignorant of the science of medicine than the people they doctored. They bled their patients unmercifully, eight, ten, or twelve times, during an illness; often in spite of the poor victims' protests. When, in the September of this same year, Madame de Coulangès was very ill with fever, the Marquise, who frequently stayed with the invalid, looked on with disgust at their barbarous methods of healing, or rather killing. "The very sight of these gentlemen is enough to deter us from putting our poor bodies in their power," she says. "I have thought of Molière a hundred times since I have witnessed these scenes. . . . However, notwithstanding their vile treatment of her, I am not without hope that our poor friend may escape."

Madame de Coulanges did escape, almost miraculously, after her sufferings at the hands of her physicians, and she and the Marquise had a good deal of faith for some time in a handsome quack doctor named Amonio. He always spoke in Italian to the Marquise, and told her amusing stories; which were two great recommendations. "It was he who advised me to dip my hands in the wine-tubs during the vintage," she says; "and after that to use the stomach of an ox; and lastly, if there be occasion for it, the marrow of a deer with Hungary water."

Corbinelli, her friend the philosopher, was undergoing a course of "potable gold," of which it was said the foundation was muriatic acid, to which some grains of gold had been added, merely for the sake of giving it an impressive name which might justify its expense. But it was some years later, when the Marquise was suffering from a bruise on her leg which persistently refused to heal, that she tells her daughter of an extraordinary number of remedies which sound ludicrous to-day. She happened to be at Les Rochers, and near by, at Rennes, was a company of monks, called the Capuchins of the Louvre, who were said to perform miraculous cures. She sent for these Capuchins to attend her at Les Rochers, but they sent word back that, owing to their enemies, they dared not leave the monastery; they would, however, be happy to apply their remędies if she went to see them at Rennes. The Marquise consequently set out for Rennes in a coach-and-six, with her maid Marie and two footmen; and a few days after she sends to her daughter an account of their methods of healing.

They first bathed the wound with "arquebusade water"; then, she says, "I do not know whether the cure is performed by sympathy, but the wound is gradually growing better as the herbs with which it is dressed, and which are afterwards buried, rot in the ground. I was inclined to laugh at this, but the Capuchins tell me that every day they experience good effects from this practice."

When the wound apparently gets a little better, the monks give her some "essence of emeralds" to apply to it, which had probably nothing of emeralds about it except its name or its colour. But these Capuchins knew that there was a good deal in a name. For the Abbé's indigestion they ordered "powdered crabs' eyes" to be taken in a spoonful of milk. They also dispense "sympathetic powder," and a precious "serene balsam," of which the Marquise can only send her daughter half a bottle, as the Capuchins have no more of it.

Even the young Baron de Sévigné was affected with this rage for taking the Capuchins' medicines, and suggested to his sister a remedy for M. de Grignan, her brother-in-law, who was nearly a cripple with gout. "These viper medicines are excellent," he writes, "they temper and purify the blood, they refresh and invigorate, but they must be taken whole and not in powder. Ask M. de Boissi to send for ten dozen for you. Take two every morning, let their heads be cut off, then skin them and cut them in pieces, and with these stuff a chicken. Continue this for a month at least, and if M. de Grignan is not better, blame your brother."

The prescriptions at this period for moral ills were, like the remedies for physical ills, severe and brutal. When Madame de Sévigné was back again in Paris, after her course of the waters of Vichy, she found the whole town occupied with the trial of the Comtesse de Brinvilliers, who had poisoned her father, her brothers, and several other people. On the day of her execution Paris apparently turned out *en masse* to view the terrible sight, and the Marquise, with her friend M. d'Escars, went to the bridge of Notre Dame, where she waited to see the cart pass. Never was Paris in such a commotion, never was its attention so completely occupied by one thing, she says. "At length all is over, la Brinvilliers is in the air; after her execution, her poor little body was thrown into a large fire, and her ashes were dispersed by the wind; so that now, whenever we breathe, we shall inhale some particle of her, and by reason of these atoms we may all be infected with the desire of poisoning, to our own astonishment.... At six o'clock she was carried in a cart, with no other covering than one garment, with a cord round her neck, to the Church of Notre Dame, to perform the *amende honorable*; after which she was put again into the cart, where I saw her, with a confessor on one side and the hangman on the other. The sight made me shudder. She mounted the ladder and the scaffold alone, barefooted, and the executioner was a quarter of an hour dressing, shaving, and preparing her for execution. This caused a great murmur among the crowd, and was certainly cruel. The next day her bones were gathered up as relics by the people, who said she was a saint."

CHAPTER XXIX

The Marquise at Versailles—Madame de Montespan at cards with the King—
The Hôtel de Carnavalet—The reckless extravagance of the Grignans—A clever
stepmother—A sarcastic letter

THE Marquise did not often go to the "wicked court," as she frequently called it to her daughter, but when she did occasionally go she sent to the Comtesse in Provence the most lively descriptions of what she heard and saw. For some years the King had been enlarging and beautifying Versailles, and though it was not yet finished, nor in its full splendour, it was so different from the time when she and her daughter had gone there together, that she gives the latter a minute and brilliant description of what passes in this changed Versailles. Things are no longer as they were when Mademoiselle de Sévigné danced in the *ballet royal*. The young Queen, under the protection of Anne of Austria, had then a semblance at least of power; Madame de la Vallière was her rival, it is true, but unrecognised and ashamed of her position; and Mademoiselle de Mortemart was a haughty young beauty, with no special position at Court. Now, however, Louise de la Vallière is among the Carmelites, hoping to atone for her sins by a life of rigid devotion, while the brilliant brunette, Madame de Montespan, is the veritable Queen of France, with the nominal Queen for her admiring friend.

"PARIS, *July* 29, 1676

"We have here, my dear, a change of scene which will appear as agreeable to you as it does to everyone else. On Saturday I was at Versailles with the Villars, and this is what happened. You know the ceremony of attending the Queen at her toilet, at mass, and at dinner; but there is no longer any necessity for being stifled while their Majesties are at table, for at three o'clock the King and Queen, Monsieur and Mademoiselle, the Princes and Princesses, Madame de Montespan and her train, all the courtiers, all the ladies, in fact, the whole Court of France, go to that fine apartment of the King's which you know. It is furnished most beautifully, most magnificently; they do not know what it is to be inconvenienced by the heat, and are able to pass from one room to another without being crowded. A game of *reversis* gives form to the assembly, and settles everything. The King and Madame de Montespan keep a bank together. Monsieur, the Queen, and Madame de Soubise are at one table, Dangeau and Langlée, with their companies, are at other tables. The baize is covered with a thousand louis d'or; they use no other counters. I saw Dangeau play, and I could not help observing how foolish we other people appeared by comparison. He thinks of nothing but his game, and gains where others lose. He seizes every advantage; he profits by everything; nothing distracts him, his close attention defies fortune. Thus two hundred thousand francs in ten days, a hundred thousand crowns in a month, are added to his book of receipts. He said that I was his partner in the game, and as a result I was seated agreeably and comfortably. I bowed to the King in the way you taught me, and he returned my salutation as politely as if I had been young and pretty. The Queen talked to me a long time about my illness, and she also spoke to me of you. Monsieur de Lorges attacked me in the name of the Chevalier de Grignan; and, in short, *tutti quanti*, you know what it is to receive a word from everyone who passes. Madame de Montespan talked to me of Bourbon, and asked me to tell her how I liked Vichy, and whether it did me any good. She said that Bourbon, instead of curing her knee, had given her a pain in both. I saw that her back was very flat, as Madame de la Meilleraye had told me; but seriously, her figure is as surprising as her beauty, she is not half so stout as she was, and yet neither her complexion, eyes, nor lips have suffered in the least. Her dress was entirely of French point-lace, her hair was in a thousand curls, and the two from her temples hung very low on the cheeks; her head-dress was composed of black ribbons, intermingled with the valuable pearls that once belonged to the Maréchale de l'Hôpital, some exquisite diamond pendants, and three or four bodkins; in fact, she was a triumphant beauty, and the admiration of all the foreign ambassadors.

"She has heard that people complained of her having prevented all France from seeing the King; she has restored him, as you see, and you cannot imagine the delight this has occasioned, nor the splendour it has given to the Court. This agreeable confusion without confusion of all the principal people in the kingdom lasted from three o'clock till six. If any couriers arrive, the King retires to read his letters and then returns. Music is played continually, to which he listens, and which has a very good effect. He speaks to those ladies who are accustomed to have that honour. They leave off their game at the hour I mentioned without the trouble of reckoning, because they use no counters or marks, and the pools are of five, six, or seven hundred louis d'or.

"At six o'clock they took the air in *calèches*; the King and Madame de Montespan, Monsieur and Madame de Thianges, who had the good d'Heudicourt upon the box-seat, which to her is a place of paradise. The Queen was in another with the Princesses, and the whole Court followed in different equipages according to their different fancies. They went on the canal in gondolas, where they heard music; they returned at ten for the comedy; at midnight they finished with the *media noche*; and this is how Saturday passed.

"If I were to tell you how many times people spoke to me of you; how many inquired after you, how many asked questions without waiting for an answer, how many I neglected to answer; how little they cared and how much less I did; you would recognise that I have given a very natural description of the *iniqua corte*. However, it never was so agreeable, and everyone wishes it may continue."

Madame de Sévigné for many years cherished the hope that M. de Grignan might some day obtain a place at Court; but the Comtesse was not desirous of returning to Paris to live. She had known the Court well, from the time that, as a girl of sixteen, she had been taken there by her mother, till she married, at the age of twenty-three; and she well knew its intrigues, its jealousies, its falsities, and the worth of its most brilliant successes. Sometimes she vexed her mother by declaring that she preferred her position as wife of the Vice-Governor of Provence, and undoubtedly she was of infinitely more importance there, where she was received like a queen whenever she went to the States with her husband to the cities of Aix, Marseilles, or Lambesc. When the Marquise visited her daughter, she was obliged to confess that life could not be pleasanter anywhere than in the beautiful Château de Grignan, where, besides the family of the Comte and Comtesse, there were relatives of M. de Grignan in the neighbourhood, and a constant succession of pleasant guests.

Madame de Sévigné's chief complaint against Providence was that she and her daughter were obliged to live so far apart from each other. "Search the Court," she says, "and you will not find a mother who loves her daughter as I love you, and is compelled to live away from her." The obvious solution of the difficulty would have been for the Marquise to have shut up her house in Paris, and to have gone to live at the Château de Grignan. But here came the question of her duty to the Bien-Bon; and, just as she had stayed in Paris to nurse her aunt, the Marquise de la Trousse, she now felt it her duty to make her home with the Abbé as long as he lived, though her heart was always yearning to be with her daughter. In 1676, Madame de Grignan stayed for a year with her mother, and the following year, when Madame de Sévigné thought of moving to a larger house, so that Madame de Grignan might have more room and conveniences for her household on her next visit, she heard of the Hôtel de Carnavalet, a large and handsome mansion in the Marais quarter, which they agreed to take jointly; and d'Hacqueville, the always good and obliging d'Hacqueville, was commissioned to secure it. "I think it will be equally convenient for both of us," the Marquise tells her daughter, "as well as saving a great deal of trouble in looking farther. People who live in the same house have certain hours morning and evening, that are lost in the hurry and bustle of visits. We shall be very well accommodated there; and nothing looks better, or is more economical for us, than to live in the same house."

The Hôtel de Carnavalet is still standing, in good repair, and is one of the few large mansions of that district that have been spared in a practically unchanged condition. It is now the

Municipal Museum of Paris, but it is not difficult to imagine all the memorials of bygone Paris swept away, and the households of Madame de Sévigné and of Madame de Grignan installed in its rooms. One "cabinet" on the first floor is still pointed out as that belonging especially to the Marquise. It was here that she wrote her letters; on the wall is Mignard's beautiful portrait of her daughter, and another of herself; and the adjoining room is said to have been occupied by her daughter, so that these two had the delight of frequent and uninterrupted intercourse. The ground-floor was reserved for Monsieur de Grignan and his two daughters by his first wife, the young girls who till then had been educated in a convent in Paris; there was also an *appartement* for the Bien-Bon; and as one wanders from room to room of the mansion, one understands how even the large, combined households could be accommodated without the least crowding.

The Hôtel de Carnavalet is eloquent of the sixteenth century, when it was built. There are fine spacious rooms, some of which have big oaken rafters; the fireplaces are cavernous, some of the floors are of stone, and there is one, at least, of the charming old wooden staircases, with wide shallow steps, in short easy flights, that were there in the time of the Marquise. The exterior, too, is very handsome, and of a style unusual in French architecture. There are fine sculptures, said to be by the famous Jean Goujon; and the building has such a magnificent effect from the courtyard, that one can quite readily enter into the satisfaction of the Marquise at having secured such a handsome and convenient dwelling.

"It is an admirable place," she tells her daughter; "there is room for all of us, and it is in a healthy situation. As one cannot have everything, we must be satisfied without parquet floors, and the small mantelpieces that are now so fashionable. But we shall at least have a fine courtyard, a large garden, and be in the best quarter of the town."

How that last little phrase of satisfaction reminds us of the inevitable ebb and flow of fashion as Time silently and relentlessly pursues its work of eternal change! The Hôtel de Carnavalet is now in the midst of a congeries of old-world, evil-smelling streets, in whose decayed and rickety tenements the poorest citizens of Paris seek a shelter, a *terra incognita* to most of those who live in the now fashionable parts of the town. But we know that it was a "select neighbourhood" in the seventeenth century. The great Hôtel de Lamoignon, now a factory, is only a few paces away; and the Place Royale, or rather the Place des Vosges, may be seen from its windows; and in Madame de Sévigné's day the brown, narrow streets were brilliant with the life and colour, the comings and goings of the fashionable world: sumpter-mules, litters, negro pages carrying the trains of Mesdames the wives of men of the law; big glass coaches conveying beauties and their cavaliers to or from Court gaieties; flambeaux, lantern-bearers, men of the watch; with the under-current of clamorous street-hawkers, artisans, and the loathsome beggars whose haunts were near-by in that dreadful stronghold of thieves and mendicants and street-assassins, the rue des Francs-Bourgeois.

In the early summer of 1677, Madame de Sévigné, whose hands were not yet quite free from rheumatism, again visited the baths of Vichy, and on her return to Paris she went to the house of the Coulanges, where she stayed while her people were moving into the Hôtel de Carnavalet. Emmanuel de Coulanges gives a brilliant little description of his cousin, who had evidently benefited by the waters. The Marquise was then just over fifty, and was said by others, as well as her cousin, to be still very handsome.

"We have her back at last, that incomparable *mère-beauté*," he writes, "she is more incomparable, and more beautiful than ever. Do you think that she was tired when she arrived? Do you think that she stayed in bed to rest? Nothing of the kind. She did me the honour to alight at my house, looking handsomer, younger, more radiant than I can describe; and though since then she has been continually occupied, this does not injure her health in the least. As for her mind, it is with us, only to talk of that rare Comtesse in Provence."

All October, Madame de Sévigné was eagerly preparing the rooms of the Carnavalet mansion for her daughter, whom she was expecting on a visit in November. She tells her she need not bring any tapestries with which to decorate the rooms, as she has sufficient. She mentions, too, that the house is in such a state of chaos that she was obliged to receive the Princesse de

AN OVER-ANXIOUS MOTHER 285

Tarente and the Rochefoucaulds in the courtyard, on the pole of her carriage.

When the Comtesse did arrive, early in November, the joy of welcoming her was mingled with much grief to see her daughter so thin and delicate. The Comtesse intended to stay a year with her mother, but when, after having been away from her husband a year and a half, she declared she must go, the Marquise complained almost querulously to Bussy, " I wish my daughter could stay with me all the summer; I think it would be good for her health, but she reasons somewhat severely, and prefers her duty to her life." As usual, however, the Marquise gained her point, and, notwithstanding the natural objections of the Comte de Grignan, and her daughter's ideas of wifely duty, the Comtesse was induced to stay till September 1679, an almost two years' separation from her husband.

Strangely enough, the mother who always wanted to have her daughter with her, and the daughter who loved her mother with more than ordinary filial affection, did not always agree very well when they were together. The very excess of Madame de Sévigné's love made her over-anxious concerning her daughter, it caused her also to shrink from a hasty word, or to be wounded to the heart by some unconscious or thoughtless remark; and then there were tears, reproaches, repentance, and reconciliation. The Comtesse, whose nature it was to be much more reserved, much less expansive in the expression of her affection, frequently thus grieved her mother, though one cannot believe that she was entirely to blame. Charles de Sévigné on one such occasion, when the mother and daughter had so jarred on each other that it had seriously affected the latter's health, wrote these kindly, sensible words, which really contained a lesson to both. While he was an invalid, home from the army with a wound in his heel, he described to his sister the care he and his mother took of each other, without either inflicting the least suffering, or wounding unconsciously by an exaggerated affection.

" We take care of each other," he says. " We allow ourselves, however, an honest liberty; no little, womanish remedies. ' You seem to be in good health, my dear mother. I am delighted to see you so well. You slept well last night? How is your head? No giddiness? God be praised. You must go out to-day; go to Saint-Maur; sup with Madame de Schomberg; take a walk in the Tuilleries, you have nothing to prevent you. I give you full liberty to do as you please. Will you have strawberries or tea? Strawberries are best. . . . Adieu, my dear mother; my heel is painful. I shall stay with you from twelve till three, and then we can each do as we wish.' This, my dear sister, is the way in which reasonable people behave."

There were, however, more than imaginary troubles hanging over the Grignans, and, by reflection, over the Marquise, for ever since their marriage in 1669 the Comte and Comtesse had been living at a ruinously extravagant rate. They had gambled from the beginning, and Madame de Sévigné was constantly warning them of what the result would be. "My hair stood on end," she exclaimed, "when the Coadjutor told me that the other day at six he saw M. de Grignan playing at *hoca*! What madness! In the name of God, do not allow it."

Play, however, was only one item, though not a small one, in their expenses. M. de Grignan, aided by his brothers, had been making additions and improvements to the Castle, and in answer to one of her daughter's letters, Madame de Sévigné gives a glimpse of the luxury and ostentation which kept the Grignans for ever on the verge of bankruptcy.

"You describe Grignan to me as being surprisingly beautiful; well, am I to blame when I say that M. de Grignan, with all his mildness, does exactly as he pleases? In vain we cried out 'Poverty.' The furniture, pictures, and chimney-pieces, all went on at the same rate, and I do not doubt that everything is as complete as possible. That is not what we object to, but where did he find the money for this? He certainly must study the black art!"

It seemed impossible for these extravagant people to economise in anything. They kept fifty servants, and, says the Marquise, "we had some trouble in counting them all"; and even on those days when they were dining quietly, a hundred people sat down to dinner! The only economy they practised was apparently that of placing their poor baby Blanche in a convent to save her dower; and had it not been for Madame de Sévigné's repeated persuasions, the charming little Pauline would have been sacrificed also. But the Marquise, who pleaded so successfully for one of her little granddaughters, had nothing to say except in approval when Mademoiselle de Grignan, the eldest daughter of the Comte, was declared to have a "vocation" for the religious life.

The two demoiselles de Grignan had each inherited large fortunes from their mother, who had been a daughter of Madame de Rambouillet. But during their minority their father, who was always plunged in debt, had borrowed large sums from their inheritance, and as they grew up it probably began to be a disturbing question as to how this money was to be refunded. When the eldest, Colette, as they called her, showed signs of a "vocation," it seemed to those so nearly concerned a particularly lucky stroke of fortune. When she eventually decided to live the life of a nun at the Feuillantines, she gave all her possessions to her father; and to her sister, Mademoiselle d'Alerac, who, her mother's family thought, should naturally have profited by the elder's renunciation, she gave nothing.

This is the most unfortunate episode with which Madame de Sévigné was ever connected. She is hardly her own upright, honest self on the occasion. Her love for her daughter so blinded her that she actually boasted of Madame de Grignan's influence in bringing this affair to such a successful issue. "My daughter," she says, "has so effectually contributed to this little manœuvre, that it affords her a double satisfaction. The Chevalier de Grignan has also done marvels." When, some years later, she blamed herself for calmly looking on at wrong-doing by those she loved, when she should have protested, was she thinking, one wonders, of how Mademoiselle d'Alerac was despoiled of her natural inheritance? The cynical Bussy, who could analyse so clearly the interested motives of others by reason of his own baseness, was lightly ironical on the occasion, and even gives Madame de Grignan the credit, which she may not have deserved, of fostering the religious aspirations of her stepdaughter.

"You have given me much pleasure, my dear cousin, by telling me of the care the Belle Madelonne has taken to inspire noble sentiments in her stepdaughter, and the happy results of her efforts. I am not surprised, for is it possible to refuse anything to Madame de Grignan? I am delighted, and so also is my daughter, who adds that God has granted her a great favour in not having given her such a stepmother, for, had this been the case, she would, without doubt, now be in a convent, and for that she feels very little inclination."

And for once it is possible to approve cordially of the Comte's ironical comments.

CHAPTER XXX

The Marquise visits Les Rochers with the Bien-Bon—The rough roads of Brittany—Madame de Grignan comes to Paris for a long stay—Company at the Hôtel de Carnavalet—The marriage of Charles de Sévigné—The death of the Bien-Bon in 1687

THE rising in Brittany in 1675 had been a disastrous affair for the province, and in the years that followed, the Marquise, like other landowners, found incredible difficulty in collecting her rents and other dues·; consequently, in 1680, the good Abbé de Coulanges, who had watched over her interests so long, decided that her presence at Les Rochers was absolutely necessary if she meant to recover what was due to her. The Marquise was now beginning to find that she was considerably less wealthy than formerly. Owing to bad times her property had yielded much less, while both her son and her daughter, in their thoughtless extravagance, had made frequent calls on their mother's purse. The Abbé, who was then seventy-three, set out from Paris with Madame de Sévigné in May, and as they travelled from one estate to another they found her affairs in terrible confusion. The Marquise, in a letter to her daughter from Nantes, gives a little idea of the miserable state into which things had fallen.

"I am here," she says, "in the midst of the worry of the accounts for nineteen years, which my son had merely glanced over. They try to make some of my letters pass for receipts; it is pitiful to see the mean subterfuges of a bad debtor. We are going to settle everything. We hope to recover certain fines from some lands belonging to us, but we want two thousand francs immediately. We have plenty of advisers; the only thing that vexes me is being obliged to distress anyone. But I am playing a desperate game, and when I play at drowning and ask who shall be drowned, M. de la Jarie or myself, I say, without hesitation, M. de la Jarie, and that gives me courage."

It was a rather melancholy journey for the Marquise, and it must have been exceedingly painful to the Abbé de Coulanges, with his positive passion for finding and keeping accounts in good order. The Marquise puts some of her melancholy into another letter, written at Nantes on her way to Les Rochers. "I was yesterday at Buron, and came here this evening. I thought I should have wept when I saw the desolation of the place. Those woods used to be the oldest in the world, and my son, in his last journey here, caused the trees to be felled; he even wished to sell a little copse which was the greatest ornament that remained. He received four hundred pistoles for this, of which not one penny remained a month after. It is impossible not to be annoyed with him; he has found out the art of spending a great deal of money without making any display; of losing without playing; of paying his debts without discharging them. In peace or war he is for ever demanding money; he is a perpetual drain, and what he does with his money I cannot think, for he seems to have no particular fancy for anything. But his hand is a crucible in which money melts."

The Marquise had, however, recovered from this sad mood by the time they reached Les Rochers, for on the 31st of May, the morning after her arrival, she gives her daughter a very gay description of the difficulties they found in traversing the four short miles between Vitré and Les Rochers. The Duc de Chaulnes had been making good roads between Rennes and Nantes, but in the less frequented ways, heavy rains made travelling in the country a serious business, as the Marquise and her uncle proved.

"LES ROCHERS, *May* 31, 1680

"We arrived at Rennes on the Eve of Ascension Day, and that good Marbœuf was fit to devour me, and greatly wished me to stay at her house, but I would neither sup nor sleep there. The next day she gave me a grand breakfast-dinner, at which the Governor, and every person of quality in the town, came to see me. We set out again at ten o'clock, though everyone said there was plenty of time, for the roads were 'just like this room,' which is always the comparison; but the roads were so much 'like this room' that we did not get here till midnight; and all the time were nearly up to our axle-trees in water. From Vitré here, a road which I have travelled a thousand times, the place was entirely unrecognisable. The causeways were impassable; the ruts were sunk to a frightful depth; the little inequalities in the road were higher and deeper than they were; and therefore, seeing that we could no longer find our way, we sent to Pilois for help. He soon came, bringing with him about a dozen country-men, some of whom held up the carriage, while others went in front with wisps of lighted straw, and all talking in their Breton jargon, which made us fit to die with laughing. By the help of that illumination we arrived here, our horses jaded, our people dripping with water, our carriage broken, and ourselves tired out."

While the Marquise was at Les Rochers, engaged with the Abbé in the sorry business of trying to get her arrears paid, she took her usual walks among her avenues and woods, and, as always, was thinking of her daughter. This time she was indulging in a pleasant little day-dream. The young Duc de Vendôme, now grown to manhood, talked of taking up his position as Governor of Provence, and M. de Grignan was making arrangements for resigning the office of Vice-Governor, which he had held with so much magnificence and expense for ten years. Madame de Sévigné was delighted at the prospect. After this long period of waiting it now seemed probable that she would at last have her dear daughter back again with her in Paris. There was the serious question of an appointment for M. de Grignan, it is true; but when, while at Les Rochers, she heard of the death of Sanguin, the chief *maître-d'hôtel* to the King, his seemed to her exactly the post that would suit M. de Grignan, with his good manner and imposing figure; and, as she told her daughter, "it was the only position in which they would be able to re-establish their fortunes, and at the same time live as well as the King."

It was a charming prospect, for Madame de Sévigné had not yet lost the hope of seeing her daughter again at Court, and some day, perhaps, who could tell? Madame la Duchesse de Grignan. It was nothing but a day-dream, however, for the Comte de Grignan still kept his place as Vice-Governor of Provence, though the Duc de Vendôme came that year of 1680 to open the States in person. One part of the dream came true, nevertheless, for in November of that same year Madame de Grignan came to stay at the Hôtel de Carnavalet, and there made her home for the next eight years, during which time M. de Grignan came from Provence when he could be spared from his duties as Vice-Governor. There were probably various reasons for this arrangement. Madame de Grignan, during her stay in Paris, went several times to Versailles, and asked from the King—and received—large sums of money for the expenses which her husband had incurred in the King's service. It was probably, also, much less expensive for the Comtesse to be living quietly at Paris with her mother, than to be keeping up the ruinous state of Madame la Gouvernante de Provence at Aix, Lambesc, Marseilles, or even in her own chateau at Grignan. But whatever the reasons may have been, Madame de Sévigné had an intense satisfaction in the arrangement ; and she herself writes how happy she felt in having the daily delight of her daughter's society. With this prospect so near, she did not stay longer at Les Rochers than was necessary. Her son Charles was in Brittany, but he was not often at Les Rochers; he was still living a life that was far from satisfactory to his mother or profitable to himself. He was trying to sell his commission, but his mother warned him that their circumstances would not allow him to sell it at a loss. There had been several projects for his marriage, but they had all fallen through, and the Marquise was no longer in a position to settle him so advantageously, nor able to satisfy the demands of the possible father-in-law, as she had been ten years before, at the time of her daughter's marriage.

She and the Abbé stayed for five months at Les Rochers, and during this visit she had the words *soli Deo honor et gloria* graven in letters of gold over the high altar of her chapel, words which, as she remarked, would make no one jealous. It was a kind of confession of faith, the result of her ripe understanding and experience, for the absurd differences of Jansenists and Jesuits revolted her wise heart and mind, and appealed to her quick sense of humour, which so readily saw the weak side of each. It was at this time she praised the Sisters of the Visitation at Rennes for their single-minded piety, their good lives, and their freedom from the grosser superstitions. " M. de Grignan," she wrote to her daughter, " would call them Jansenists, but, for my part, I call them good Christians."

In October she returned to Paris and busied herself in preparing her daughter's rooms. Madame de Grignan, so used to every luxury in Provence, could not endure the thought of the big, old-fashioned fire-places, nor the unfashionable stone floors; and the Marquise before her departure from Paris had arranged that these should be altered. "They are working at your suite of rooms," she writes; "everything is arranged; the partitions, the mantelpiece, the parquet of the bedroom, and the windows"; and by the time Madame de Grignan arrived in Paris at the latter end of November, everything in her rooms was probably as nearly perfect as the loving care of her mother could make it.

It is pleasant to know that for nearly four years, from 1680 to 1684, Madame de Sévigné enjoyed a period of almost uninterrupted happiness with her daughter, and that the Hôtel de Carnavalet was a centre of much interesting society. The great mansion was so well occupied by members of her family and intimate friends, that, when she is writing to the President Moulceau, she says she must go from apartment to apartment to collect "kind remembrances" to send to him. In addition to their own large family, there was the philosopher Corbinelli, who often paid long visits, sometimes staying for a year at a time. Mademoiselle de Méri, too, the daughter of her aunt the Marquise de la Trousse, frequently had rooms at the Carnavalet mansion; and there were, besides, almost daily visitors driving into the great courtyard with a resounding clatter and pleasant bustle. The Duc and Duchesse de Chaulnes, who had had such a warm friendship for Madame de Sévigné ever since they became so intimate at the Brittany States in those bright days of 1671, were frequent visitors; and the ailing Madame de la Fayette, who loved the Marquise better than anyone in the world, came often to see her dear friend, who consoled and comforted her as well as she was able after the death of the Duc de la Rochefoucauld; the witty and vivacious little Madame de Coulanges would bring the latest story from Court, or the news that Madame de Maintenon now stood better than ever with the King, who conversed with her seriously every day for quite two hours! And this intelligence was of tremendous import to the Marquise and her daughter, both of whom vaguely and vainly hoped so much from favour at Court.

There were bright little suppers too, when the President Lamoignon and his wife would step across from their own great mansion, which was only a few paces away; when the witty little Emmanuel de Coulanges would make the evening brilliant with his jests and stories and sparkling repartee; when the beautiful Comtesse would entertain the fashionable young men from Court—and even now the hospitable mansion is not so altered that one cannot picture its rooms aglow with great fires on the cavernous hearths, and brilliant with candles on festive evenings; the coming and going of guests, the stir of lackeys and waiting-women; and, above all, the Marquise, still the *mère-beauté*, with her gracious, cordial manner, her social gift of making each of her guests feel happy and especially welcome, and intensely happy herself because of the daily presence of her idolised daughter.

In 1683, Madame de Sévigné experienced a fresh satisfaction in hearing that her son Charles, who had left the army, and had been for some time living in Brittany, was on the point of marriage with a young lady of his own province, Mademoiselle de Brehant de Mauron, the daughter of the Baron de Mauron, conseiller au Parlement de Bretagne. The Marquise reveals a good deal of her satisfaction in writing the news to her cousin Bussy.

"My son is in Brittany," she says, "and on the point of marrying a young woman of noble family whose father is a counsellor in Parlement, with an income of more than sixty thousand a year. He gives his daughter two hundred thousand francs; and, as times go, this is an excellent match. . . . We should never despair of good fortune. I thought my son's situation quite hopeless, after so many storms and shipwrecks, without employment, and out of Fortune's way; and while I was

THE MARQUISE DE SÉVIGNÉ
FROM A PORTRAIT AT VERSAILLES

indulging in these melancholy reflections, Providence had destined for us such an advantageous marriage that I could not have wished for a better. It is thus that we grope in the dark, taking good for evil and evil for good in utter ignorance."

There were some difficulties with the prospective father-in-law. He knew that Madame de Sévigné had given more than forty thousand crowns to her daughter since her marriage, in addition to her wedding portion, and he now desired some security that Charles de Sévigné should have fair treatment in the matter of sharing his mother's fortune. It was then that the generous Marquise showed herself to be a good *mère de famille*, by stripping herself of almost everything to ensure her children's happiness. She made over to her son the chief part of her property to satisfy M. de Mauron's demands, leaving herself only a very small life-annuity, in case the Baron should die before she did. To her daughter she gave her castle of Bourbilly, on account of what still remained unpaid of her *dot*; and this good mother, who a few years ago had been so wealthy, had now scarcely anything left of all her possessions.

All this had not been done without some irritation and ill-feeling on both sides. M. de Mauron resented Madame de Sévigné's too evident preference for her daughter when it was expressed by giving her material advantages over his future son-in-law, and in downright Breton fashion he did not hesitate to say so; at which Madame la Comtesse de Grignan declared herself insulted; and the Marquise, whether in right or wrong, was always on her daughter's side, and had evidently shown annoyance to the Baron, who, in spite of his failures in every other direction, had always been such a loving and devoted son. A letter to his mother on the occasion reveals something of the friction that the marriage had caused.

"My heart is heavy when you speak of your room at Les Rochers as your former room. Have you then given it up entirely, my very dear Madame? Will you then have no more intercourse with your son after having done so much for him? Will you deprive him of your company, and punish him as if he had failed in everything he owes you? My marriage could not compensate for this misfortune, and I love you a thousand times better than anything in the world. Write and tell me, I beg of you, something concerning this, for in truth my heart is so full, that if there were not just now some people in my room I could not refrain from weeping. Good-bye, my dear Madame ; do not renounce your son ; he adores you, and wishes you all happiness with as much sincerity as he hopes for his own salvation."

Madame de Sévigné loved her son too well to renounce him, but neither she nor his sister was present at the wedding, which was quite an event in the neighbourhood. It was solemnised at Rennes on the 8th of February 1684, and two days later the young Baron and his wife drove to Les Rochers, with a procession of carriages in which were a number of the bride's friends following them from Rennes. Many of the nobility in the neighbourhood of Les Rochers came out to meet them on horseback or in carriages, and at the chateau they were received by a thousand armed vassals, the honour that the Baron had missed some twelve years before because of the Abbé's forgetfulness.

In the September of that same year the Marquise paid a visit to her newly-married son, taking with her, as usual, the Bien-Bon, who never liked to be long away from his niece. Madame de Sévigné wrote to her daughter her first impressions of her daughter-in-law soon after her arrival. "We lead a very dull life here," she tells her; "my daughter-in-law has few moments of gaiety; she is overwhelmed with the vapours, and her expression changes a hundred times a day, yet she never looks well. She is extremely delicate, and scarcely ever goes out of doors ; she is always cold, and by nine o'clock at night she is exhausted."

It was not an attractive portrait, but the Marquise could never be long with anyone without drawing forth or discovering their good points, and she soon began to find that this delicate, cold, sad little wife was a very good woman, wishing to be loved by her mother-in-law, and by the beautiful Comtesse of whom she must have heard a great deal. She proved an excellent wife for the Baron, and was so devout that, under her influence, his thoughts turned to religion, and many years later they ended their lives in a religious retreat in Paris.

After a year's absence from her daughter, the Marquise returned to the Hôtel de Carnavalet again in 1685, and two years later the good Abbé de Coulanges died at the age of eighty; and she writes to her cousin Bussy with grateful recollection of the kindness, the good training, the tender care she had received from him, ever since, on that fortunate day for her, she became his ward.

"You know," she says, "that I was under infinite obligations to my dear uncle the Abbé. It was to him that I owed the comfort and happiness of my life; it is to him you owe the pleasure you have had in my society; but for him, we should never have laughed together. You are indebted to him for all my gaiety, my good-humour, my vivacity, the gift of sympathising with you, the intelligence which made me understand what you had said, and what you were going to say; in short, the good Abbé, in drawing me from the abyss in which I was left at the death of M. de Sévigné, made me what I was, and what you have seen me—worthy of your friendship and esteem. I draw a veil over your wrongs; they are indeed great, but I must forget them, and tell you how keenly I have felt the loss of this beneficent source of all the happiness of my life. He died after a fever of seven days, like a young man with the most Christian sentiments, which touched me deeply, for God has given me principles of religion which made me able to view properly this last scene of his life. His life had lasted for eighty years; he lived in honour, and died as a Christian; God grant that we may do the same. It was towards the end of August that I mourned his loss. I should never have left him, had he lived as long as I myself, but about the middle of September, finding myself only too free, I determined to go to Vichy to cure my imagination, at least, of a kind of vapours."

CHAPTER XXXI

The young Marquis de Grignan at Philipsburg—Madame de Sévigné at the performance of *Esther* by the young ladies of Saint-Cyr—Her last visit to Les Rochers—The marriage of the Marquis de Grignan—The marriage of Pauline—The death of Madame de Sévigné

NOW that the good Abbé de Coulanges was dead, and the Baron de Sévigné married, the Marquise was, if possible, more than ever devoted to Madame de Grignan and her family. Madame de Sévigné declared that she was "steeped" in Grignans, and it is evident from her correspondence that the smallest event that happened to any of the Grignans was full of interest for her, even when it merely concerned the brothers or the sister of her son-in law.

The year following the death of the Abbé de Coulanges, Madame de Grignan left Paris after a stay of eight years, and returned to her home in Provence, just at the time that her only son, the young Marquis de Grignan, went to his first campaign. Louis XIV, who for years had been making war on Holland and other countries of Europe, often for mere vanity and the display of his prowess, now found himself at war with all the neighbouring countries. The revocation of the Edict of Nantes had aroused much indignation, and the valiant Prince of Orange was taking up the cause of the Protestants.

Louis Provence, the young Marquis de Grignan, was only sixteen, but boys as well as girls began life early in those robust days, and his mother had carefully chosen and equipped a company for him, in her own clever and determined fashion. The little captain was sent to the siege of Philipsburg, and was under fire just as the Comtesse was on her way to Provence, in the October of 1688.

Madame de Sévigné, judging of her daughter's anxiety by her own, remained in Paris, and sent word to her daughter all the news she could gather of the young Marquis, and every detail that she heard from others of what was passing in the camp; and in answer to her daughter's overwhelming maternal fears, she tells her that "all the good women of Paris who have husbands, brothers, sons, cousins, or what you please, engaged in the same war, eat, drink, laugh, sing, visit, chat, reason, and hope soon to behold again the objects of their affection."

This is the example that she wishes her daughter to follow, instead of brooding in melancholy loneliness over the thought of the dangers to which her son may be exposed; but even while she sends this bracing advice, she tries her utmost to relieve her daughter's anxiety. Indeed, Madame de Coulanges declared afterwards that the Marquise slept at the post, so as to get the earliest news possible to send to her daughter.

Her letters during this period of anxiety are not brilliant, but she has never written anything more tender, or shown herself more lovingly eager to give strength and courage and consolation to that other mother away in Provence, whose heart is torn with anxious fears, whose only desire just now is for tidings of her son; whose one absorbing thought is whether he is safe. The Marquise gives very little of the news she usually sends; there is no brilliant gossip from Versailles; and once, when she has written a few words about English affairs, she says with the intuition of her own loving heart, "You do not listen to me; you are thinking only of your child."

Fortunately the suspense was not long, as on the 30th of October Philipsburg was taken. Madame de Sévigné, immediately on hearing the news, wrote joyfully to her daughter, beginning her letter, "*Philipsburg is taken and your son is safe.* I have only to turn this phrase in twenty different ways for I do not intend to change my theme. Your son is safe and Philipsburg is taken. Sleep then, my dear one, sleep soundly on this assurance. If you are covetous of grief, as we used to say, seek another cause for it, for God has given you back your dear son."

The little captain came back to Paris, and the news had to be sent to his mother that he had a slight wound, and, knowing the black "dragons" of fear and apprehension that will assail her daughter, she makes as light as possible of the affair. It is a mere bruise, she says, but she explains that it has brought this young hero into such notice at Versailles, that Madame de la Fayette declared that "it was a thing to be bought if money could procure it"; while Madame de Maintenon, when talking to the Chevalier, who said it was nothing, replied, "Monsieur, it is better than nothing."

Then she describes his reception at Versailles; but her letters, however delightful they may have been to the fond mother who received them, are scarcely so interesting to us. There is a deeper interest and significance attached to her frequent mention of the little sister Pauline, who for eight years had been in a convent while her mother was away in Paris at the Hôtel de Carnavalet, the big house where she would have been warmly welcomed by her affectionate grandmother if her mother had allowed her to come. When Madame de Grignan returned to Provence, the Marquise continually asked about Pauline, and to the mother's cold complaints about her temper and little girlish faults, the grandmother sends the sagest advice, the most loving wisdom, under which one divines the fear that the pretty and clever little Pauline will perhaps be found to have a "vocation" like her stepsister, or be immured without one, like her sister Marie-Blanche; quite evidently her fate hangs in the balance, for the child has already expressed herself as willing to obey her mother if she desires her to go into a convent. Almost every letter mentions Pauline: "I love Pauline; you describe her as pretty and good-humoured; I can see her running everywhere and telling everyone of the taking of Philipsburg. Love, love your daughter, my dear child; it is the most natural and delightful occupation in the world." Indeed, one can scarcely doubt that Madame de Grignan, who was ready to sacrifice everything that her son, the Marquis, might fitly carry on the honour of the Grignans, would have placed Pauline in a convent but for the constant and wise intervention of Madame de Sévigné.

The year 1689 began pleasantly for the Grignans, for the Comte de Grignan received the distinction of the Order of the Holy Spirit, which, however, he was permitted to receive by proxy, to spare the expense of a journey to Paris. The Marquise, in sending him a little badge, a "Saint Esprit," on the occasion, writes cheerfully; but there is an undercurrent of pathos too, when one remembers the beautiful gift of pearls that she had been able to send to her daughter only a few years before.

"These are strange presents, a ribbon, a little dove, a trifle, this is what we give when we have nothing left to give. I have resigned all; I contemplated the effects and consequences, but it did not shake my resolution, and I said to myself, 'Well, if I am slighted or ruined, God may turn this ingratitude to my advantage, and make it the foundation of my salvation'; and with this thought I have never repented of what I have done, and your friendship and tenderness make my life too happy."

The following month Madame de Sévigné had her own little distinction, an invitation to see the performance of *Esther*, that play by Racine in which Ahasuerus and the heroine are the King and Madame de Maintenon under a very thin disguise. There were hundreds of people desiring invitations to this celebrated performance; for was it not given by the pupils of Saint-Cyr, the school that had been founded and supervised by the most important lady in the land, Madame de Maintenon? It was only a few years before, that Madame Scarron used to sup with Madame de Sévigné every evening, and to keep in her good graces talked continually to the Marquise of her daughter, but she apparently had a very slight remembrance of her former friendship, for it was Madame de Coulanges who received her chief marks of favour. Madame de Sévigné describes the evening to her daughter—

"We went on Saturday. We found places were reserved for us, and an officer told Madame de Coulanges that Madame de Maintenon had ordered a place to be kept for her next herself; you see what honour is paid to her. 'You, Madame,' said he, 'may choose.' I placed myself with Madame de Bagnols in the second row, behind the duchesses. Maréchal de Bellefond came, and sat on my right, and he and I listened to the tragedy with an attention that was noticed, and said some praises in a low voice that were very well chosen. . . . I was delighted with the play, and so was the Maréchal, who left his place to tell the King how much he was gratified, and that he was seated next to a lady who was worthy of the honour of seeing *Esther*. The King came up to where we sat, and having turned round, addressed himself to me: 'I am told, Madame, said he, 'that the piece has given you satisfaction.' I replied, with perfect self-possession, 'Sire, I am delighted beyond the power of words to describe.' The King continued, 'Racine has great talents.' I answered, 'He has indeed, Sire, and so have these young ladies; they enter into the subject as if it had been their only occupation.' 'Ah, that is very true,' he replied, and then retired, leaving me the object of universal envy. The Prince and Princess came and spoke a word to me; Madame de Maintenon flashed upon me like lightning, and then retired with the King. We returned at night with torch-bearers, and I supped with Madame de Coulanges."

Two months after this distinction, in April 1689, Madame de Sévigné set out for Brittany on a last visit to Les Rochers. She had no fine cavalcade of her own now; on her return from her last visit she had been obliged to hire post-horses from Mans, and even in Paris she was dependent on the kindness of her friends. "I have no carriage now," she wrote, "but I am at the same time embarrassed with too many carriages"; the carriages of her devoted friends, who were all so eager to offer her the use of theirs.

The Duchesse de Chaulnes, who had a deep affection for the Marquise, happened to be going to Brittany in April, and suggested that she should travel with her. Madame de Sévigné accepted the kind offer, and she and Madame de Carman, who at the States in 1671 had been the "Murinette beauty," set out with the Duchesse "in the best carriage, drawn by the best horses, with a great retinue, caravans, outriders, and every possible convenience, with every possible precaution." They stayed at Chaulnes for ten days, and then went on to Rennes; and the Duchesse was so charmed to have Madame de Sévigné's company, that the Marquise only reached Les Rochers after a month of travelling from place to place in Brittany.

The Baron de Sévigné and his wife came for Madame de Sévigné to Rennes, and carried her off to Les Rochers with much delight at having her with them again. And the Marquise was scarcely less happy at finding herself once more among those gardens and avenues which had held so large a part in her life; the Solitaire, the sunny Place de Coulanges, the Place Madame, the Labyrinth, were all visited and inspected, with the same fresh delight and tranquil happiness that she always experienced amid the silence of this green retreat.

It was a very peaceful and serene existence that they all spent at Les Rochers; her son and his wife were so devout, that the Marquise declared she was the most wicked of the three. They were not without their little innocent pleasures, however; they had visitors; they read books—neither Rabelais nor the novels of Calprenède now!—Nicole's *Essais*, the Life of Theodosius, and other devotional works; or they played cards; and one is sure that on Twelfth-night they had the usual rejoicings. The Marquise gives a vivid little picture of how they kept the Carnival; it is a delightful peep across two centuries into the simple pleasures of that day; it is the more idyllic and charming when one thinks of the maskings in Paris, and the extreme licence that was carried on under the disguise of the *loup* and domino.

"I ask Pauline," writes the Marquise, "how she enjoyed her Carnival."

"Last night, without any preparation, my daughter left us a few minutes before supper, and immediately after, the servant who sets the table entered, disguised very prettily, and told us supper was ready. We went into the dining-room, which was brilliantly illuminated, and found my daughter-in-law, in the midst of her servants and ours, all in complete masquerade. Those who held the basins, those who handed the napkins, all the officers, and all the lackeys were masked, making a troop of more than thirty people, all most amusingly dressed. We were so surprised at all this, that it caused quite an outcry of laughter and confusion, which lasted the whole of supper-time, for we did not know who waited upon us. After supper, some music was provided, and they all danced *passe-pied*, minuets, *courantes*, and country dances. At length twelve o'clock struck, and Lent began." A Lent which they kept at Les Rochers by "eating bread-and-butter strewed with fine herbs and violets."

But Madame de Sévigné's friends in Paris were anxious that she should not spend another winter amid the cold and damps of Brittany, and urged her to come back among them again. Madame de la Fayette, who was weaker and more ailing than ever, urged it especially; and, yielding to the entreaties of her friends, she left Les Rochers and joined her daughter in Provence. To her cousin Bussy she writes: "When you see the date of this letter, my dear cousin, you will take me for a bird. I have passed courageously from Brittany to Provence. If my daughter had been in Paris, I should have gone there; but as she was spending the winter in this beautiful country, I determined to pass it with her, and to come and enjoy her beautiful sunshine." This was almost her last letter to Bussy, and she says with a touch of sadness, "Love me always; it is not worth while to change after all these years."

All that summer she stayed in Provence, happy in the presence of her daughter, enjoying the company of the charming little Pauline, and appreciating the luxurious life at the Château de Grignan; which always seemed to her, in its magnificence, something like life in a fairy-tale, the more especially as its grandeur rested on a foundation of debt which might at any time give way and involve them all in ruin. At the end of 1691 they all returned to the Hôtel de Carnavalet, where they spent the next two years. Madame de la Fayette shed tears of joy at seeing her friend again, the friend to whom she wrote with deep emotion: "Believe me, you are the person in the world I have most truly loved."

Change and death had been busy among her friends for many years; her later letters so frequently record the passing of some old acquaintance. The good d'Hacqueville had gone long before; the Duc de la Rochefoucauld; the Duc de Lude, who had been her admirer in her brilliant youth; her uncle the Cardinal de Retz; and now two others of the few that remained were called away, the Comte de Bussy and Madame de la Fayette. Both of these died in the same year, 1693, and Madame de Sévigné's letters are very sad as she writes her tender reminiscences.

A few months after the death of Madame de la Fayette, early in 1694, Madame de Grignan went to Provence to arrange her son's marriage, and the Marquise soon followed her daughter; her last journey to Provence, as it proved to be. The next year was occupied with negotiations for the marriage of the young Marquis de Grignan, whose mother was torn between the desire of marrying her son into a family of high rank, and that of providing him a rich bride whose money should place the tottering grandeurs of the Grignans on a more solid foundation: "stones or gold," as Madame de Sévigné expressed it. Wisdom prevailed, and the young Marquis was married to Mademoiselle Saint-Amand, the daughter of a financier, who brought her husband a rich dowry: four hundred thousand francs, and linen, dresses, laces, and jewels to the value of fifty thousand francs.

The charming little Pauline had no such dower. Madame de Sévigné prophesied truly when she said that Pauline's wit and beauty would serve for her dowry, and it was fortunate it was so, for she had no other. The Comte de Simiane and his family were more generous than was usual in French families. "Nothing could be better," wrote the Marquise, "everything is noble, convenient, and advantageous for a daughter of the house of Grignan, who, in her husband and his family, have found those who value her worth, her person, and her name, and care nothing for her fortune."

Pauline's marriage was celebrated on the 29th of November 1695, a gloomy time of year, and under circumstances which were still more gloomy, for her mother was too ill even to be carried to the chapel of the Château de Grignan. The bride, however, was not taken far away from home, for the estates of the Simianes adjoined those of the Grignans.

Madame de Sévigné had been a tender nurse to her daughter in her long illness, but, as she complained to Emmanuel de Coulanges, it was wearing out her strength and endurance. "I own to you, my dear cousin, that I am dying of this, and I am hardly able to support all the bad nights that she causes me to pass."

This was written in October, and though in the following spring Madame de Sévigné seemed quite well, there is no doubt that when she was stricken by the small-pox in April, her strength had been so exhausted by her continual anxiety for her daughter that the disease found her an easy prey. It is sad to think of her lonely deathbed; she, who had loved her daughter with such rare devotion, was denied that dear daughter's presence in those last mournful hours. Madame de Grignan was in a room close by, but still dangerously ill, and unable to go to her mother; Charles de Sévigné was hundreds of leagues away in Brittany; and that bright spirit, which had so dreaded the thought of death, was obliged to face it alone, without either of her children to minister to her wants, or to sustain her courage as she set out on the last drear journey. It is a satisfaction to know, however, that, in spite of the terror which this dreadful disease always caused, especially in those days when it so frequently proved fatal, she was nursed with devoted care and affection by Mademoiselle de Martillac, and Montgobert, one of her daughter's dependants, who is often mentioned familiarly in the letters.

The Marquise died on the 17th of April 1696, at the age of seventy, and her tombstone records that she received "all the sacraments" in her last hours; a fact that must have given much solemn happiness to her devout mind. Her friends in Paris, when they heard the sad news, "met together to weep." Madame de Chaulnes, Madame de la Troche, Madame de Coulanges, and others; and her frivolous cousin Emmanuel for once wrote with a sad sincerity of his loss that is peculiarly touching from such a gay society trifler. M. de Grignan in reply wrote to him a letter that, as it not only expresses his grief but gives a few details of her illness as well, is one of the many written on the occasion that is most worth quoting.

"GRIGNAN, *May* 23, 1696

"You, sir, can understand better than anyone the magnitude of the loss we have sustained, and my just grief. Madame de Sévigné's merit was perfectly known to you. It is not merely a mother-in-law that I regret, this name does not always command esteem, it is an amiable and excellent friend, and a delightful companion. But it is a circumstance more worthy of our admiration than regret, that this noble-minded woman contemplated the approach of death (which she expected from the beginning of the attack) with astonishing firmness and submission. She, who was so tender and timid respecting those she loved, displayed the utmost fortitude and piety when she believed that she ought to think only of herself; and we cannot but remark how useful and important it is to fill the mind with sacred subjects, for which Madame de Sévigné appears to have had a peculiar taste, by the use she made of these excellent provisions in the last moments of her life. I relate these particulars to you, sir, because they accord with your sentiments, and will be gratifying to the friendship you have borne for her whom we lament, and at the same time my mind is so full of them that it is a relief to me to find a man so willing to listen to the recital, and to take pleasure in hearing it."

Her daughter was overwhelmed with grief, and in a few heart-broken sentences reveals how terribly she realised the extent of her loss. To the President Moulceau she writes: "What perfections did she not unite, to be to me in different ways more dear and precious? A loss so complete and irreparable does not dispose one to seek consolation except in tears and lamentations. I have not the strength to lift my eyes to the place whence comfort comes, I can as yet only cast them around me, where I no longer see her who loaded me with affection, and had no other care but to give me every day fresh proofs of her love. You lose a friend of incomparable merit and fidelity; and I, Monsieur, what do I not lose?"

INDEX

Adhémar, François. *See* Grignan, Comte de
—— Marie Blanche d', 190, 217, 250-252
—— Pauline d', 252, 258, 286, 300, 305
Albret, Chevalier d', 81, 82, 84
Amonio, quack doctor, 276
Andilly, Arnauld d', 138, 175, 189, 210
Angennes, Angélique d' (Comtesse de Grignan), 40, 41, 150, 179
—— Julie d'. *See* Montausier, Marquise de
Anjou, Duc d'. *See* Orléans, Philippe, Duc d'
Anne de Bourbon. *See* Longueville, Duchesse de
Anne of Austria, Queen Regent, 9, 15, 29, 33, 63, 64; and the Fronde, 66, 72; 86, 109, 133
Arnauld, Abbé, 92, 151
Arpajon, Madame d', 213-214
Artagnan, M. d', 142, 145, 148, 149

Ballets at the Court, 155-159
Balzac, Jean L. G., 44, 45
Beaufort, Duc de, 51, 66, 67, 73, 170
Bellefond, Maréchal de, 301
Benserade, Isaac, 156-159
Boileau-Despréaux, Nicolas, 174, 215, 254
Bondi, Forest of, 15-17
Bossuet, Jacques Bénigne, 44, 212, 213
Bouillon, Cardinal de, 261, 263
—— Duc de, 68
—— Duchesse de, 67, 68
Bourbilly, 10, 258, 295
Bouteville de Montmorency, Marquis, 1-7, 87
Brinvilliers, Comtesse de, 278
Brissac, Duc de, 106
—— Duchesse de, 157, 273, 274
Brittany, revolt in, 264-265; the States of, at Vitré, 224, 227-246
Bussy d'Amboise, 5, 6

Bussy-Rabutin, Roger, Comte de, 3, 13, 24, 27; marriage of, 28; 33; and Madame de Sévigné, 54-56, 74-78, 93-95, 98-103, 109-113, 124-129, 138-139, 160-168; and Madame de Miramion, 56-60, 61, 62, 69, 71; gives a fête in the Temple Gardens, 94-95; his *Histoire amoureuse*, 128-129, 160-161, 166-167; and Madame de Grignan, 154, 172, 180-182; 288; death of, 304

Cadaval, Duc de, 203
Caderousse, Duc de, 175
Calprenède, Seigneur de la, 182, 224
Candia, Expedition to, 184
Capuchins of the Louvre, 277
Carman, Madame de. *See* Murinais, Mademoiselle de
Chabot, Henri de. *See* Rohan, Duc de
—— Mademoiselle de, 90
Chalais, Prince de, 5
Champmeslé, Mademoiselle, 215, 216
Chantal, Celse Bénigne, Baron de, 1-8, 10, 11
—— Baronne de, 1, 4-9
—— The Blessed (Jeanne Françoise Frémyot), 7-12, 143
Chantilly, Fête at, 218-220
Chapelain, Jean, 14, 18, 22, 23, 46, 137
Charles II, King of England, 195
Châtillon, Duchesse de, 49, 52, 73, 86
Chaulnes, Duc de, 224; at the Brittany States, 228-246; 264-265, 275, 290, 293
—— Duchesse de, at the Brittany States, 228-246; 293, 302
Chésières, M., 235, 242
Chevreuse, Duchesse de, 5, 49, 52, 73, 87
—— Mademoiselle de, 79, 80
Christina, Queen of Sweden, 76, 114-116
Clément, Père, 57
Coëtlogon, M. de, 234, 237
Colbert, Jean Baptiste, 131-132, 135, 140, 147

Condé, Henri, Prince de, 36, 43
—— Louis, Prince de (The Great Condé), 42, 58, 61, 62; and the Fronde, 65, 69, 72–73; 75, 87; at the Battle of Saint Antoine, 92; 95, 195; gives a fête at Chantilly, 218–220
—— Dowager Princesse de, 41, 65, 72
Condom, M. de. *See* Bossuet
Conti, Prince de, 36, 43, 52; and the Fronde, 67, 72; 96–97, 99
Corbinelli, Jean, 129, 164, 165, 276, 293
Corneille, Pierre, 174, 253, 254
Cornuel, Madame de, 45, 46, 47, 49
Coulanges, Christophe de, Abbé de Livry, 13–16, 24, 28, 85; and Ménage, 107–108; 126, 180, 221, 223, 238, 249, 256, 270, 282, 283, 289, 290, 292; death of, 296–297
—— Emmanuel de, 18, 193, 221, 232, 249, 250, 254, 284, 294, 306
—— Henriette de. *See* La Trousse, Marquise de
—— Madame de, 257–259, 276, 294, 301, 302
—— Marie de. *See* Chantal, Baronne de
—— Philippe de, 4, 8, 9, 13
Cours-la-Reine, 51, 54
Créance, Comte de, 232, 233, 253

Dangeau, Marquis de, 280
Daughters of the Visitation of Saint Mary, Order of, 12
Des Chappelles, M., 5, 6
Du Chastellet, Paul Hay, 29
Du Plessis Argentré, Mademoiselle, 153, 223, 270
Du Plessis-Guénégaud, Madame, 144, 146, 174, 175
Du Vigean, Mademoiselle, 42, 43

Elbœuf, Duc d', 68
—— Madame d', 261, 263
—— Mademoiselle d', 158
Enghien, Duc d'. *See* Condé, Louis, Prince de
Etauges, Comte d', 176

Fiennes, Mademoiselle de, 212
Fiesque, Comte de, 74
—— Comtesse de, 47, 49, 87
Foire Saint-Germain, 50
Foucquet, Nicolas, 97–98; and Madame de Sévigné, 111–112; 116–118; his last fête at Vaux, 131–135; arrest of, 135–136; Madame de Sévigné's letters to, 136–139; trial of, 140–150; 174

Fouesnel family, 225, 226
Fougères, 53
Francis de Sales, Saint, 10–12, 143
Frémyot, Jeanne Françoise. *See* Chantal, The Blessed
—— President, 10, 11, 182
Fronde, The, 6, 62–74, 91, 92, 95, 105

Gêvres, Duchesse de, 213, 214
Gondi, Paul de. *See* Retz, Cardinal de
Gondran, Madame de, 79, 80, 81, 83
Gourville, Sieur de, 218–220
Grignan, Comte de, 41; his first wife, 150; betrothed to Mademoiselle de Sévigné, 176, 177; family of, 178; marriage of, 179–181; appointed Lieut.-General of Provence, 185; letters of Madame de Sévigné to, 186–192; and Madame de Sévigné, 202–203; 283; extravagance of, 286; receives the Order of the Holy Spirit, 300; letter on Madame de Sévigné's death, 306
—— Comtesse de (Françoise Marguerite de Sévigné), birth of, 33, 41; childhood of, 151–154; at Court, 155; dances in the *ballet royal*, 157–159; and her suitors, 169–170, 175–176; and the King, 171–173; betrothal of, 176–177; marriage of, 178–181; 183; remains in Paris with her mother, 186; birth of a daughter, 190; 193; goes to Provence, 202–205; character of, 206–209; 214; at Marseilles, 226; birth of a son, 248; letter of Emmanuel de Coulanges to, 250; and her daughter Blanche, 252; visits her mother in Paris, 259, 282, 285; birth of youngest son, 270; and her step-daughter, 287; in Paris, 292; returns to Provence, 298; and her daughter Pauline, 300; in Paris, 304; returns to Provence, 304; illness of, 305–306; on her mother's death, 307
—— Mademoiselle de, 287
—— Mademoiselle d'Alerac de, 287
—— Marquis de, 76, 298–300, 304–305
Guirlande de Julie, La, 40

Hacqueville, M. d', 92, 204, 258, 282, 304
Harcourt, Mademoiselle d', 203
Harouys, M. d', 232, 235, 237, 241, 242
Hébert, Madame de Sévigné's servant, 218
Henriette, Duchesse d'Orléans, 133, 157, 159, 171

INDEX

Hôtel de Carnavalet, 282-284, 293, 296, 304
—— de Lamoignon, 284
James II, King of England, 46
La Baume, Marquise de, 129, 160, 164
Lacger, M., 80, 81, 84
La Fayette, Marquise de (Marie de la Vergne), 17, 19; her "portrait" of Madame de Sévigné, 25; 35, 46; and the diamond earrings, 79-80; 86, 106; and Ménage, 108; 173-175, 205, 213, 215; and the Duc de la Rochefoucauld, 252-253; 257, 259, 293, 303; death of, 304
La Fontaine, Jean de, 98, 117-119, 169, 174, 214
La Grande Mademoiselle. *See* Montpensier
Lambesc, Madame de Sévigné at, 257
La Meilleraye, Maréchal de, 106-107
Lamoignon, Madame, 96
—— President, 294
La Mousse, Abbé de, 152, 171, 184, 217, 221; at Les Rochers, 224, 239, 248; 256
La Rochefoucauld, Duc de, 17, 46, 52, 67, 72, 174, 205, 217, 252-253, 304
La Sablière, Madame de, 212
La Trousse, Marquise de (Henriette de Coulanges), 85, 90, 103, 137, 138, 211, 255, 256
Lauzun, Duc de, 194, 196-201
Lavalée, Foucquet's servant, 148, 149
La Vallière, Louise de, 133, 135, 158, 171, 172, 272, 279
Lavardin, Marquis de, 222, 224, 232, 235, 237
—— Marquise de, 22, 112
La Vergne, Marie de. *See* La Fayette, Marquise de
L'Enclos, Ninon de, 74-77, 79, 115, 212, 213, 214, 215, 216
Lenet, M., 33, 70
Le Féron, President, 68
Lesdiguières, Duc de, 74, 122
Les Rochers, 29-32, 163, 237, 247-248, 302-303
Le Tellier, Michel, 147
Livry, the Abbaye de, 15-17
—— Abbé de. *See* Coulanges, Christophe de
Locmaria, Marquis de, 234, 237, 244
Longueville, Charles Paris, Duc de. *See* Saint-Paul, Comte de
—— Duc de, 67, 68, 72
—— Duchesse de (Anne de Bourbon), 23, 40-42, 46, 65, 67, 68, 72
Loret, Jean, 73, 85

Louis XIII, 4
—— XIV, 56, 121-122; at Vaux, 133-136; 137, 140, 141, 147; and Court Ballets, 155-159; and Mademoiselle de Sévigné, 171, 172; and la Grande Mademoiselle, 198-199; at Chantilly, 218-220; 259, 280, 281, 301
Lude, Duc de, 52, 91, 304

Maintenon, Marquise de (Madame Scarron), 74, 117, 137, 144, 172, 254, 258, 259, 294, 301, 302
Malicorne, 222, 249
Mancini, Mademoiselle de, 35, 109
Marie Thérèse, Queen of France, 272, 279-281
Marigny, Jacques Carpentier de, 69, 90
Marseilles, 226, 256
—— Bishop of, 185, 190-192, 258
Marsillac, Prince de. *See* La Rochefoucauld
Martillac, Mademoiselle de, 306
Maskers in Paris, 122-123
Mauron, Baron de, 294-295
—— Mademoiselle de Brehant de, 294
Mazarin, Cardinal, 63-65, 97, 116, 117, 131, 132, 141, 195
Ménage, Gilles, 14, 15, 18-22, 46, 78, 107-108, 137, 169
Méri, Mademoiselle de, 293
Mérinville, Comte de, 175
Miramion, Madame de, 57-60, 96
Molière, Jean Baptiste Poquelin de, 20, 35, 118, 129-130, 134, 156, 172, 174, 254
Montausier, Marquis de, 40, 198, 259
—— Marquise de (Julie d'Angennes), 40, 97
Montbazon, Duchesse de, 73
Montespan, Marquise de, 157, 158, 172, 259, 271-272, 275, 279-281
Montglas, Madame de, 94, 111, 112, 126, 128, 160
Montpensier, Duchesse de ("La Grande Mademoiselle"), 39, 50, 52, 65, 86, 87, 92, 95, 112; projected marriage of, 194-201; 213-214
Montreuil, Abbé de, 48, 53, 54
Mortemart, Mademoiselle de. *See* Montespan, Madame de
Motteville, Madame de, 39, 64, 155, 175
Moulceau, President, 293, 307
Murinais, Mademoiselle de, 232, 233, 240, 244, 302

Nantes, Madame de Sévigné at, 289-290
Neuchèze, Jacques de, Bishop of Chalon-sur-Saône, 29, 61, 126, 164

Nicole, Pierre, 189, 222, 227, 303
Noirmoutier, Marquis de, 68

Orléans, Gaston, Duc d' ("Monsieur"), 52, 65, 95, 195
—— Henriette, Duchesse d', 133, 157, 159, 171
—— Philippe, Duc d' ("Monsieur"), 33, 122, 133, 158, 195, 280, 281
Ormesson, Olivier d', 29, 62, 144, 145, 147, 148

Paulet, Mademoiselle, 43
Pecquet, Jean, 148, 149, 218
Pellison, M., 118, 137
Philipsburg, Siege of, 298-299
Pignerol, 149, 150, 201
Pilois, Madame de Sévigné's gardener, 223, 225, 241, 248, 249, 291
Pisani, Marquis de, 37
Place de Grève, 2, 3
—— des Vosges. *See* Place Royale
—— Royale, 4-6, 8
Pomenars, Marquis de, 232, 233, 239, 241, 244, 253
Pommereul, President de, 74
Pomponne, Marquis de, 138, 140, 142, 148, 151, 152, 174, 175, 260
Pont-Gibaud, M., 1, 2
Précieuses, Les, 35, 129-130

Rabutin, Guy de, 10
—— Hughes de, 33, 56, 94
—— Roger de. *See* Bussy-Rabutin, Roger, Comte de
Rabutin-Chantal, Christophe de, 10
Racine, Jean, 174, 215, 301
Rambouillet, Hôtel de, 22, 23, 35-39, 40, 41-46, 130
—— Marquis de, Charles d'Angennes, 37
—— Marquise de (Catherine de Vivonne), 22, 34, 36-44, 130, 287
Rennes, 265; Capuchins of, 277
Retz, Cardinal de (Paul de Gondi), 28, 33, 52, 66, 67, 72-74, 95, 97, 105-108, 179, 254, 304
Rhé, Isle of, 7
Richelieu, Duc de, 1, 3, 5-7, 43, 45
Rohan, Duc de, 46, 88-91, 224, 230, 237
—— Duchesse de, 88-91, 232, 235
Romilly, Abbé de, 80
Rossan, Marquis de, 158, 159
Ruelles, 38

Saint-Amand, Mademoiselle, 305
Saint-Antoine, Battle of, 92, 195
Saint-Germain, 65
Saint-Hérem, M., 256, 273, 274

Saint-Paul, Comte de (Duc de Longueville), 68, 170, 184, 196, 250
Saint-Pavin, Denis, 18, 53, 169
Saint-Simon, Mademoiselle de. *See* Brissac, Duchesse de
Sainte-Geneviève, procession of, 91-92
Sainte-Hélène, M., 147, 148
Sarrazin, Jean François, 44
Scarron, Madame. *See* Maintenon, Marquise de
Schomberg, Henri, Comte de, 4
Scudéry, George de, 45
—— Mademoiselle de, 39, 45, 46, 117-120, 130, 137, 144, 146
Segrais, Jean Regnault de, 39, 53
Séguier, Chancellor, 115, 136, 142, 143
Sévigné, Charles de, 30; birth of, 55; 76, 151-152; character of, 182-183; goes to Candia, 184; his dissipated life in Paris, 211-212, 214-217; at Les Rochers, 222-224; 226, 265; and his mother's illness, 269-270; 277, 285, 290, 292; marriage of, 294-296; 302-303
—— Françoise Marguerite de. *See* Grignan, Comtesse de
—— Henri, Marquis de, 28; marriage of, 29; 33; neglects his wife, 49; 53; in Normandy, 68,; 74; and Ninon de l'Enclos, 75, 76, 77, 79; leaves his wife at Les Rochers, 78; and Madame de Gondran, 79, 80, 81; killed in a duel, 81, 82
—— Marquise de (Marie de Rabutin-Chantal), parentage, 1; birth, 5-6; death of her parents, 7-8; early childhood, 8-9; her guardian, 13; education, 14-15; at Livry, 15-18, 109-110; and Ménage, 19-22; "portrait" of, by Mme. de la Fayette, 25; marriage, 29; at Les Rochers, 30-32, 56, 78, 83-85, 105-108, 115, 136, 163, 222-249, 264-271, 276-277, 290-292, 296, 302-304; birth of a daughter, 33; and the *précieuses*, 35; neglected by her husband, 49; and the Comte de Bussy, 54-56, 69-71, 74-78, 93-95, 98-103, 109-113, 160-168, 181-182; birth of her son, 55; and the Fronde, 66, 69-70, 73; death of her husband, 82-83; "portrait" of, by Mademoiselle de Scudéry, 119; Bussy's "portrait" of, 128-129, 162, 164-165; her letters to Foucquet, 136-139; and Foucquet's trial, 140-150; and her children, 151-152, 183; at Versailles, 171-172, 279-281; and her daughter's marriage, 176-180;

INDEX

her letters to the Comte de Grignan, 186–192, 202–203; and La Grande Mademoiselle, 193–194, 198–201, 213–214; her daughter's departure for Provence, 204–206; character of, 207–208; her journey to Brittany, 221–222; and her son, 212, 214–217, 226; and the Brittany States, 224, 227–246; birth of a grandson, 248; sends her daughter a pearl necklace, 254–255; at Bourbilly, 258; her pet dog, 266–267; at Vichy, 271–275, 284; visits her daughter in Provence, 256–258; and the death of Turenne, 260–263; illness of, 269–271; visits Vaux, 276; and the Capuchins of the Louvre, 277; and the Hôtel de Carnavalet, 282, 293–294; at Nantes, 289–290; and her son's marriage, 294–296; visits her son at Les Rochers, 296; at the performance of *Esther*, 301–302; in Provence, 304; her last illness and death, 305–307

Sévigné, Renaud de, 68, 79, 90, 106, 151
—— Madame Renaud de, 86
Simiane, Comte de, 305
—— Comtesse de. *See* Adhémar, Pauline d'
Soyecour, Marquis de, 81, 84

Tallemant des Réaux, G., 21–23
Tarente, Princesse de, 266–267, 285
Têtu, Abbé, 258–259
Thianges, Madame de, 258, 271, 281
Toiras, Marquis de, 5, 7, 8
Tonquedec, Marquis de, 88–90, 232
Toulongeon, Comte de, 3
—— Gabrielle de, 28
Turenne, Vicomte de, 92, 112, 113, 147, 260–263
Twelfth-night at the Court, 64

Vassé, Comte de, 53, 77, 91
Vatel, *maître d'hôtel*, 117, 133, 219–220
Vaux, 116–118, 132–135, 276
Vendôme, Duc de, 185, 291–292
Versailles, 171–172, 279
Vibraye, Madame de, 158
Vichy, 271–275, 284
Villeroy, Marquis de, 158–159, 253
Vincent de Paul, Saint, 96, 143
Vitré, 30; the States of Brittany at, 227–246
Vivonne, Catherine de. *See* Rambouillet, Marquise de
Voiture, Vincent, 43–44

Walpole, Horace, Earl of Orford, 15

Ytier, M., 212, 251

THE END

www.ingramcontent.com/pod-product-compliance
Lightning Source LLC
Chambersburg PA
CBHW020325240426
43673CB00039B/919